David
Biblical Portraits of Power

Studies on Personalities of the Old Testament

James L. Crenshaw, Series Editor

David
Biblical Portraits of Power

Marti J. Steussy

University of South Carolina Press

Published in Columbia, South Carolina, by the
University of South Carolina Press

Manufactured in the United States of America

03 02 01 00 99   5 4 3 2 1

Library of Congress Cataloging-in-Publication Data

Steussy, Marti J., 1955–
    David : biblical portraits of power / Marti J. Steussy.
        p.   cm. — (Studies on personalities of the Old Testament)
    Includes bibliographical references and index.
    ISBN 1-57003-250-5
    1. David, King of Israel.   2. Bible. O.T. — Criticism,
interpretation, etc.   I. Title.   II. Series.
BS580.D3 S64   1999
222'.4092 — ddc21   98-19683

CONTENTS

CONTENTS

EDITOR'S PREFACE

Critical study of the Bible in its ancient Near Eastern setting has stimulated interest in the individuals who shaped the course of history and whom events singled out as tragic or heroic figures. Rolf Rendtorff's *Men of the Old Testament* (1968) focuses on the lives of important biblical figures as a means of illuminating history, particularly the sacred dimension that permeates Israel's convictions about its God. Fleming James's *Personalities of the Old Testament* (1939) addresses another issue, that of individuals who function as inspiration for their religious successors in the twentieth century. Studies restricting themselves to a single individual—e.g., Moses, Abraham, Samson, Elijah, David, Saul, Ruth, Jonah, Job, Jeremiah—enable scholars to deal with a host of questions: psychological, literary, theological, sociological, and historical. Some, like Gerhard von Rad's *Moses*, introduce a specific approach to interpreting the Bible, hence provide valuable pedagogic tools.

As a rule, these treatments of isolated figures have not reached the general public. Some were written by outsiders who lacked a knowledge of biblical criticism (Freud on Moses, Jung on Job) and whose conclusions, however provocative, remain problematic. Others were targeted for the guild of professional biblical critics (David Gunn on David and Saul, Phyllis Trible on Ruth, Terence Fretheim and Jonathan Magonet on Jonah). None has succeeded in capturing the imagination of the reading public in the way fictional works like Archibald MacLeish's *J. B.* and Joseph Heller's *God Knows* have done.

It could be argued that the general public would derive little benefit from learning more about the personalities of the Bible. Their conduct, often less then exemplary, reveals a flawed character, and their everyday concerns have nothing to do with our preoccupations from dawn to dusk. To be sure, some individuals transcend their own age, entering the gallery of classical literary figures from time immemorial. But only these rare achievers can justify specific treatments of them. Then why publish additional studies on biblical personalities?

The answer cannot be that we read about biblical figures to learn ancient history, even of the sacred kind, or to discover models for ethical action. But what remains? Perhaps the primary significance of biblical personages is the light they throw on the imaging of deity in biblical times. At the very least, the Bible constitutes human perceptions of deity's relationship with the world and its creatures. Close readings of biblical personalities therefore clarify ancient understandings of God. That is the important datum which we seek—not because we endorse that specific view of deity, but because all such efforts to make sense of reality contribute something worthwhile to the endless quest for knowledge.

James L. Crenshaw
Duke Divinity School

ACKNOWLEDGMENTS

I owe much to many for their help in birthing this book. James L. Crenshaw encouraged me to undertake the project. I hope my work is worthy of all I have learned from him. I did most of my research and writing during a year-long research leave, for which I thank the trustees of Christian Theological Seminary and faculty colleagues who covered for me during my absence. Loren D. Crow, M. Patrick Graham, John Endres, S. J., Joyce Krauser, and especially Jon L. Berquist and David M. Gunn rendered invaluable assistance in reading and commenting on the work in progress. Special thanks goes to Joseph A. Walters for his work on the scripture index. The programmers of NotaBene 4.5 (NotaBene, 1996) and BibleWorks for Windows 3.0 (Hermeneutika, 1995) also had a hand in making my work easier.

I fear I am not easy to live with while I wrestle words and ideas. "Thank you" most of all to my patient, cooperative children and to my husband, Nic, who not only cooked for me but also insisted that I have top-notch computer equipment in good working order. I dedicate this book to David Steussy, who is as charming as his biblical namesake but has (in my expert motherly opinion) a far less problematic character.

ABBREVIATIONS

Torah

Genesis	Gen
Exodus	Ex
Leviticus	Lev
Numbers	Num
Deuteronomy	Dt

Former Prophets

Joshua	Josh
Judges	Jdg
1 Samuel	1 S
2 Samuel	2 S
1 Kings	1 K
2 Kings	2 K

Latter Prophets

Isaiah	Isa
Jeremiah	Jer
Ezekiel	Ezek
Hosea	Hos
Joel	Joel
Amos	Amos
Obadiah	Ob
Jonah	Jon
Micah	Mi
Nahum	Nah
Habakkuk	Hab
Zephaniah	Zeph
Haggai	Hag
Zechariah	Zech
Malachi	Mal

Writings

Psalms	Ps (plural Pss)
Job	Job
Proverbs	Prov
Ruth	Ruth
Song of Solomon	Cant
Ecclesiastes	Eccl
Lamentations	Lam
Esther	Esth
Daniel	Dan
Ezra	Ezra
Nehemiah	Neh
1 Chronicles	1 C
2 Chronicles	2 C

New Testament

Matthew	Mt
Mark	Mk
Luke	Lk
John	Jn

Miscellaneous

BCE	Before the Common Era (equivalent to BC)
CE	Common Era (equivalent to AD)
n.	note
KJV	King James Version
NRSV	New Revised Standard Version
RSV	Revised Standard Version

PART 1

THE ISSUES

CHAPTER 1

AN INVITATION

I have found my servant David;
with my holy oil I have anointed him;
. . . .
Forever I will keep my steadfast love for him,
and my covenant with him will stand firm.
I will establish his line forever,
and his throne as long as the heavens endure.
(Ps 89:20, 28–29, NRSV)

Who is this David? His name appears more times in the Hebrew Bible
than that of any other human person.[1] Why are God and people so smitten
by him?

One might expect a man of heroic proportions, a paragon of gifts and
virtue. Indeed David appears a talented fellow—"skillful in playing, a man of
valor, a warrior, prudent in speech, and a man of good presence; and the
LORD is with him," says the courtier who recommends David to Saul (1 S
16:18). Yet we also see him—especially in 2 Samuel—as fearful, querulous,
arrogant, and outright sinful. "What I like about David," announced a
woman in a church Bible study group, "is that if God can love him, God can
surely put up with me."

David's complexity accounts in part for his appeal. He is vulnerable
enough to identify with—as he embraces a friend, suffers persecution from
his boss, quarrels with his wife and sons, and finally lies abed as an impotent
old man—yet glorious enough to make such identification appealing. If
David were either merely heroic or merely flawed, he would be just one more
good or bad example for religious education texts and sermon illustrations.
But the mixture gives David the unpredictable mystery of a living person.

David's complexity does not entirely account for his prominence in a Bible
full of realistic, interesting characters. David, like that other looming presence, Moses, is also a nexus of power. He wields it in the obvious forms of
military might (both personal and strategic) and political authority. He also
displays more subtle powers of personal charm and artistic acumen.

3

In and through these worldly powers shimmers divine power. "The LORD, the God of hosts," say the biblical writers, "was with him" (2 S 5:10). Yet the Bible, especially the books of Samuel and Psalms, will not let us simply identify David's power with God's. Sometimes David acts over against God. Thus David's story further becomes a study in the interaction of divine and worldly power.

LOCATING THE BIBLICAL DAVID

So far, I have spoken as if "David's story" were a single unified narrative. This is not the case. The Hebrew Bible offers four broad portraits of David:

1. The most detailed and realistic-seeming picture occurs in the great historical narrative which runs from Genesis through Kings (excluding Ruth). In this primary history—more specifically in the books of 1 and 2 Samuel—we find such familiar incidents as David's triumph over Goliath, his vow of friendship with Jonathan, his narrow escapes from Saul, his affair with Bathsheba, and his mourning for Absalom. We also find references to God's support for David and his dynasty.

The overall scale, perspective, and coloring of this portrait are so persuasive that people sometimes mistake it for a photograph. Yet close examination shows that many details are missing from the picture: we aren't even sure how tall David is, much less how he feels when Samuel anoints him in 1 S 16. Different parts of the picture are drawn from different angles: in 1 S 17:4–10 we view Goliath from the Israelite lines, but later in the chapter (17:42) we look back toward those lines and David from Goliath's standpoint. In a few places the artist sketches something that would not have been visible to a camera at all, such as God's opinion of David's adultery and of his murder of Uriah (2 S 11:27).

For the most part these different perspectives blend smoothly, but in a few places their juxtaposition leaves us dizzy and disoriented. We see David's predecessor, Saul, as an obedient and successful king who strikes down even the hated Amalekites (1 S 14:47–48). But he also appears as a bedeviled fool who hesitates when he should plunge, plunges when he should hesitate, and is dogged by Amalekites even in death (the dominant portrayal from 1 S 13 onwards). David especially seems to shift and change when we look closely at him. The noble shepherd boy who turns down the king's armor (1 S 17:39–40) has one eye on God, but the other watches greedily for reward (17:26).

Above all, the artistry of the picture appears deliberate. Every line and dot, every subtle nuance of color interacts with other details near and far. Our imagination is drawn in; we lose ourselves in the picture which haunts us even when we turn away.

2. Chronicles, especially 1 C 10–29, also tells the story of David's reign. In many places its wording is almost identical to that in the book of Samuel. But Chronicles leaves out many incidents, especially ones that place David in a bad light. It also adds material that we do not find in the books of Samuel. In particular, it tells how David provided plans and materials for the temple that Solomon eventually built and how David organized the temple's music ministry.

If we were to offer a visual analogy for Chronicles, we might call it a rendering in stained glass. It shows some of the same scenes as the picture in 1 and 2 Samuel, but in brighter colors and more heroic style. Here we do not find confusing and unflattering angles of vision. Around the window's depictions of former times appear names of the present congregation's founders. We know their children will ponder the stained glass, absorbing dreams for the future.

3. The book of Psalms presents us with poetry rather than connected narrative. David appears in the psalms in three ways. Some psalms talk about David, especially as recipient of special promises from God. Second, many psalms are marked *lĕdāvid* (NRSV "of David"), a phrase which could have many meanings but has often been understood to mean that David wrote the psalm in question. Some psalms bear additional captions that tie them to events in David's life. For reasons we will explore later, it seems unlikely that David actually wrote all the psalms bearing his name. Literarily, however, the titles function to make Psalms a diary of David's prayers. Finally, tradition has come to understand David as the guiding voice of the entire book of Psalms.

This book offers a huge collage of dissociated scenes in a style resembling that of Picasso—an impassioned rendering of the soul's perception with warped connections to ordinary physical reality. A victim wriggles limbless on the ground, abandoned by family and friends, body at once melting and crumbling into dust. A dog-pack of leering opponents with lion mouths circles, ready to impale the sufferer with swords which are oxen's horns (Ps 22:1–21). What is "really" the problem? Illness, economic ruin, legal trouble, war? We can no longer discern; we know only the subject's horror and eventual jubilation over deliverance (22:22–31). To make it all worse, the iconography is ancient; the canvas displays gods (Ps 82:1–7) and dragons (Ps 74:13–14) which seldom stir in our own culture's mythology. Here and again David's face peeks out at us, sometimes as if copied directly from one of the other pictures, but we are hard put to tell where he is himself and where he appears as a figment of the artist's tortured imagination. This powerfully evocative picture requires a flexible, image-sensitive interpretation; it will be hard to know whether we have got it "right."

4. Miscellaneous references to David appear in the prophetic books (referred to in Jewish tradition as the Latter Prophets), especially Isaiah, Jeremiah, and Zechariah. Genesis may also contain veiled allusions to David. The Genesis allusions concern events in David's reign—like movie scenes that echo current events using different names and faces—whereas the prophets more often use David as a symbol of God's promise for the future, flashing his name as a stylized logo.

Elaboration of David in art and literature continues to the present day. (For an interesting discussion examining the canonical portraits of David in connection with one by Chagall, see David Petersen's article "Portraits of David.") In this book, however, we will confine ourselves to material in the Hebrew Bible. We will first study each of the major portraits (Samuel, Chronicles, and Psalms). I will discuss the Genesis allusions briefly in connection with Samuel and survey the other miscellaneous references in Chapter 16. We will then ask how the portraits combine into an overall picture of David.

WAYS OF APPROACHING THE BIBLE

Very broadly speaking, there are three ways to approach the Bible. I will label these approaches dogmatic, critical, and artistic. Dogmatic approaches (*dogma* is the Greek word for an opinion or belief) align the Bible with a given set of religious beliefs, interpreting in a manner that will not contradict these assumptions. For instance, dogmatic readers usually assume that God keeps promises. If God declared an eternal throne for David's line (as in the quotation at the beginning of this chapter) then that throne must still exist. But because no heir of David sits on a physical throne in Jerusalem today, dogmatic readers will tend to reinterpret the promise in terms of a heavenly throne or one to be established in the future.

A common and important dogmatic assumption—so common that we sometimes fail to recognize it as an assumption—is that scripture proclaims a single, consistent system of beliefs, or at least that interpretation of scripture should yield such a system of beliefs.[2] When a reader working under this assumption encounters materials which appear to conflict with one another, he or she automatically sets about ignoring, explaining or reinterpreting some of the material to eliminate the conflict. Dogmatic approaches typically seek the meaning of scripture for the believer's life *today*.

Critical approaches (*critical* in the sense of skillfully judging rather than fault-finding) seek to answer questions about the Bible on the basis of available evidence, whether or not the answers fit with traditional dogmatic assumptions. Critical readers also tend to read each piece of the text on its own terms. Asked whether the biblical God keeps promises, a critical reader might answer, "Psalm 18:30 says yes, but 1 S 2:30–31 shows God declaring a promise void."

Most—not all—critical scholars try to understand what texts would have meant to their original audiences. Such historical-critical inquiry has the goal of "objectivity" in the sense that one's assessment of ancient events should be controlled by evidence rather than one's own subjective wishes. The word *objective* has become suspect, however, as we come to understand how inevitably a scholar's own circumstances influence his or her assessments. For instance, men and women often see different issues in David's confrontation with his wife Michal (2 S 6:16–23). Admitting scholarly "subjectivity" does not necessarily mean giving up the search for an honest understanding of the ancient world. It does mean that people of different backgrounds and interests need to be drawn into the discussion to compare notes and criticize (again in the sense of skillfully judging, which may or may not involve fault-finding) each other's work.

Both dogmatic and critical approaches tend to assume that there are right and wrong answers to questions about the Bible. Artistic approaches use visual, musical, and/or verbal media to explore the Bible's stories and symbols, probing associations within the biblical material and between it and our own world. Such associations do not as easily lend themselves to judgments of right or wrong. One artist may portray David as the ideal king, a worthy recipient of God's promise; another may prompt reflection on God's grace by calling attention to David's unworthiness; and yet a third may concentrate on David's response, inviting us to put ourselves in David's shoes. In fact, the same artist may experiment with all these approaches without identifying an only or final answer. Some artists emphasize the distance between biblical subjects and our own world, but more often artistic interpretations create bridges between ancient material and the contemporary world. Although most people in the United States associate religious Bible study with dogmatic approaches, Christians and Jews through the centuries have found creative exploration of biblical images to be an important way of nourishing spirituality.

Partisans of these approaches—especially the dogmatic and critical—can be quite harsh in their assessments of one another. Critical readers may accuse dogmatic ones of wrenching the text out of shape to make it agree with religious beliefs. Dogmatic readers respond that because their beliefs are drawn from the Bible itself, they are simply reading it on its own terms. In turn they may attack the critical community's claims of open-mindedness. Is it open-minded, they ask, to assume that God does not do miracles or give us predictions of the future?[3] Neither dogmatists nor critics are quite sure what to do with artists, except to praise portrayals that agree with their own views and ignore or attack those that do not.

We must not let this bad-tempered rhetoric obscure our view of the shared ground between approaches. Although the word *scholarship* most commonly appears in connection with the critical approach, knowledgeable and insightful interpreters may be found in all three groups. All interpreters have beliefs and assumptions which shape their understandings of the Bible. All also find themselves shaped in one way or another *by* the Bible, creating a circular, chicken-and-egg sort of relationship between the Bible and our understandings of it.

Each broad approach covers a range of options; for instance, one finds both historical and literary options within the "critical" approach. Options within a group may be less compatible with each other than with those in a completely different group; for instance, adherents of different Christian dogmatic approaches often find it easier to live with textual critics than with each other.

Thus the lines between these approaches are not—repeat, *not!*—hard and fast. Yet it remains useful to distinguish between them and to declare one's own affinities. This book will speak primarily out of the critical tradition. I embrace that tradition's historical curiosity and its ideal of uncensored exploration, and it is this tradition which has given me my scholarly training. But my literary approach (which I will explain more fully in Chapter 2) unavoidably brings aesthetic considerations into play. I am also an educated white clergywoman in an ecumenically oriented Protestant denomination. What influence that exerts upon my interpretation remains to be seen.

ENTERING THE WORLD OF BIBLICAL SCHOLARSHIP

This book addresses readers who are interested in critical biblical scholarship but do not necessarily have advanced training in it. I have tried to avoid or explain scholarly terms, spell out background assumptions, and emphasize English-language resources. Many footnotes contain additional explanation, so if you have questions about something and there is a note, check it. I give references in brief author-title-page form (if page numbers are not given, the idea in question is discussed throughout the article or book). You will find full publication information on these sources in the bibliography at the end of the book. Literary biblical study inevitably draws us into conversation about Hebrew words, but I use English letters[4] and provide translation. I hope you will read with a Bible at hand and look up verses if you do not remember what they say. I have based my discussion on the New Revised Standard Version (NRSV, which I cite unless otherwise indicated), although occasionally I will challenge its choice of words.

Too often, books for nonspecialists focus on the "bottom line," presenting conclusions without explaining how they were reached. Here I offer something different. I invite you into a Bible scholar's world, to rummage among minute details and complex arguments for a better understanding of words written far away and long ago. I hope you finish not only with a freshened sense of David's importance and appeal but also with an understanding of the ways in which the Bible has created these portraits.

CHAPTER 2

LOOKING FOR DAVID

This book focuses on the Bible's portraits of David—their artistic techniques and distinctive features—rather than seeking a "historical David" behind the portraits. But my very distinction between the portraits and the man suggests reservations about the Bible's historicity, and readers may well be curious about the relationship of my literary approach to a historical one. In this chapter I will briefly sketch the historical controversies which swirl about David and about the Bible texts through which we know him. I will then discuss my literary approach and its relationship to historical-critical scholarship.

DAVID IN HISTORY

Questions about the historicity of the Bible's David rose initially not from archaeology but from inconsistencies in the biblical materials themselves. I have already mentioned that the Samuel books' version of David's story is generally considered the most realistic: it contains few flashy miracles, many familiar psychological dynamics, and a believably fallible David.

Yet even within the Hebrew text of the Samuel narrative we must grapple with historical questions. Take for example David's famous fight against Goliath (1 S 17). In this chapter Saul does not seem to know who David is (17:55–58), in conflict with the previous claim that David entered court as Saul's personal musician (16:14–23). Furthermore, the verses in which Saul does not know David, along with 17:12–31—which explain how David came to be with Saul at the battlefield—are missing entirely from the ancient Greek translation of the book, as if they were not in that translator's Hebrew text. Verse 54 speaks as if David took the Philistine's head to Jerusalem before he put the armor in his tent, but David did not capture Jerusalem until many years later (2 S 5:6).

A bigger problem rises in connection with 2 S 21:19: "Then there was another battle with the Philistines at Gob; and Elhanan son of Jaare-oregim, the Bethlehemite, killed Goliath the Gittite, the shaft of whose spear was like a weaver's beam." *Who* killed Goliath? Elhanan?

One might square this with 1 S 17 by supposing that there were two Philistine champions named Goliath whose spears were like weaver's beams. But the descriptions in both chapters allude to the spear shaft as a defining characteristic—"yes, *the* Goliath, the one who had a spear like a weaver's beam!" They suggest not that this was a common type of Philistine warrior, but that this one was exceptional, one whom everyone would remember.

Alternatively, one might suppose that Elhanan is another name for David. Although a king might well have both a personal name and a throne name (perhaps this explains the dual names Solomon and Jedidiah in 2 S 12:24–25), we would also have to suppose that David's father (who was not a king) had two names.[1] And why would David's name be given as Elhanan in 2 S 21:19 when it appears in the usual form, David, two verses previously and two verses later? Furthermore, 2 S 21:17 tells us that Elhanan's victory occurred after David quit going out to battle, whereas 1 S 17 presents the Goliath fight as the beginning of David's military career.

A more likely explanation is that we have conflicting reports on who killed Goliath. The first (David kills Goliath) may seem more convincing because it is longer and more detailed. On the other hand, stories have a well-established tendency to gravitate to famous people. If David killed Goliath, it would be unlikely for a writer to attribute the victory to an aide, but one can easily imagine a subordinate's victory drifting into David's legend. A storyteller might have assumed that an anonymous Philistine killed by David must have been *the* Philistine champion Goliath. Whichever explanation we choose, however, at least one of the Goliath-killing reports must be faulty.

A more subtle kind of historical question concerns David's wife Ahinoam (first mentioned in 1 S 25:43). The Bible knows of only one other Ahinoam, and *she* was Saul's wife (1 S 14:50). Are these the same person?[2]

Some, to use Diana Edelman's words, reject the suggestion because it "would require David to have run off with the queen mother while Saul was still on the throne."[3] Yet such an action would account for Saul's persecution of David as well as provide a reasonable antecedent to God's statement (via Nathan), "I gave you [David] your master's house, and your master's wives into your bosom" (2 S 12:8).[4] It would explain why the statement that Saul gave David's wife Michal (1 S 25:44) to someone else follows immediately after the report of David's marriage to Ahinoam (Saul's action is a retaliation). It might also explain why Saul calls his son Jonathan—at precisely the moment of David's final departure—the "son of a perverse, rebellious woman!" (1 S 20:30). It fits with David's pattern of politically advantageous marriages.[5]

Thus several details in the text support the possibility that David's wife Ahinoam was formerly Saul's wife Ahinoam. This understanding runs counter to protests that David was blameless in all his dealings with Saul (for instance, 1 S 19:5; 24:9–15; 2 S 22:24). Yet does the narrator protest too much? In the end, the evidence is suggestive rather than irrefutable, and we have no outside witnesses to settle the argument for us.

These examples (Goliath and Ahinoam) illustrate that even within a single biblical portrait we do not get a consistent, problem-free account. Rather we are left trying to decide which hypothetical reconstruction of events best explains the mixed accounts that have come down to us.[6] Some find a David who only erred once in his life (the Bathsheba/Uriah affair described in 2 S 11). Such interpretations are especially attractive to dogmatic readers who assume identity between Samuel's David and the very positive David in Chronicles. If God is with David, they reason, David must be virtuous. Such a reader is likely to suppose that David *did* kill Goliath himself and that Saul's Ahinoam and David's are different women.

Critical readers have tended to assume that 1 and 2 Samuel present pro-David propaganda, so most take complimentary details with a grain of salt while giving credence to negative points. In a fairly typical example of such analysis, P. Kyle McCarter dismisses the anointing and giant-fighting stories of 1 S 16–17. Noting, however, that younger sons typically made their way by learning professions and entering someone's service, he gives credence to the story in 1 S 16:14–23 that David entered Saul's court as a musician and warrior. After separating from Saul, according to McCarter's read of the biblical evidence, David gathered a refugee gang which "lived on booty taken in raids on various villages and settlements" and "by extortion, offering 'protection' to local landowners in return for goods and favors." David's band later hired out to a Philistine king. David gave plunder from his raids to Judean chiefs (1 S 30:26–31). The support of these chiefs, David's marriage to the widow of a powerful landowner (Abigail, 1 S 25), and the personal army David had built allowed him to become king in Hebron and eventually Jerusalem. Although the success of his son Absalom's revolt shows that "there must have been wide dissatisfaction with David's rule," support from his palace staff and personal army kept him on the throne until his death.[7]

Not all scholars find the stories of 1 and 2 Samuel so believable. Archaeology has come no closer to David's individual life than a single Aramaic inscription, from at least a century after David's presumed lifetime, which mentions a *bytdwd*—possibly, but not necessarily, "the house (*byt*) of David (*dwd*—ancient writing used only consonants, and the letter which we pronounce 'v' was probably then pronounced 'w')." Even if the inscription does refer to a Davidic dynasty (it could mean several other things), it hardly illuminates David as a person.[8]

If archeologists have not found David's personal diaries, could they at least tell us whether biblical tales of David's reign fit the general social, technological, and economic conditions of the tenth century BCE? Considerable discussion has taken place around this question in the last fifteen years, but experts disagree, vehemently, over the answer.

Those who respond "yes" often point to Samuel's picture of a David who gathers influence through alliances, marriages, threats, and bribes. This pattern of power acquisition is typical of "paramount chieftains" in diversified, nonstate societies. James Flanagan has explored this point in detail; he compares David's career to that of Ibn Saud, founder of Saudi Arabia.[9] McCarter's already-discussed reconstruction draws on Flanagan's work. Robert Coote's book *Early Israel*, written for a nonspecialist audience, also uses archaeological and sociological arguments to reconstruct a chieftainlike David from details of the Samuel texts.

Others find the Samuel narrative less compatible with the region's history as archaeologically reconstructed. First, although we do see a change in settlement patterns at about the time we would expect "Israelites" to be moving in, "there is no evidence whatsoever in the material culture that would indicate that these Iron I villagers originated outside Palestine, not even in Transjordan, much less in Egypt or the Sinai."[10] Did "Israel" really exist around 1000 BCE as a twelve-tribe group, religiously and ethnically distinct from surrounding "Canaanites," or is that identity projected backward by later writers? (Compare the way in which modern Americans tend to speak of early colonists coming "to establish a new nation" with "liberty for all." In fact, the different colonies had quite varied purposes, were often suspicious of and at odds with one another, usually excluded dissidents, and certainly had no idea at the outset that they would be incorporated into a single new nation.) The idea that "Israel" only gradually became aware of the identity eventually ascribed to it also explains some features in the Bible itself, such as the widespread opinion that religious practices prior to Jerusalem's fall did not meet Torah standards (note the practices Josiah suppresses in 2 K 23:1–14 and 24–25). Although the present text presents this as willful disregard of God's commands, more likely those commands as we know them hadn't yet been set out.

A second question concerns the existence of a united monarchy embracing the territories of both (northern) Israel and Judah with Jerusalem as its capital around 1000 BCE. One of the more recent books to detail this challenge is Thomas L. Thompson's massive *Early History of the Israelite People*. (Davies presents a similar thesis in more accessible form in *In Search of Ancient Israel*.) After extensive discussion of archaeological evidence, Thompson concludes it likely that Jerusalem became capital of a regional state only during the seventh century (600s BCE)[11]—a far cry from the biblical claim that in the 900s BCE David and Solomon ruled from Jerusalem over not only Judah but the northern Israelite territory and an assortment of vassal states.

Thompson's claims are by no means universally accepted. The debate would be complex enough if it only involved interpretation of the archaeological data, a notoriously tricky business. But people's reactions are further colored by deeply held religious and political commitments. Parties on various sides of the debate may claim that the historical facts are obvious, but the same "facts" are not obvious to everyone.

THE HISTORIES OF DAVID'S PORTRAITS

If we cannot find a historical David or even the united kingdom which he is supposed to have ruled, might we at least say something about the history of the texts that present him?

Twenty years ago a significant consensus seemed to have been reached on this question. Scholars saw David's story in Samuel built around two large blocks: the "History of David's Rise," from 1 S 16:14 to 2 S 5:10 (less a few verses), and the "Succession Narrative," including primarily 2 S 9–20 and 1 K 1–2.[12] These narratives were thought to have been written during or soon after David's lifetime for political propaganda purposes. As late as 1986 a popular college Bible textbook could say of the succession narrative, "Here we have a firsthand historical writing, so vivid and reliable that it must have come from one who was a contemporary of David and probably a member of his court."[13]

These ancient stories, scholars believed, were eventually woven into the "Deuteronomistic History," a much larger story running from Joshua through 2 Kings (excluding Ruth, which the Jewish canon groups with other short stories). Deuteronomy is either the first chapter of or a preexisting prologue to the history. This work, scholars believed, was compiled to show how the principles of Deuteronomy worked themselves out in history. A first edition, late in the monarchy, might have been intended as a warning that Judah must mend its ways. The completed version was exilic, for it knew of the Judean king's release from prison but showed no awareness of an eventual return to the land (2 K 25:27–30).

Some time later, most scholars thought, a new priestly oriented history had been issued in Chronicles and Ezra-Nehemiah (seen as compatible in interest and agenda and often as parts of a single work). Chronicles, the theory went, had used the deuteronomistic history as a source (accounting for significant stretches of duplicated material), but its compilers had also left out important portions including sections that reflected negatively on David. Meanwhile they had added new chapters which credited to David the temple staffing arrangements of their own time.

Scholars make their living (and their reputations) by questioning old ideas and proposing new ones, so perhaps it should not surprise us that these apparent condenses have begun to crumble. Particularly interesting for our study are debates over the intents of various narrative complexes. Rost saw the succession narrative as a justification of Solomon's accession. His student Delekat argued the opposite: "the main points of the story—Bathsheba, the woman of Tekoa, the palace intrigue, Solomon's murders—do not *explain* why the kingship is established in Solomon's hand but on the contrary leave this key fact unexplained, an apparent scandal." According to Delekat, the writer wishes that Absalom had taken Ahithophel's advice and brought David's reign to an early end (2 S 17:1–3). Delekat agrees that the story asserts divine backing for David and his dynasty, but "where the narrator asks about Yahweh's position in regard to David's history, an overall deep-seated grudge of the narrator against Yahweh is unmistakable."[14] Others have questioned whether the succession narrative is political propaganda at all, suggesting for instance that it might have been written as educational material or "serious entertainment."[15]

Similarly contrasting positions have been taken with respect to the larger complex of the deuteronomistic history. Martin Noth, original proponent of the history's unity, thought its author saw no further hope for the Israelite/Judean people but merely documented the reasons for their decline. An equally weighty scholar, Gerhard von Rad, responded that the history does contain hope—centered in God's promises to David. On the Chronicles and Ezra-Nehemiah side, Sara Japhet and H. G. M. Williamson argued that these books were not companion volumes by the same author but that Chronicles and Ezra-Nehemiah disagreed rather pointedly with each other on central issues.[16]

These arguments might be easier to resolve if we remained confident about the dates of the varying complexes of literature, but on that matter, too, new proposals have been advanced and old ones revived. For instance, Gunn points to markers typical of folk/traditional composition in the succession narrative, a strike against its presumed early date. Its "realism" may be a mark of the teller's style and skill rather than proof of closeness to the source. Flanagan questions whether the two incidents which concern Solomon (the murder/adultery story of 2 S 11–12 and the succession drama in 1 K 1–2) were originally part of the sequence at all. Van Seters proposes that the entire Succession Narrative was a late (postexilic) addition to Samuel.[17]

15

A late dating of material in the Samuel books has consequences for Chronicles study. McKenzie has shown that the versions of Samuel and Kings used by the Chronicler probably did not contain everything that our present versions of those books have;[18] in fact, even the ancient Greek translators and the Qumran library knew a Samuel scroll (not yet split into two books) different from today's Hebrew text. Debate continues over just how different the Chronicles source was. Auld pushes the question to its logical limit, portraying Chronicles and Samuel as independent developments of a source document containing *only* the material they have in common. (He presents a tentative reconstruction of this document, in English translation, in Chapters 3 and 5 of *Kings Without Privilege*.) Because the shared material includes the tale of Judah's last rebellion against Babylon and lacks such well-known stories as the battle with Goliath and the Bathsheba/Uriah debacle, he argues that these must have been added after the monarchy's fall. Although Auld's position has not won a widespread following, it reminds us to be cautious in our assumptions about what material the Chronicler did or did not have at hand. Davies' *In Search of Ancient Israel* reviews historical problems and gives a readable, although hypothetical, account of how late-date composition of both the primary history (Genesis through 2 Kings, excluding Ruth) and Chronicles might have taken place.

The book of Psalms presents a rather different set of historical problems. Individual psalms are notoriously hard to date. Most are so stylized that we cannot tell what particular situations, if any, prompted their composition. Psalm 74 describes an attack on the temple, but we don't know what attack and aren't even sure which temple: perhaps a psalm about the fall of a northern sanctuary such as Bethel or Dan has been adapted here for Jerusalem. Psalm 22 might describe an illness, a military attack, persecution by demonic forces, or some other problem. Indeed, psalmic language may be purposely vague in order to widen the range of situations to which each psalm speaks.

Even though individual psalms are difficult to date, we have reason to suspect that David did not write all (or even most) of the psalms which bear his name. Many of them refer to events occurring after David's time. Psalm 51, for instance ("a Psalm of David, when the prophet Nathan came to him, after he had gone in to Bathsheba") pleads, "Do good to Zion in your good pleasure; *rebuild* the walls of Jerusalem" (51:18). Yet the Bible reports no problems with Jerusalem's walls in David's time.[19] Other psalms attributed to David use theological language typical of periods much later than the tenth century.

A further reason for questioning Davidic authorship is the fact that the Greek translation of Psalms (probably done early in the second century BCE) assigns more psalms to David than does the traditional Hebrew text. The

Greek Psalter also gives headings with Davidic "life setting" information to more psalms than the Hebrew book of Psalms does, and it includes an additional psalm (151, found in the apocrypha section of Protestant Bibles) attributed to David after the fight with Goliath. Ancient Syriac and Aramaic translations expand heading statements even further.[20] This suggests that new psalms were still being ascribed to David and to particular occasions in his life almost a thousand years after his death. Although some "of David" psalms may actually come from the tenth century, the Psalter's editors have widened David's role well beyond what most historical scholars find credible.

What about the editorial history of Psalms as a book? Very roughly speaking, older psalms seem to occur toward the front of the Psalter and more recent compositions toward the back. One also sees a shift from individual laments (the prominent psalm type early on) through communal laments to songs of trust and praise, but again the general trend contains many exceptions. Other structural features include clusters of psalms with similar headings (such as "of Asaph" or "A Song of Ascents"), similar themes (such as God's kingship), or distinctive phrases (such as "praise the LORD!"). Blessing/amen formulas in 41:13, 72:18–19, 89:52, and 106:48 divide the Psalter into five "books." Psalms scholar Gerald H. Wilson has pointed out that royal psalms (2, 72, and 89) occur at some key junctures between these books. This and other observations about the Psalter's overall structure will play an important role as we explore the David of Psalms.[21]

THE BIBLE'S DAVID AS A LITERARY FIGURE

Whatever the truth about a historical David and the development of the Bible's writings about him, we can say with confidence that at some point those writings reached the form we have now. In recent decades an increasing number of scholars have been asking, How do these texts work *in their present form*? Rather than treating the Bible as a window through which to discern the historical David (or at least the history of his story), these scholars approach it as if it were a painting or picture—something to look *at* rather than *through*.[22]

For the historical scholar, conflicting information about who killed Goliath signals warping or obstruction in the window. For the literary scholar, varying accounts do not obstruct the view: they *are* the view. The question changes from, Which (if either) account tells what really happened? to, What effect does their joint presence create? Literary criticism offers the tools to attempt an answer.

At first glance one might attribute this interest in final-form literary study to frustration with the uncertainties of historical criticism. Some also see in it, for better or worse, a way to avoid historical challenges to dogmatic interpretation. Although both these elements may be present, interest in literary criticism of biblical texts also arises from the observation that these historical texts are composed of words. Someone has decided what to tell and how to tell it, and we do well to attend to the nuances of their choices.

Let's look at an example, the first verse of 2 S 11: "In the spring of the year, the time when kings go out to battle, David sent Joab with his officers and all Israel with him; they ravaged the Ammonites, and besieged Rabbah [the capital city of Ammon]. But David remained at Jerusalem." The chapter continues with the adultery/murder story of David, Bathsheba, and Uriah.

Let us suppose, for the sake of argument, that the factual assertions of 2 S 11:1 are correct—that spring was the traditional season for military campaigns, that the army under Joab did attack Ammon and besiege Rabbah, and that David meanwhile remained in Jerusalem. What role does this information play when given at this point and in this way? Well, asks biblical literary critic Meir Sternberg, what do kings do in the spring? Go out to battle. What are David's general and his officers and "all Israel" doing? Battling the Ammonites and besieging Rabbah. Where is Israel's king? Sitting in Jerusalem! He may be enthroned, but he is not behaving as either a king or a member of "all Israel." This opening verse, so often overlooked by interpreters eager to get to the scandal, foreshadows the problem of a king misusing his privilege.[23]

A literary approach to the Bible thus does not require (although it may accompany) a negative judgment about the Bible's factual reliability. What it does require is careful attention to the given text. We may not dismiss odd phrases or unexpected statements with a cavalier "what they really meant to ·say was . . ." as if the problematic words are mere blots obscuring our otherwise clear view through a window. Rather we assume that what we have is what the author meant to say; it's our job to make sense of it. We may still occasionally conclude that a text is garbled (for instance, when the Hebrew text of 1 S 13:1 tells us that "Saul was one year old when he reigned, and he reigned two years over Israel"[24]), but not before we have given it all the benefit of the doubt.

Careful attention to the Bible's words is of course not new. Centuries of dogmatic interpreters—both Jewish and Christian—have worked carefully with the final form of the text. Historical-critical scholars have also paid close attention to exact phrasings. Indeed, inquiry into the Bible's compositional history was long called "literary criticism" because of its attention to plot structure, characterization, and prose style. Today's literary critic can therefore garner important insights from both the dogmatic and historical-critical interpretive traditions. However, the literary critic differs from the historical-critical scholar in asking how various features function in the final text rather than what they may tell us about its history, and she tends to be more open to textual disunity and unorthodoxy than is the dogmatic interpreter.

The differences between literary-critical and dogmatic readings emerge most sharply with respect to God, who is almost always assumed by dogmatic readers to be omnipotent, omniscient, and good. Such a reader, encountering language that suggests limitations on God's part, usually classifies it as poetic or figurative. A literary critic asks, What kind of character does this text portray God as? and, in theory, answers on the text's own terms, whether or not the critic likes or personally endorses them. I have done this for the books of Samuel in "The Problematic God of Samuel." Jack Miles's book *God: A Biography*, which shows God gradually learning to come to terms with humanity and then withdrawing, also exemplifies such an approach. On the other hand, Meir Sternberg, another final-form literary analyst, retains the assumption of divine omnipotence.[25]

The general category of literary criticism covers a variety of more specific approaches.[26] Some focus on broad conceptual dynamics in the text, often drawing on models from anthropology, psychology, and folklore studies. Psychologically oriented critics use the terminology of their own favorite theorists to describe biblical characters and relationships. Some critics look for "deep structure," "oppositions," and "transformations," taking special interest in the text's handling of concepts such as life/death, male/female, and insider/outsider.

Other literary critics focus more on precise details of wording (vocabulary choice, order of words in sentences, and patterns of individual sounds). Such analysts may describe their work as close reading, rhetorical criticism, or composition analysis. They have helped us to see beyond traditional Western dismissals of the Bible's literary style as "primitive" and "unimaginative" and to appreciate the artistry of biblical writers, who may now be praised as the equals of Shakespeare.[27]

I have found composition analysis an especially fruitful approach to biblical texts. Robert Alter's *Art of Biblical Narrative* provides a good introduction to it; Berlin's *Poetics and Interpretation of Biblical Narrative*, Bar-Efrat's *Narrative Art in the Bible*, and more recently Gunn and Fewell's *Narrative in the Hebrew Bible* are also helpful in orienting to the field. The Samuel books have been favorites for such analysis. Sternberg, Fokkelman, and Polzin have taught me a great deal through their work, as has Walter Brueggemann. David Gunn, David Clines, Lyle Eslinger, Peter Miscall, and Danna Nolan Fewell have been even more helpful as they question traditional interpretive assumptions about Saul, the prophet Samuel, David, and especially God.[28]

19

Chronicles and Psalms have received less attention from specifically literary interpreters (although some studies, such as Duke's *Persuasive Appeal of the Chronicler*, do exist). Fortunately, some of the historical-critical interpreters of these books show great literary sensitivity. H. G. M. Williamson, Sara Japhet, and to a lesser extent Roddy Braun have profoundly influenced my understanding of Chronicles. I do not entirely agree with Eaton's work on royal psalms, but it and Gerald Wilson's studies on the final shape of the Psalter were wonderfully helpful in developing an approach to David in the book of Psalms. I also found the individual psalm discussions by Craigie, Allen, and Tate in the Word Biblical Commentary volumes on Psalms to be highly compatible with my methods. The bibliography cites many additional scholars who have contributed to my understanding.

To follow discussions which deal intimately with the Hebrew text, non-Hebrew readers need translation which proceeds word-by-word, rather than thought-by-thought, and which maintains a consistent relationship between Hebrew words and English renderings. For instance, translators usually render the verb *hištaḥweh* as "worship" if the object is God (for instance, 1 S 1:3) but "bow down" if the object is a king (for instance, 1 S 25:41). A non-Hebrew reader receives no clue that these terms actually translate the same word. This obscures a possible concern that "bowing down" (*hištaḥweh*) to a king might violate the commandment to "worship" (*hištaḥweh*) God alone.[29] I will supply the reader with word-by-word translations at appropriate points.[30] When exact details of Hebrew wording are not at issue, I will simply quote the NRSV translation.

Application of literary criticism to biblical texts has profited from current developments in literary criticism. Whereas earlier generations tended to celebrate unity as a primary virtue of artistic works and sometimes spoke of literature as a rarefied phenomenon above politics and religion, many of today's literary critics work from "poststructuralist" or "postmodern" standpoints that emphasize—on the one hand—the consciousness-shaping, social/ideological functions of language and—on the other—its cracks, disunities, and continuing processes of disruption and transformation. The former aspect sensitizes us to the interests and values promoted (openly or covertly) by the writing. It provides a helpful corrective to our tendency to assume that the text promotes the same values as later religious traditions which call upon it. For instance, many supposedly critical scholars interpret the reports of Saul's and Ahithophel's deaths (1 S 31:4 and 2 S 17:23) as negative because (they say) Hebrew people regarded suicide with horror. But no support is offered for this assertion; in fact, the Hebrew Bible has practically nothing to say on the subject. The assumption is an unexamined remnant of the dogmatic heritage in biblical studies. In its place we need a thoughtful examination of tone: just how do the narrators feel about these deaths?

The other side of postmodernism—its attention to disunity—also suits the qualities of biblical text. Our David stories were not all written by a single person at a single time with a single purpose, and even sections traditionally ascribed to a single source (such as the succession narrative) can often be read in contradictory directions (either pro or con David).[31] In Psalms we will encounter multiple voices speaking through a single set of poetic lines. Postmodern approaches, which see disunity as a normal condition, are well suited to exploring the dynamics of such multivoiced writing.

A special word is in order here about intertextuality. Because we discern the meaning of words from how they are used, no single text can stand alone; its word meanings depend on prior usage in other places. Intertextuality describes this cumulative quality, especially within literary traditions. When one work quotes another, the quotation acquires two meanings: its meaning from the original work and the one given by the newer context. Thus God's self-description to Moses, "a God merciful and gracious, slow to anger, and abounding in steadfast love" (Ex 34:6), takes on different accents when Jonah cites it as a reason for running from God (Jon 4:2). Intertextual echoes will be of importance to us in several arenas: links between Samuel and other portions of the primary history (Genesis–2 Kings), citations shared by Chronicles and the primary history, references in Psalms to other portions of the Bible and, finally, psalmic use of material from the more general sphere of ancient Near Eastern religion and royal ritual.

In addition to intertextually established multiple meanings, we will encounter sentences with meanings at different levels within their own stories. "As the LORD lives, not one hair of your son shall fall to the ground," David tells the wise woman from Tekoa (2 S 14:11). He believes his promise concerns her fratricidal child (one level of meaning). He will shortly be called to apply it to his own son Absalom (second level of meaning). Yet for Absalom, hair not touching the ground will mean death with his head caught in a tree (third level of meaning).

Multiple meanings create a special problem when meanings ironically oppose one another. Consider God's promise with respect to David's heir that "I will not take my steadfast love from him, as I took it from Saul, whom I put away from before you" (2 S 7:15)—a promise that may well be quoted from ancient royal traditions. Is it reverently quoted as reassurance of God's ultimate support for David's line? Or does the narrator mock reliance on supposedly eternal promises from God (a possibility supported by the reference to God's turn against Saul)?

21

Mikhail Bakhtin, a Russian literary critic who studied the development of multivoiced literature from ancient to modern times, observes that sometimes we simply can't know which way the irony cuts. The possibility of inversion (interpreting reverential words as ironic or vice versa) is always present. However, Bakhtin suggests, "There is no crude violation of the author's will. . . . Such conditions [of inversion] merely actualize in an image a potential already available to it."[32] We may misjudge the balance, but the tension itself is real. Shifts between reverence and irony may already have occurred during the period of the text's formation. The worst misreading, according to Bakhtin, is not an inversion but failure to hear the dual voices in an image, squashing a complex multidimensional structure of meaning into a flat one.

Some literary critics emphasize ancient historical context in their interpretation, whereas others make little reference to particularities of time and place. An example of the former is Robert Polzin, who interprets Nathan's confrontation with David after Uriah's death (2 S 12) in context of the history which runs from Deuteronomy through 2 Kings. He notes that the ewe-lamb parable (2 S 12:1–4) refers to three different characters as "the man." Nathan's "you are the man!" (12:7) does not specify *which* man David is. Polzin believes that the ensuing oracle compares David to all three. "The scope of Nathan's parable embraces the entire career of David and the history of his house, not just the immediate situation. . . . David *was* the wayfarer, 'the one who comes,' insofar as his past dealings with God are concerned (12:7–8); he *is* the rich man when his present crimes are brought into the picture (12:9–10); and he *will be* the poor man when God's punishing future for him and his house arrives (12:11–12)."[33]

Polzin then adds a third layer to the parable—an interpretation of Israel's history in light of Jerusalem's fall. Israel (as wayfarer) receives Canaan (lamb), which God (the rich man) has taken from the Canaanites (poor man). But then Israel (as rich man) refuses to use its own traditions (flocks and herds) and instead takes the institution of kingship (lamb) from the Canaanites (poor man). In response, God (rich man) takes the land (lamb) from Israel (poor man) and gives it to "the one who comes," first Assyria and then Babylon.[34] Polzin supports his proposal by pointing to a network of thematic and verbal ties between the parable and other parts of the larger history.

We may contrast Polzin's interpretation of the parable with that offered by J. P. Fokkelman. Fokkelman notes that the parable "grabs" David because he would rather locate himself with the poor man than the rich: "David is a good listener who puts his heart into the matter, gets very involved, and feels pity. In this fashion Nathan mobilizes the good forces in David." He then moves, as Polzin did, from the parable's significance for David to its significance for the reader. "On this level, the city where the neighbours live is the soul, David's life and our life. Everyone has the choice to live either as the poor man or as the rich man and to change his course at any moment."[35]

Fokkelman's interpretive methods are no less rigorous than Polzin's; he attends in excruciating detail to patterns of word and sound and cross-connections between related texts. Like Polzin, he offers specific, publicly accessible arguments to undergird his interpretation, including its relation to themes running through the larger body of literature in which the parable is embedded. But Fokkelman interprets in terms of universal human psychodynamics, whereas Polzin thinks of specific concerns about the meaning of Judah's history.

We can see by now that different literary approaches may bring out different meanings in a given text. This does not mean that only one is "right," for we may have multiple "right" insights about a given work. David's response in 2 S 12 may show realistic psychodynamics, while the chapter also provides a complex metaphor for Judah's history. Tolerance for multiple readings gives literary criticism an artistic as well as critical aspect (with reference to Chapter 1's dogmatic/critical/artistic framework). It does not, however, make every opinion "right." We still have room to assess how well each interpretation fits the text.

At this point, historical uncertainties come back to haunt us, for literary analyses and their assessments involve assumptions about historical context. In biblical studies, this quickly becomes a circular process: we know the history from the text, then date the text in terms of that history, then further characterize the history on the basis of the texts dated to it.[36]

In theory, my proposal to discuss the David portraits as they appear in the finished Hebrew Bible (with corrections of a few copying mistakes which seem to have accumulated over the centuries) could mean accepting a Roman date for the whole complex, dating it to the time when the entire collection seems to have been finished and its boundaries determined. However, it seems to me that the form of the final collection, which presents portraits of David in three separate books (Samuel and Chronicles—each of which was originally a single scroll—and Psalms) in two separate divisions of the Hebrew canon (Samuel in the Prophets, Chronicles and Psalms in the Writings), invites us to consider them separately as well as together.

I further consider the Chronicles and Samuel portraits *literarily* connected to the books of Ezra-Nehemiah and the deuteronomistic history, respectively. Samuel is also connected, more loosely, to the Torah—the first five books of the Bible. These links are established by juxtaposition in the final form of the Hebrew canon but also and more importantly by narrative continuity and intertextual echoes of vocabulary and theme. Note well: These are the same features on which historical-critical interpreters have based their arguments for close relationship or even identity between the producers of Ezra-Nehemiah and Chronicles and from which they have argued that the deuteronomistic history should be considered a unified work. I owe a heavy debt to those historical scholars for their keen observations, and at first glance it may look like I am simply accepting their results. However, I am working with the connections as a *literary* feature rather than claiming them as a *historical* feature. Whether or not the deuteronomistic history was produced from fragments as the unified document of which we felt so confident fifteen years ago, the links which gave rise to that hypothesis continue to require literary attention.

One may further observe that the literary matrices of our three major David portraits each suggest a horizon for interpretation. Psalms and the Ezra-Nehemiah/Chronicles complex explicitly draw our attention to the life of the Second Temple community, thus inviting us to interpret David as part of that community's history. The books of Samuel, however, contain little to make us look beyond David's own lifetime—which partially accounts for the tendency to understand them as eyewitness accounts—although an occasional phrase such as "formerly" or "in earlier times" (1 S 9:9; 2 S 13:18) suggests distance between the story and the events it narrates. Samuel's context—the great history running from Genesis through 2 Kings—only hints at anything beyond the deportation of Judean leaders to Babylon in the sixth century BCE.

Many historical-critical scholars have dated this "Primary History" to exile and Psalms and Chronicles to the Persian period on the basis of these horizons. However, these literary complexes may have reached their present form substantially later than the latest events they mention. When I use these horizons in interpretation, I do so as a response to the reading cues offered in the texts, not as a claim about compositional dates.

It may seem that in accepting historical horizons suggested by the literature I have succeeded in sidestepping the problem of actual historical setting. Unfortunately, such sidestepping can lead to serious misjudgments about literary tone. For instance, references to "the War to end all wars" in the war's own time might have a determined and hopeful tone, but to refer to World War I in this way now, in light of the subsequent wars of the twentieth century, has a sad or cynical ring. Thus I do not think we can escape historical questions entirely. In discussing Chronicles, and later in my final summary, I will raise some issues connected with probable circumstances of composition.

When we have differing portraits of a character, the order in which we study them makes a difference, for we tend to accept the first as our reference point and judge others in terms of variance from it. One might make a case from the composition-history picture sketched earlier in this chapter for beginning with Chronicles as the default picture of David—because it resembles a hypothesized common source more than Samuel does—or with Psalms, on the principle that liturgy precedes systematized historical accounts. In both the Jewish and Christian canons, however, the Samuel portrait takes precedence by virtue of its position in the massive foundation narrative which begins both collections. (This may in fact have influenced our tendency to date it earlier than Chronicles.) I will follow this canonical lead and deal first with Samuel, next with Chronicles, and third with Psalms, which presents a complex picture related to both Samuel and Chronicles.

Having dealt with the major David portraits independently, I will ask in the final chapter about the implications of their juxtaposition—to one another and to scattered references elsewhere in the Hebrew canon. At that point we will revisit the question of Samuel's priority and raise some additional questions about its life in historical context.

PART 2

THE POWER OF KINGS AND GOD
David in the Primary History

CHAPTER 3

SAMUEL'S DAVID: PRELUDE

The books of Samuel and Kings present David not simply as a human individual, but as the founder of a nation's government and its religious traditions. The meanings of David's kingship derive in part from the preceding story of Israel's journey toward monarchy, especially as developed in the books of Deuteronomy through the beginning of 1 Samuel. We now survey that story as a prelude to our discussion of Samuel's David.

If you have not recently read the books of Samuel, it will be helpful to do so at this point (read also the first two chapters of 1 Kings). Remember that we will deal with the story as written, not with events as reconstructed by historical critics. For instance, in the story Moses preaches Deuteronomy to the people before their entry into the land. We will accordingly consider him to have done so, although historically speaking Deuteronomy seems to have been written hundreds of years after the period talked about in the book. Remember also that when I make statements about God in this discussion (for instance, "in 1 S 16 God tries to shift the blame") the statements concern God as a literary character in the passages at hand, not my own beliefs about God or what may be said about God in other parts of the Bible.

"OUT OF THE HOUSE OF SLAVERY"

The primary history defines God above all as the one who liberated Israel from Egypt (the exodus) and guided the people through the wilderness. God introduces the Ten Commandments, for instance, by saying, "I am the LORD your God, who brought you out of the land of Egypt, out of the house of slavery" (Dt 5:6). Although the deliverance and giving of land fulfill promises reported in Genesis, those promises receive surprisingly little attention in the subsequent narrative. The history mentions Abraham's name only four times in the six books relating events after the wilderness period (Joshua through 2 Kings).

The exodus archetypally demonstrates God's power vis-à-vis all other claimants, be they putative gods or human powers. "Has any god ever attempted to go and take a nation for himself from the midst of another nation, by trials, by signs and wonders, by war, by a mighty hand and an outstretched arm, and by terrifying displays of power, as the LORD[1] your God did for you in Egypt before your very eyes?" (Dt 4:34). So long as God chooses to defend Israel, no other nation can harm it.

The exodus story not only tells who God is but also defines Israel's relationship to God. Having been delivered from service to Pharaoh, the Israelites must never again serve anyone but this God. They must not worship other gods. They must not fear other nations nor submit to them. And they must not credit their good fortune to their own strength or virtue. "Do not say to yourself," Moses warns in Dt 8:17, " 'My power and the might of my own hand have gotten me this wealth.' "

At some points, especially when speaking of past history, the story presents God's love for Israel as sheer unmerited favor. At other points, especially when speaking of how the people should behave in the present and future, it emphasizes that God will reward obedience and punish disobedience. Often God's attitude seems somewhere between these extremes.

PROPHETS, ELDERS, AND JUDGES

Israel's service to God clearly excludes service to foreign gods and kings. Does worship of God leave room for human leaders within Israel? What might the acceptable parameters of such leadership be?

Initially of course we have Moses, God's chosen agent. Yet even Moses has his limits, and in the end he is not allowed to enter Canaan. Before he dies, he promises the people that their special relationship with God will result in blessing—*if* their society is just and *if* they remain faithful to God. This speech takes up most of the book of Deuteronomy. In Joshua and Judges, the tribes, with God's aid, invade and settle Canaan. But repeatedly they stray after their neighbors' gods. In response God sends foreigners to oppress Israel. When the people cry out, God appoints a deliverer—a judge—to quell the foreign oppression. When the judge dies, trouble begins all over again.

The Israelites also oppress one another, often under the leadership of the very judges who deliver them from foreigners (for instance, in Jdg 12:4–6 Gideon arranges the slaughter of forty-two thousand people from the Israelite tribe of Ephraim). By the end of the book of Judges, the phrase "there was no king in Israel" (Jdg 21:25) describes a distinctly problematic situation.

JUDGE VERSUS KING

What is the difference between one of these judges and a king? Because the story lays such stress on God's appointment of judges, people sometimes jump to the conclusion that a judge is divinely appointed, whereas a king is humanly chosen. This is not correct. According to Samuel and Kings, God personally designates Saul, David, David's line, and even rulers for the breakaway north. Both judges and royal dynasties are divinely selected.

Others think of judges as democratically chosen leaders and kings as totalitarian rulers. This understanding is especially common in the United States, where people have been taught to see monarchy in a very negative light. But judgeship, being neither democratic nor national, is not a democratic form of national government. The narrator tells us that God chooses the judges. Stories show them building factional alliances (sometimes against other Israelite factions!) and seldom exercising more than regional authority. There is a significant gulf between this pattern and modern democratic ideals.

The key difference between a judge and a king seems to be that a judge's authority is personal, built upon a shifting structure of connections, favors, and alliances, cemented by divine charisma. It is also ad hoc, usually born out of some special need. A king's authority, on the other hand, is institutionalized, backed by administrative structures for taxing, conscription, and enforcement. This is why kings have capital cities; they need to headquarter their bureaucracies. The narrative shows Saul and David developing support networks in judgelike fashion, but, according to the Bible, each—especially David—finally consolidates power in a manner that earns the title"king." A handy rule of thumb is this: "judgeship" must be established anew in each generation. "Kingship" is sufficiently regularized that it can be bequeathed to an heir or seized in a coup. Kingship thus offers greater stability and continuity—and is, by the same token, more difficult to control or overturn.

KINGS AND PROPHETS

Deuteronomy anticipates that when the people have settled in Canaan they will want to have a king "like all the nations that are around" (Dt 17:14). God permits this (Dt 17:14–20), provided that (1) the king is not a foreigner; (2) he bridle his desires for horses, wives, and money; and (3) he study and observe Moses' teaching. The king is apparently to be chosen by both God (17:15a) and the people (17:16b), a requirement met by both Saul and David.

An early experiment with kingship in Shechem (Jdg 9) turns out disastrously for all concerned. Yet the stories in Judges reveal increasing problems with nonmonarchic leadership. Monarchy becomes a central theme in Samuel, introduced somewhat unexpectedly at the climax of Hannah's celebratory song in 1 S 2:

The LORD will judge the ends of the earth;
he will give strength to his king,
and exalt the power of his anointed.

(1 S 2:10)

This seems a very positive presentation, especially because the preceding themes of God's warfare and uplifting the humble are already familiar from exodus poetry. The poem's parallelism equates the king's strength with God's own judging of the earth, suggesting that the anointed is a legitimate embodiment of God's governance.

But Polzin suggests that Hannah's story embodies a parable.[2] Her desire for sons, he says, expresses Israel's desire for kings. Her husband Elkanah expresses God's wistful reaction to Israel's discontent: "Why is your heart sad? Am I not more to you than ten sons?" (1:8). If Polzin is correct, we must take Hannah's celebration with a grain of salt. Perhaps Hannah/Israel should be more careful what she prays for.

Although hereditary kingship has not been established in the early chapters of Samuel, there is a hereditary priesthood, which provides context for some dark brooding on questions of leadership and succession. Eli's sons Hophni and Phinehas abuse their privileges. God harshly rejects them, along with their father (who tried to correct his sons, but they would not listen because God had already condemned them, 1 S 2:25). " 'I promised that your family and the family of your ancestor should go in and out before me forever'; but now the LORD declares: 'Far be it from me' " (1 S 2:30). Instead, God says, "I will raise up for myself a faithful priest, who . . . shall go in and out before my anointed one forever" (2:35).

Three items of importance lurk here. First, we see the importance of ensuring that heirs merit the offices they inherit. Second, we see that even a "promise . . . forever" can be broken. Third, like Hannah's song, the oracle looks forward to a new era associated with an "anointed one" (messiah). (Christians tend to think that messiah means Jesus, but "messiah" is simply a spelling-out of the Hebrew word *māšîaḥ*—"anointed one"—and in the passages we will study it usually refers to an ordinary human king.) Hannah's song associated the messiah with God's judgment/rule of the earth. Now we hear of a faithful priesthood serving under the messiah.

Like most biblical prophecies, God's promise of a faithful priest can be applied in several ways. At this point in the story, it seems fulfilled in Hannah's child, Eli's apprentice, Samuel. (Later it will be applied to Abiathar's displacement by Zadok in 1 K 2:27, 35; much later in biblical tradition it prompts hope for a "messianic" priest to accompany the "messianic" king.) Samuel's words and deeds play an important role in the establishment of Israelite monarchy. But in order to evaluate them correctly, we need to take a hard look at Samuel's own position. We will find that we cannot simply equate Samuel's opinions with God's.

Samuel is a prophet, to be sure. He is also a human person—and a flawed one, at that. Hannah's delay in fulfilling her vow about him (1 S 1:22) may already be a hint that Samuel's story is not an idealized example of service to God. With respect to the next major episode in the temple at Shiloh (1 S 3), pro-Samuel commentators have said that Eli is spiritually as well as physically blind; they contrast his blindness with Samuel's youthful virtue. But Samuel does not recognize God's voice; it is old Eli, rejected and blind though he may be, who identifies the caller and gives instructions for reply. Perhaps Samuel does not even believe Eli's identification, for he answers the next call with a simple "speak," rather than "speak, LORD," as Eli had instructed (3:9–10).

Samuel learns, however. "As Samuel grew up," the narrator tells us, "the LORD was with him and let none of his words fall to the ground. And all Israel . . . knew that Samuel was a trustworthy prophet of the LORD" (1 S 3:19–20). The term "trustworthy" (*ne'ĕman*) increases our suspicion that Samuel is the "faithful" (same Hebrew word, *ne'ĕman*) priest promised earlier. We must be careful, however. Is a *ne'ĕman* prophet the same as a *ne'ĕman* priest?[3] We should also notice that *ne'ĕman* is Israel's opinion of Samuel, not necessarily the narrator's, although the report that "the LORD was with him" seems to support Israel's opinion.

In 1 S 4–6, Israel's defeats—read against the thesis of God's power to save—suggest that all is still not well. Even the ark's homecoming makes trouble in Israel (1 S 6:19). Two decades lapse (!) before the people, in response to a call from Samuel (why did he wait so long?), "put away the Baals and the Astartes" (Canaanite deities) and confess sin (1 S 7). When the Philistines muster again, Samuel intercedes and God routs the Philistines.

The closing paragraphs of 1 S 7 mark the end of an era for Israel. Once more the cycle of judgeship has turned: oppression, outcry, deliverance, and now peace under Samuel's leadership, which is described three times by the Hebrew verb *špṭ*[4] (7:15–17). NRSV translates this as "judged" (7:15–16) and "administered justice" (7:17). This translation links Samuel to the heroes of Judges and also suggests that the demand for a "just" society was met by

Samuel's leadership. However, the word also means "govern" (and is so translated in 8:5). Samuel governed Israel. We need that information to make sense of the subsequent chapter.

Given the rule of thumb that judgeship must be negotiated anew in each generation, although kingship can be bequeathed to an heir, it surprises us to see Samuel appoint his sons Joel and Abijah as judges/governors (the *špṭ* word family again). (How ironic that Samuel, who will soon oppose kingship so forcefully, has himself attempted to introduce dynastic governance![5]) But Samuel has the same problem as had Eli: "His sons did not follow in his ways, but turned aside after gain; they took bribes and perverted justice" (1 S 8:3). Their *špṭ* is corrupt.

Eli had been disowned for his sons' corruption, even though he tried to correct his sons in 1 S 2:23–25. No such attempts at correction are recorded for Samuel, but he suffers no curse. What accounts for this inconsistency in divine standards? It forms part of a recurring pattern in which God legislates, severely punishes disobedience, and then—perhaps realizing that more has been asked than fallible humans will deliver—softens expectations. A good example of this pattern occurs in Joshua, where booty taking is forbidden (6:17–19). Achan transgresses (7:1) and is executed along with his family (7:19–26), after which the rules concerning booty are relaxed (8:2). This pattern should be kept in mind as we ponder God's rejection of Saul and David's subsequent rise to power (with forbidden/permitted booty among the stakes).

Israel's elders do not want to be ruled by Samuel's corrupt sons; Eslinger suggests that they fear being punished by God for the sons' misdeeds.[6] The elders appeal instead for a king (1 S 8:4). Preachers and commentators often regard the desire to be "like other nations" (8:5) as self-evidently sinful, but such an evaluation errs on two points. It ignores the stated premise of the elder's request; Samuel is old and his sons are corrupt! Further, Miscall reminds us, Dt 17:14 regarded a king "like all the nations" as an appropriate next step for a people taking their place among those nations.[7]

Commentators typically allege that Samuel is displeased because the nation is rejecting God. In fact, the narrator does not explain Samuel's displeasure, but juxtaposition with 7:15–8:2 suggests pique at his family's loss of influence. As Gunn points out, God's response assumes that this is Samuel's objection: "They have not rejected you" (1 S 8:7).[8] God—not Samuel—introduces theological considerations:

> "They have not rejected you, but they have rejected me from being king over them. Just as they have done to me, from the day I brought them up out of Egypt to this day, forsaking me and serving other gods, so also they are doing to you." (1 S 8:7–8)[9]

Yet God opens and closes this speech by telling Samuel to "listen to the voice of" the people, which is the biblical Hebrew way of telling Samuel to obey them (in 1 S 15:19, 20, 22, 24, NRSV translates the same expression with "obey"). What are the tone and intent of God's words? Is God terribly upset at being rejected by the people? Or does God allude to their fickleness primarily in order to console Samuel—"Welcome to the club, Sam"?

Miscall argues that the speech focuses on consolation for Samuel. He suggests that God's talk of rejection "does not refer specifically to the people's demand for a king but rather to their consistent abandonment . . . from the time of the exodus."[10] This removes an apparent contradiction between God's statement that "they have rejected me from being king" and God's order to provide a king for them. God, who has been patient and loyal to Israel even when rejected, recommends similar patience and loyalty to Samuel.

Polzin (like most people) does relate God's statement that "they have rejected me from being king" directly to the people's request for a human king. But like Miscall he finds God's attitude "disinterested and remarkably magnanimous." The conversation shows "a God who reveals his love in spite of being rejected, in contrast to a judge who fails to conceal his selfish reluctance to become the maker of kings."[11]

Fokkelman hesitates over the interpretation of God's words (noting the deuteronomistic history's reticence about referring to God as "king") but does conclude that God "is specific about the request for a king being apostate." He hears a note of discord in God's tone: "Samuel is advised to brace himself and to be sure not to feel under personal attack. But these words of consolation and support come from a character who does not take his own advice." Given this assessment of God's attitude, the order to appoint a king is "an astonishing turn" in the conversation.[12]

All these interpretations see the king as in some sense a favor granted to Israel. Others hear an offended God snarl, "give them a king then, if that's what they want!" In this reading, God brushes off Samuel's own distress: "what are *you* upset about? Look what they've done to *me!*" Petulant anger dominates God's tone, and God gives the people a king as punishment rather than indulgence. Gunn proposes an ironic tone: "Make them a king—and let us see what we shall see!" Polzin suggests that God is "reluctantly pedagogic." Eslinger comes at the question from a slightly different angle. In his view, the people want to be free of theocratic government, but God intends for the proposed monarch to remain accountable to God: "Yahweh tries to appease them by giving them a king, but not such as they desired."[13]

On occasion I meet people who are offended to hear a biblical text read "with expression," especially if the expression is playful or sarcastic. They fail to consider that reading in a ponderous monotone is also an interpretive

35

choice that may seriously distort the meaning of some passages (see for example Amos 4:4). Augustine counseled long ago that "the first thing to consider is whether we have punctuated the passage wrongly or mispronounced it in some way."[14] Our discussion of 1 S 8:7–9 shows why decisions about the text's "tone of voice" are not an optional literary exercise but a crucial step in understanding.

Unfortunately (with respect to our longing for certainty), all of the possibilities described are credible. Readers make tentative decisions based upon their overall evaluations of God's character especially as developed in Samuel, but if God changes and learns in the course of the story—which I believe to be the case—then God's attitude in other passages is not entirely decisive for the one in question. We noted above that as early as Dt 17 provision has been made for a king, and we will see that even the relationship with Saul has some bright spots at the outset (1 S 9:16–17 and 11:4–11). This makes me doubtful about the harshest "king as punishment" readings. But Miscall's assertion that "the Lord gives no evaluation of the request" also seems questionable, in light of God's statement that "they have rejected me from being king." The teeter-totter of meaning is delicately balanced. This may be a good place to invoke Bakhtin's dictum that choosing the "right" option may be less crucial than recognizing the existence of multiple options.[15]

In any case, God does order a disgruntled Samuel—thrice over—to obey the people (8:7, 9, 22). Along with this, Samuel is to "solemnly warn" them about the "ways of the king"—a phrase which could also be translated "the justice of the king" or "the law of the king." (These variations involve a derivative of the verb *špṭ*—to—to judge/govern. NRSV renders the same word as "rights and duties" in 1 S 10:25.) One would expect Samuel to respond with something like Dt 17:14–19. Instead he delivers a noticeably one-sided tirade. He does not mention the king's service in governing. He also does not say that having a king is sinful. He does suggest, repeatedly, that a king's characteristic activity is to "take."

"Samuel is being portrayed here," Polzin remarks, "as trying to delay or subvert the LORD's command even as he wants to appear fulfilling that command. . . . His motivation is clearly self-interested."[16] The upshot: Samuel does not obey the elders (as God commanded), but first tries to dissuade them and then simply sends them home (8:22). The people are quite justified when they refuse to obey ("listen to the voice of . . ." 8:19) this disobedient prophet. The surprise is that God tolerates Samuel so patiently.

Because Samuel dallies in seeking out and anointing a king, God sends the king to Samuel (1 S 9). Some interpreters make a great deal of the fact that 1 S 9 uses the term *nāgîd* (prince or ruler) rather than *melek* (king). They conclude that it is all right to have a human prince, but only God may be king.

Others point out that *nāgîd* is used in Samuel and Kings for persons who have been chosen but not yet assumed office (for instance, 1 S 10:1) or when emphasizing to a reigning king that his authority derives from divine designation (for instance, 2 S 7:8).[17] If it points specifically to the designation of a king, whether or not he has actually been installed in office, then speaking of a divinely approved *nāgîd* ("prince") does not mean that God opposes the office of *melek* ("king").

There has also been a great deal of discussion about Saul's personal merits or lack thereof. We will return to this issue in Chapters 5 and 6. For now, suffice it to say that God clearly supports Saul's ascent to office. Samuel's role is (as we might by now expect) less clear. He tells Saul, "do whatever you see fit to do, for God is with you" (1 S 10:7), but still expects Saul to take orders from him (10:8).

Saul's reign gets off to a glorious start when, in a manner strikingly like that of the old judges, he delivers the citizens of a besieged city. Samuel takes the victory celebration as occasion for a farewell speech which drips with indignation (1 S 12). "Whom have I wronged?" he asks. The people refrain from reminding him about his appointment of corrupt sons to judgeship. Samuel then reviews Israel's history from the exodus onward. This time he does stress that God is the people's proper king (12:12). But the same verse shows that Samuel's perception is skewed: the people had asked for a king and received Saul (1 S 8 and 10:17–24) *before* the incident with Nahash in 1 S 10:27–11:11.

Samuel eventually concedes a possible legitimacy to kingship, but in a manner that stresses his own power. He calls upon God for a thunderstorm. God obliges. A terror-stricken crowd pleads, "Pray to the LORD your God for your servants, so that we may not die" (12:19). Samuel assures them that they may depend (!) upon his intercession.

Note the relational dynamics. Overtly Samuel asks that both people and king cleave to God. But his rhetoric and demonstration create a cleavage *between* people/king (on the one hand) and Samuel/God (on the other). "Pray to the LORD *your* God," they say to him, going on to describe themselves as "*your* servants" (12:19, emphasis added) rather than God's! Samuel unhesitatingly seizes upon the power they thus offer him: "I will instruct you in the good and the right way" (12:23).

Why does God underwrite Samuel's manipulations? The conventional answer assumes that God is fair and that a prophet's speech always faithfully represents God. Samuel's position is then justified: he *does* stand beside God—over against the people and their king—and he *is* uniquely qualified to instruct them, therefore they *should* fear and obey him, granting him authority to mediate between themselves and God. (This explanation comes especially from people holding church offices they consider equivalent to Samuel's.)

But we know that Samuel and God do not always see eye-to-eye: we saw it from their conversation in 1 S 8 and will see it again in the story of David's anointing (1 S 16). We also know, if we take the history's presentation of God at face value, that God plays favorites. God supports an Israel who often doesn't deserve it and also supports individuals of questionable merit (Jacob is a good example).

We go back to an odd phrase from early in Samuel's story: "As Samuel grew up, the LORD was with him and let none of his words fall to the ground" (1 S 3:19). How peculiar! Shouldn't the prophet guard God's words, rather than vice versa?[18] I submit that 1 S 12 illustrates the relationship of 1 S 3:19; God is "with Samuel" and will "let none of his words fall to the ground." This divine loyalty holds even when Samuel behaves inappropriately. Thus the silence about Samuel's corrupt sons, and thus the present thunderstorm.

Why is God so forebearing with Samuel? Recall God's "welcome to the club" statements in 1 S 8. Perhaps, God pities Samuel because God has been in Samuel's position. The reader who has attended carefully to God's relationship with Moses knows that God gets lonely at the top and reaches out to interact with someone in a similar position.

By now you may be wondering why I am so eager to debunk Samuel. I offer three points to ponder.

1. Samuel's words are not necessarily a straightforward statement of the narrator's, or God's, opinions on kingship. According to the prophet Samuel (in 1 S 12), for Israel to ask for a king is for Israel to spit in God's face. But Samuel has his own investments. The narrative shows him resisting God where monarchy is concerned. To understand what is at stake in monarchy, we must heed Samuel's lectures, but we must also look beyond them. When we do, we find a mixed and confusing picture. Kingship creates both practical and religious difficulties. It also offers practical and religious advantages.

2. Prophetic authority and kingly authority coexist in uneasy relationship. At the very beginning of Israel's monarchy we find a highly problematic relationship between two types of authority. Both prophet and king enjoy divine sanction. Both also show a human tendency to let personal agendas influence their public work. The prophet argues that the king should obey him; we have no proof that this is God's initiative rather than the prophet's. We must not simply equate the prophet

with God and the king with sinful mortals (although on occasion that analysis may be accurate).

3. God does not always act with impartial consistency; certain individuals enjoy special favor. In particular, God backs Samuel despite the prophet's grumbling and delays. Ironically, the God Samuel depicts in his sermons to Israel and to Saul would never show such patience. On the other hand, God does sometimes strike out with surprising harshness; witness the rejection of faithful Eli.

Our survey of kingship issues reminds us that we must pay careful attention to who says what and how they say it. Such attention raises questions about things that seem obvious—or are entirely overlooked—in a casual first reading. How many of us have stopped to think about Samuel's conflicts of interest? How many have noticed that Samuel rewrites history in his farewell speech? Many of these discrepancies can be (and have been) explained as evidence of multiple sources. But in the final text they create an engaging and highly nuanced picture in which none of the human characters—including Samuel—can be taken as a simple mouthpiece for God.

CHAPTER 4

SAMUEL'S DAVID AS INNOCENT AND ATTRACTIVE HERO

We now sketch David as commonly perceived—an innocent and attractive hero, a man after God's own heart, who falters only once and in that case contritely repents. Some parts of this picture come straight from the books of Samuel; other parts are not present in Samuel but are filled in by the observer, who at the same time screens out certain material which *is* present in Samuel. For instance, this sketch will characterize Saul as "anointed by a reluctant Samuel at the people's insistence." It overlooks the character of Samuel's reluctance and God's firm instructions vis-à-vis the anointing. I include such interpretive elements because they are prompted by suggestions in the text; not by accident do so many people understand David in this fashion. In Chapters 5 and 6 we will return to challenge these rosy assumptions.

We have seen that Israel needed a king. Saul, anointed by a reluctant Samuel at the people's insistence, had kingly height but not a kingly heart. From the start he showed a disturbing lack of confidence (1 S 9:21; 10:16, 22). His excitability and impulsiveness prompted gossip (for instance, when he began to "prophesy," 1 S 10:10–12), although it also helped him defeat an Ammonite oppressor (11:5–11). No sooner does Samuel declare the need for kingly obedience (1 S 12) than Saul's lack of faith leads him to ignore Samuel's instructions (1 S 13). LORD withdraws support from Saul; Samuel delivers the message of rejection followed by news that "LORD has sought out a man after his own heart; and the LORD has appointed him to be ruler over his people" (1 S 13:14).

Saul still manages to achieve major victories (14:47–48), but his increasing instability shows in his persecution of his own son Jonathan. He brazenly ignores divine orders (1 S 15). In his second rebuke of Saul, as in the first, Samuel throws a still anonymous David in Saul's face: "The LORD has torn the kingdom of Israel from you . . . and has given it to a neighbor of yours, who is better than you" (1 S 15:28).

LORD then sends Samuel to Bethlehem to anoint a new king (1 S 16). This one will be chosen not by humans, but by LORD, who "looks on the heart"

(16:7). In keeping with the biblical theme of chosen younger sons, Jesse's eldest seven pass by Samuel without a "hit." The eighth and youngest must be summoned home from the fields, where he dutifully tends his father's sheep. "Now he was ruddy, and had beautiful eyes, and was handsome. The LORD said, 'Rise and anoint him; for this is the one'" (16:12). Samuel obeys, "and the spirit of the LORD came mightily upon David from that day forward" (16:13).

An evil spirit meanwhile torments the rejected king Saul. His servants suggest musical therapy; indeed, they recommend a specific musician. One of them says, "I have seen a son of Jesse the Bethlehemite who is skillful in playing, a man of valor, a warrior, prudent in speech, and a man of good presence; and the LORD is with him" (16:18). David proves as good as advertised and becomes Saul's healer.

The pagan Philistines continue to press Israel (1 S 17). A huge giant, Goliath, swaggers out twice daily to taunt Saul's frightened troops. David, bringing supplies to his older brothers, cannot understand why God's people tolerate this insult. He volunteers for single combat against the human tank, mentioning almost in passing that with God's help he has already fought lions and bears.

A grateful Saul offers armor and weapons, but the boy politely declines after discovering that he cannot even walk in the cumbersome battle gear. David skips out to meet the Philistine with only his shepherd's equipment. "There was no sword in David's hand," the narrator reports (17:50). A well-slung stone topples the giant, producing a classic underdog victory. Saul, astonished, signs the new star into his army (1 S 18). Saul's son Jonathan embraces David at first sight—a friendship that will endure through Saul's ugly persecution of David and beyond. Jonathan strips off his own royal gear and bestows it on David, in recognition of the lad's obvious destiny.

Israel's women welcome Saul and David with exuberant song, but Saul cannot stand to share the limelight. Mad with jealousy, he tries to kill his harper boy. David evades the flying spear and continues to distinguish himself. Soon Jonathan's sister loves David too. When ardent David doubles the requested bride-price of a hundred Philistine foreskins, Saul, who had negotiated in bad faith on a previous occasion, can only hand over the bride.

Saul's murder attempts continue, in spite of Jonathan's pleas in David's behalf (1 S 19). Saul's daughter, firmly on her husband's side, helps David escape. David takes refuge with the old prophet Samuel. Saul's mental illness by now has the better of him: his attempt to capture David ends (at least temporarily) with Saul stripping off his clothes and raving naked on the ground.

Jonathan, loyal to both his father and his friend, cannot quite believe how bad things have gotten. He and David arrange a final test of Saul's disposition (1 S 20); this time the deranged Saul attempts to kill his own son. Warned by Jonathan, David flees, after renewing his vows of eternal friendship with Saul's noble son.

Divine support for David materializes once again in the form of weapons and food from LORD's sanctuary at Nob (1 S 21). David tries to find refuge with a Philistine king, but the Philistine nobles share Saul's opinion—this man is dangerous. David cleverly feigns madness and escapes. He hides in the wilderness (1 S 22). Men dispossessed by Saul's harmful policies begin gathering to David. Fearful of Saul's revenge, David sends his family to a neighboring country.

Saul—by now completely paranoid—accuses his whole staff of conspiring against him and with a heathen's aid slaughters Nob's entire priestly clan. The sole survivor flees to David, who nobly takes responsibility for the disaster. Saul must now operate without any religious support, while the good relationship between David and LORD leads to David's asking for and receiving tactical advice from God (1 S 23).

A providentially timed Philistine advance foils Saul's next attempt to hunt David down. When Saul returns to the chase (1 S 24), he wanders into a cave occupied by David and his men. Unseen, David snips off a corner of Saul's cloak, although even this small irreverence for LORD's anointed bothers David's conscience. David presents the cloth to Saul as proof of his goodwill and loyalty. Saul's mercurial temper undergoes yet another change. Regretstricken, he acknowledges not only David's righteousness but his claim to the throne.

David (who has experienced other changes of heart from Saul) wisely remains in the wilderness (1 S 25). He protects the flocks and shepherds of a wealthy landowner. But Nabal ("churl"[1]) allows David's band no part in a shearing feast; he sneeringly dismisses them as runaway slaves. David loses his temper, but Nabal's wise and beautiful wife intervenes. She warns David that vengeance is best left to God and further comments that LORD will establish "a sure house" for him (25:28, the first statement of this promise to David). God strikes down Nabal. Faithful, valiant David then marries the suitably beautiful, discerning Abigail.

Saul, despite his promises, hunts David yet again (1 S 26). This time, David and a companion slip into Saul's camp at night to remove the spear and water jar which stand beside Saul's bed. The companion proposes a swift spear thrust through Saul's body, but a horrified David forbids it. From a safe distance, David displays the trophies. He rebukes Saul's general for poor protection of LORD's anointed. Saul apologizes for misjudging David and calls him "son." David again protests his righteous intentions toward Saul, but makes it clear that he feels safer in LORD's hand than Saul's. Saul pronounces a blessing as David departs.

David, now sure that he cannot trust Saul, goes once again to the Philistine city of Gath (1 S 27). This time King Achish installs David in a southern desert stronghold. From there, the king believes, David will raid the Judean people and related tribes (27:10). In fact, David attacks only foreigners such as Saul's foes the Amalekites (27:8).

Will David's double game entrap him when the Philistines go to war with Israel yet again (1 S 28)? Achish raises the question of David's loyalty. The king takes David's ambiguous answer ("then you shall know what your servant can do," 28:2) as a promise of obedience. Meanwhile Saul gives final proof of his unworthiness. Unable to get any advice from God, he appeals to one of the mediums whom he himself has banished from the land. Samuel's ghost delivers a rebuke more crushing (if possible) than those given by the live Samuel: "LORD has torn the kingdom out of your hand, and given it to your neighbor, David. . . . Moreover the LORD will give Israel along with you into the hands of the Philistines; and tomorrow you and your sons shall be with me" (28:17,19).

In the Philistine camp, God's hand behind the scenes once again saves David: Achish's fellow Philistine lords refuse to let David participate in the battle (1 S 29). David returns to the southern desert, where he and his men rescue their families from Amalekite raiders (1 S 30). David's men—fighters and baggage-watchers alike—all get a share in the booty. He distributes the rest, Robin Hood style, to Judean towns in the region.

Saul's army is routed by the Philistines (per the prediction of Samuel's ghost); the defeated king kills himself to avoid further humiliation (1 S 31). This grim news comes to David via—who else?—an Amalekite. The messenger, doubtless anticipating a reward, claims to have slain the king himself (2 S 1). David executes him for this affrontery, then composes a moving lament in memory of Saul and Jonathan. It leaves no doubt about David's sincere grief for the fallen king.

God instructs David to return to Judah, specifically to Hebron, where the Judeans make David their king (2 S 2). Meanwhile Saul's son Ishbosheth rules the north.[2] But a quarrel develops, and Ishbosheth's general Abner defects to David (2 S 3). David pledges safe passage for Abner, but David's own general Joab assassinates the rival in connection with a private blood feud. A horrified David, who everyone knows had no part in the murder, personally leads public mourning for Abner. Ishbosheth himself is killed in his bed by scoundrels who take the head to David (2 S 4). He executes the assassins.

The northern tribes, bereft of leadership, place themselves under David's rule (2 S 5). Hebron, far to the south, will not do as capital of this enlarged domain. David cleverly captures Jerusalem. Hiram, king of Tyre to the north, sends congratulations in the form of artisans and materials to construct a palace. Enlargement of David's household signals God's favor for David. When Philistines come to fight their breakaway vassal, God miraculously strikes them down.

The time is now ripe to bring the Ark of God—that ancient symbol of God's protection for the tribes—into the capital of the newly established state (2 S 6). An unpleasant accident halts the first attempt at ark transfer, but three months later the move is safely accomplished, amidst much public celebration and feasting. The only sour note is struck by one of David's wives, Saul's arrogant daughter Michal. She watches David's selfless dance of joy through the lens of her own jealousy—and despises David. David's real motive, the desire to honor LORD at any cost, is beyond her understanding. God strikes Michal with lifelong barrenness as punishment for her faulty priorities.

Firmly settled in his rule, David wants to thank God by building a magnificent temple (2 S 7). God responds that a building isn't necessary. And God has yet more in store for David! "Your house and your kingdom shall be made sure forever before me; your throne shall be established forever" (7:16). David, properly overwhelmed ("Who am I . . . that you have brought me thus far?" 7:18), praises God's magnificence and generosity.

God's support for David yields continuing military victories (2 S 8), complete with tribute and booty. At home, David appoints officials to administer "justice and equity" (8:15). He recalls his vow to Jonathan and fulfills it by making Jonathan's lame son Mephibosheth a permanent house guest (2 S 9). He continues to show consideration for his men, allowing messengers humiliated by Ammon's new king Hanun to linger in Jericho until their beards have regrown (2 S 10).

Then David falters (2 S 11). Seduced by a beautiful woman, David gets her pregnant. He tries to cover up, summoning her husband home, but the husband stubbornly refuses to enter his own house, even after David gets him drunk. David sends him back to the front with a letter containing instructions to kill the bearer. Hard-boiled Joab takes care of the matter. After a decent interval, David brings the woman to his palace and marries her.

But God disapproves. The prophet Nathan presents David with a fictitious legal case about a greedy and inconsiderate rich man (2 S 12). David, whose heart is still in the right place, responds in outrage: "The man who has done this deserves to die . . . because he had no pity." (12:5–6) Nathan shoots back, "You are the man!" (12:7).

David, unlike Saul who always offered excuses, acknowledges his guilt immediately: "I have sinned against the LORD" (12:13). Nathan assures him that the sin has been "put away," but the illegitimate child will die (12:13–14).

The freshness and unconventionality of David's restored faith emerge in the subsequent scene of the child's illness. David mourns and prays ardently for his son's recovery. He is so concerned that his courtiers are afraid to tell him when the child finally dies. What might he do to himself? But David does not descend into suicidal depression. Instead he quits mourning: he bathes, anoints himself, worships, and eats. Why? David explains that the point of no return has passed. "Now he is dead; why should I fast? Can I bring him back again? I shall go to him, but he will not return to me" (12:23). Life must go on. Bathsheba bears another child, Solomon, whom "the LORD loved" (12:24).

If we have any doubts about David's restored sense of purpose, they are removed by the rest of the chapter. He joins Joab in the field, captures the capital of Ammon, and puts its people to hard labor for the Israelites. When he returns to Jerusalem again, it is the right way: "all the people"—or "all the army," for "people" often seems to have the specialized meaning "army" in Samuel—are with him (12:31).

Unfortunately David—like Eli and Samuel before him—has unworthy children. His eldest son Amnon rapes a half-sister, Tamar (2 S 13). Tamar's brother Absalom—who is, after Amnon, next in line for the throne—bides his time for two years, then murders the rapist and flees to his mother's family in the neighboring kingdom of Geshur.

Again years pass. David yearns for Absalom, but does not bring him home. Finally General Joab intervenes (2 S 14). Using the same strategy employed by Nathan (a fictitious legal case), Joab and an unnamed wise woman persuade David to bring his son home. The woman appeals to David's own wisdom, which she recognizes as "like the wisdom of the angel of God" (2 S 14:20; see also 1 S 29:9; 2 S 14:17 and 19:27).

But the restored Absalom, who would presumably have taken the throne when David died, is not content to wait. He acquires a royal bodyguard (2 S 15) and suggests to the people that he would serve their interests better than David. Finally Absalom's trumpet sounds in open rebellion. David responds as he did to Saul's persecution; he flees, trusting his fate to LORD's hands. As he leaves Jerusalem, key figures offer their loyalty. David allows some to accompany him and sends others back to monitor Absalom. When a relative of Saul meets him with stones and curses, David replies, "Let him alone. . . . It may be that the LORD will look on my distress, and the LORD will repay me with good for this cursing of me today" (2 S 16:11–12).

LORD indeed supports David. Solomon's counselor Ahithophel advises a course that would quickly settle matters in Absalom's favor (2 S 17). David's "plant," Hushai, offers a flawed alternative. Absalom and his advisers choose the second course, "for the LORD had ordained to defeat the good counsel of

Ahithophel, so that the LORD might bring ruin on Absalom" (17:14). Absalom's error gives David time to cross the Jordan and rally his forces.

By the time Absalom pursues, David is ready (2 S 18). The king gives strict orders that his son is not to be harmed, yet merciless Joab orders Absalom's execution. David mourns his rebellious but beloved child. "O my son Absalom, my son, my son Absalom! Would I had died instead of you, O Absalom, my son, my son!" (18:33).

Hard-bitten Joab rejects David's fatherly grief as "love of those who hate you and hatred of those who love you" (19:6). He predicts mass desertion if David fails to encourage the troops. David overcomes his personal loss to do his duty as commander-in-chief.

The Israelites—both those who had been faithful to David and those who had followed Absalom—now unite to welcome David back (2 S 19). David magnanimously appoints Absalom's supporter Amasa as general in place of the disobedient Joab. Joab assassinates this rival (2 S 20) as he long ago assassinated Abner. He then nips a second rebellion in the bud by negotiating to have its leader "neutralized."

At the end of 2 Samuel, God—angered by the people's sin—tells David to take a census of Israel. David obeys. But he knows that the census (associated with taxation and conscription) threatens the people's well-being, and he later begs God's forgiveness for taking it. Trusting in God's love, he chooses to be punished by God rather than mortals. When some of his people die in a resulting plague, David prays that he may take their place.

God responds, through a prophet, with instructions for David to buy a certain threshing floor. David does. The previous owner offers his oxen for sacrifice, but David insists on paying for them: "I will not offer burnt offerings to the LORD my God that cost me nothing" (24:24). David builds an altar and slaughters the oxen. Then "the LORD answered his supplication for the land, and the plague was averted from Israel" (24:25). The books of Samuel thus close with the king established, praying in the people's behalf.

Only two episodes remain to be told. When David is so old that he has no intercourse with the lovely virgin who warms his bed (1 K 1), his eldest surviving son assumes the trappings of power (in a manner quite reminiscent of Absalom). David, true to an earlier promise, immediately transfers the crown to Solomon. With Solomon firmly established, it remains only for David to impart his deathbed wisdom (1 K 2). "Be strong, be courageous, and keep the charge of the LORD your God," David advises (2:2). "Then David slept with his ancestors, and was buried in the city of David" (2:10).

He does not disappear from the story, however. 1 and 2 Kings invoke him as a model of faith and rightly exercised kingship. "Solomon loved the LORD, walking in the statutes of his father David" (1 K 3:3). He prays, "You have shown great and steadfast love to your servant my father David, because he walked before you in faithfulness, in righteousness, and in uprightness of heart toward you" (3:6). God promises support to Solomon, on condition that Solomon "walk in my ways, keeping my statutes and my commandments, as your father David walked" (3:14). Solomon, unfortunately, "did not completely follow the LORD, as his father David had done" (1 K 11:6), but for the sake of David, God does not take away the kingdom. The next king is even worse and loses most of the kingdom, but he retains a portion "for the sake of my servant David whom I chose and who did keep my commandments and my statutes" (1 K 11:34). God meanwhile chides Jeroboam, leader of the breakaway, for not being "like my servant David, who kept my commandments and followed me with all his heart, doing only that which was right in my sight" (1 K 14:8).

After the generation of the split of the kingdom, northern kings are consistently compared to Jeroboam, whereas David remains the yardstick for Judean kings. Rehoboam's successor is "not true to the LORD his God, like the heart of his father[3] David," but is supported for David's sake "because David did what was right in the sight of the LORD, and did not turn aside from anything that he commanded him all the days of his life, except in the matter of Uriah the Hittite" (1 K 15:3, 5).

Not all of the Judean kings get such poor marks. "Asa did what was right in the sight of the LORD, as his father David had done" (1 K 15:11). On Amaziah we get a mixed report, "He did what was right in the sight of the LORD, yet not like his ancestor David" (2 K 14:3). Hezekiah, in pleasing contrast to his wicked father Ahab, "did what was right in the sight of the LORD just as his ancestor David had done" (2 K 18:3). The book of Kings' final mention of David comes in the climactic story of good king Josiah,[4] who "did what was right in the sight of the LORD, and walked in all the way of his father David; he did not turn aside to the right or to the left" (2 K 22:2; note the intensification, *all the way* of his father David).

SUMMARY: THE INNOCENT AND ATTRACTIVE HERO

Reviewing our sketch of David as exemplary king, we identify features that contribute to our overall positive impression of David.

1. God approves of David.

    (a) The prophet Samuel says so (1 S 13:14; 15:28).

    (b) God says so (1 S 16:1, 12; 2 S 7; statements in 1 and 2 Kings). God also sends the ephod, an instrument for asking questions of God, to David (1 S 23:6).

(c) David says so (1 S 17:37, 46–47; 2 S 7:27–29; 2 S 22).

(d) The narrator tells us God was with him (1 S 16:13 and elsewhere).

(e) Other characters refer to David's election (for instance, 1 S 24:4, 20; 25:28–30).

2. People like David.

(a) People in general like David. Repeatedly we hear of the favor that David enjoys with "all the people"; for examples, see 1 S 18:16 and 2 S 3:36.

(b) Important individuals like David—including Saul (some of the time), his children Jonathan and Michal, and wise Abigail.

(c) Even foreigners like David—including King Achish of Gath (1 S 27–29), King Hiram of Tyre (2 S 5:11, 1 K 5:1), and Ittai the Gittite with his troops (2 S 15:19–22).

3. David succeeds. Instances here are too numerous to mention. In a few places we are told that David's success results from divine intervention (for example, the blocking of Ahithophel's advice in 2 S 17:14), or we see God providing crucial advice (for example, telling David to go to Hebron in 2 S 1). More often God remains unmentioned, but we infer a divine hand in the Philistine's timely move of 1 S 23:27–28, Saul's choice of cave (1 S 24:3), the Philistine objections that keep David out of battle (1 S 29), and so forth. This is one of the features that make David's story so accessible to modern audiences: we see God's favor enacted subtly rather than through flashy miracles. David's success underscores both his personal competence and God's support.

4. David refuses to harm others (except for "enemies of the LORD" such as the Philistines, whose foreskins he removes, and the wicked assassins who brag of killing Saul and his son). In particular, he never—despite extreme provocation—lifts a finger against Saul. He deals magnanimously with opposing generals (Abner in 2 S 3 and Amasa in 2 S 19). He twice forgives Shimei's cursing (2 S 16:11–12; 19:22–23). Above all, he orders his men not to kill the son who has rebelled against him (2 S 18:5). He even wishes that he could die in that rebellious son's place (2 S 18:35).

5. David's excellence stands out by contrast, especially with disobedient Saul and the bloodthirsty thug Joab. Later kings, except for Josiah and possibly Hezekiah, cannot meet the high standard David sets.

CHAPTER 5

TROUBLING DETAILS: READING DAVID'S HEART

We now move closer to Samuel's David for a detailed appreciation of the artist's technique. As we carefully survey the portrait, we will note many details that our positive overview overlooked, misstated, or assumed without proof. We will reassess not only the narrator's statements about David, but also the credibility of David's supporting witnesses and the qualities of contrasting characters.

We begin with three statements that frame our expectations for David. How valid is the anti-Saul, pro-David grid they suggest? Because they make a strong suggestion about the qualities of David's "heart," we will next attend to our glimpses of that heart. How much—and what—do we really know about David's inner life, his thoughts, feelings, and motives? (Once more, we are exploring "David" as presented in Samuel—not a historically reconstructed David or the composite David of the Bible as a whole.) Our findings about David's "heart" will guide a reexamination of his words and deeds in Chapter 6.

DAVID AND SAUL: THE RHETORIC OF EXPECTATION

The typical reader's positive impression of David is driven above all by three statements made before David's name even enters the story:

1. Samuel to Saul: "The LORD has sought out a man after his own heart; and the LORD has appointed him to be ruler over his people" (1 S 13:14).

2. Samuel to Saul: "The LORD has torn the kingdom of Israel from you . . . and has given it to a neighbor of yours, who is better than you" (1 S 15:28).

49

3. God to Samuel concerning Eliab (who like Saul is tall and good-looking): "Do not look on his appearance or on the height of his stature, because I have rejected him; for the LORD does not see as mortals see; they look on the outward appearance, but the LORD looks on the heart" (1 S 16:7).

Casual readers typically infer a contrast from these statements, as follows:

Saul	*David*
chosen by people (or Samuel)	chosen by God
on basis of appearance	on basis of heart
bad, sinful	good, virtuous

This contrast grid misleads us on two points. First, although most readers understand Samuel and especially God to be contrasting God's choice of David with somebody else's choice of Saul, 1 S 9–11 states clearly that God—not Samuel and not the people, however much they may concur—selects Saul.

> Now the day before Saul came, the LORD had revealed to Samuel: "Tomorrow about this time I will send to you a man from the land of Benjamin, and you shall anoint him to be ruler over my people Israel."... When Samuel saw Saul, the LORD told him, "Here is the man of whom I spoke to you." (1 S 9:15–17)

Lest we—or the Israelites—or Samuel—doubt this divine choice, it is verified by lot (an ancient method of discerning the divine will) in the following chapter, after which Samuel himself asks, "Do you see the one *whom the LORD has chosen*? There is no one like him among all the people" (1 S 10:24, emphasis added).

Thus, contrary to the grid's suggestion, Saul is chosen by God. This God is not merely informed about the state of Saul's heart, but specifically controls it (1 S 10:9). So what about God's rhetoric in 1 S 16:7 (quoted above)? God's speech suggests that God, by looking on the heart, can choose a *good* king, in contrast to handsome but flawed candidates (Eliab, Saul) who attract the human eye. By innuendo, without making the claim in so many words, God blames human selection for Saul's failure.

Some may object that God would never stoop to misdirection. But see God's instructions to Samuel in this same chapter: "Say, 'I have come to sacrifice'" (16:2). This may be true, but it is far enough from the whole truth to be deceptive in intent and effect. (For a more detailed discussion of troubling aspects of God's character in 1 and 2 Samuel, see my essay "The Problematic God of Samuel.")

Let us inquire further into Saul's qualifications. The narrator introduces him this way:

> There was a man of Benjamin . . . a man of wealth. He had a son whose name was Saul, a handsome young man [*bāḥûr* and *ṭôb*]. There was not a man among the people of Israel more handsome [more *ṭôb*] than he; he stood head and shoulders above everyone else. (1 S 9:1–2 NRSV, other English translations read similarly.)

This description, although positive, fits the impression we derived from our grid: Saul's qualifications are primarily external. But the vocabulary deserves another look. The phrase translated "a handsome young man" contains, in Hebrew, two descriptive terms: *bāḥûr* and *ṭôb*. *Bāḥûr* describes a young man in his prime. Its derivation from the verb "choose" etymologically suggests "a chosen one." Although in general I try to define words according to how they are used (thus, "young man") rather than etymologically ("chosen"), the Bible's fondness for puns and wordplay suggests that we should not dismiss the allusion here, especially because chosenness/rejection is such a crucial issue with regard to Saul. *Ṭôb*—used twice in this verse—means, to a first approximation, "good." (Its most famous appearances are probably when God sees that various parts of creation are "good" in Gen 1, and in the name of "the tree of the knowledge of good and evil" in Gen 2–3.) It is the *same* word (exactly) that Samuel later uses to describe David: "a neighbor of yours [Saul's], who is better (more *ṭôb*) than you" (15:28). I am not aware of anyone who translates 15:28 "more handsome than you," although this is theoretically possible. Why translate one way for Saul and another for David? Without our grid-locked assumption, retroactively imposed, that Saul's "choiceness" depends upon appearance only, his introductory paragraph might be translated as follows:

> There was a man of Benjamin . . . a man of wealth. He had a son whose name was Saul, in his prime (*bāḥûr*) and a good man (*ṭôb*). There was not a man among the people of Israel better (more *ṭôb*) than he. He stood head and shoulders over the entire people. (1 S 9:1–2, my translation)

By the time we reach the final line of this description, we read "head and shoulders over the entire people" as a figurative statement about Saul's virtue rather than rewriting the previous statements in terms of physical appearance.

Saul's initial qualifications point to a second, more subtle problem with the grid which contrasts Saul and David: it presumes that characters and relationships do not change. If Saul is rejected by God now, the thinking goes, then surely Saul was never really chosen by God to start with. If Saul sins now, Saul must never have been good.

But biblical characters do change. Recognizing this allows us to make more sense of statements about God's choice and Saul's character: God did choose Saul, but now God chooses someone else; Saul was the best man in Israel, but he is not the best man any more.

An important corollary: if Saul can go from "none more *ṭôb*" to rejected abandonment, then David's initial status of "more *ṭôb* than you [Saul]" may also be subject to change. *A positive initial assessment does not guarantee that David* (or any other character) *will remain good.* In fact, suggests Meir Sternberg, "with biblical man . . . there is usually a distance—and often a clash—between the impression produced on his first appearance and the one left after his last." Elsewhere he writes, "the reader tends to generalize character and assimilate it to type. And the Bible encourages this tendency with a view to its ultimate discomfiture."[1] One moment's "none better" may be headed for a less admirable end.

Without doubt, the books of Samuel do invite us to contrast David and Saul, especially during the period of David's rise and Saul's demise. The contrast can be traced along several thematic lines, for instance, the kings' interactions with foreign peoples.[2] Saul's first condemnation from Samuel and his death as reported by the narrator are tied to conflict with the Philistines (1 S 13, 31). His pursuit of David is frustrated by Philistine activity (1 S 23:27). David, on the other hand, first gets employment and a landholding from the Philistines (1 S 27–29), then defeats them (2 S 5), and finally enjoys the deep loyalty of Philistine troops (2 S 15). The Amalekites repeatedly bring trouble to Saul, from his final condemnation by Samuel (1 S 15) to his death as reported to David (2 S 1), whereas David scores major victories over Amalek (1 S 27, 30).

So far, the contrasts favor David. We find a different situation when we consider the Ammonites. Saul's first and most glorious victory comes against the eye-gouging Ammonite king Nahash (1 S 11). David speaks of Nahash as a friend (2 S 10:2). When war nonetheless erupts with Ammon, it becomes David's occasion for adultery and murder (2 S 10–11).

This suggests that if we were to compare Saul and David over the course of their entire careers (rather than at the moment of Saul's downfall and David's rise), the contrasts and comparisons might work out rather differently. We will undertake such a comparison in Chapter 7. Now, however, we turn our attention back to knowledge about David's "heart."

READING DAVID'S HEART

"LORD looks on the heart," we hear in 1 S 16:7, just prior to God's identification of David as "the one" (16:12). "Heart," in Hebrew, denotes not only feelings but thoughts and will—the whole inner life of a person. In some places we will find the same Hebrew word translated "mind." We infer that God has looked upon David's heart and liked the view; but we readers do not share God's insight into David. Just what *do* we know about David's feelings, motives, and plans?

The narrator gives us several kinds of clues about characters' hearts. Some clues come from external description, for instance, when we see David weep and lament at Abner's grave (2 S 3:32–33). Uncertainty creeps in when we try to extrapolate feelings and motives from such outward behavior. Does David feel bad about Abner's death? Or does his agitation arise more from fear of bloodguilt (see his initial reaction in 3:28–29) and loss of Abner's help in rallying Israel? How much of his lament is a public-relations ploy?

Similar questions arise when the narrator quotes characters' own statements about their thoughts, feelings, and motives. "I will show you kindness for the sake of your father Jonathan," David says to Mephibosheth (2 S 9:7). But numerous interpreters have noted that David's "kindness" allows him to keep Saul's surviving heir under close watch; compare the Judean king's status in Babylon (2 K 25:29). Later David shows remarkable readiness to give away Mephibosheth's estates (2 S 16:4). Should his stated motive for summoning Mephibosheth be taken at face value?

Some readers may find such questions unduly suspicious. But we *know* biblical characters can lie, because in some cases we have evidence to prove it. The Amalekite messenger lies to David about the circumstances of Saul's death (2 S 1; either that or the narrator is lying in 1 S 31). David himself lies to the priest at Nob in 1 S 21: he is not carrying out an urgent mission on Saul's behalf, and probably the "young men" do not exist (so far as we know, David flees alone from the meeting with Jonathan). He deceives Achish of Gath (via his actions) later in the same chapter. In the previous chapter, Jonathan—who may be the cleanest, most virtuous character of the entire story—knowingly lies to his father about the reasons for David's absence.

In none of these cases does the narrator report the speech as "lying." Instead he or she assumes that we are alert enough to notice what is happening. Given these certain cases of misleading speech, we may not simply assume characters' veracity in other cases. The fact that in some cases the narrator explicitly confirms characters' words—for instance, by verifying the elders' statements about Samuel's age and his sons' corruption in the opening lines of 1 S 8—is further evidence that he or she expects us to wonder about character credibility.

Because of the interpretive uncertainty surrounding actions and a character's own words, we will give special attention to those passages which actually show us David's inner life.[3] In some cases the narrator will make a descriptive statement: "David . . . was very much afraid" (1 S 21:12). Elsewhere, we enter into David's inner life by being invited to share his perception: "David and his men came to the city, and—look! burned up by fire!" (1 S 30:3, my translation).[4] In still other cases, we eavesdrop on thoughts: "David said in his heart, 'I shall now perish one day by the hand of Saul . . .'" (1 S 27:1). Even when we include all these categories, glimpses into David come seldom.

Of these glimpses, a full third[5] give insight only in the technical sense; they reflect David's point of view or inner life without improving our understanding or altering our evaluation of him. An example is the comment that "David heard him [Goliath]" in 1 S 17:23. We share David's perception but remain uncertain of how he feels about what he hears. For the purpose of understanding his character, we will focus on those insights which have greater implications for understanding David's inner life.

Rachel Paley observes that David's first *spoken* words in the story are, "What shall be done for the man who kills this Philistine?" (1 S 17:26).[6] Our first insight into David's *thoughts* (beyond the bare information that David heard Goliath) comes in 1 S 18:26: "David was well pleased to be the king's son-in-law." Not "Michal's husband" nor even "Saul's son-in-law" but "the king's son-in-law." This privileged insight reinforces the implication of David's opening words: whatever else may or may not be on his mind, David is keenly aware of political position and possibilities for his own advancement.

David's ambition is balanced by a sense of danger. What we know from his words (especially the conversation with Jonathan in 1 S 20) and his actions (Fokkelman points out how "escape" and "flee" characterize the David of 1 S 19–27, especially 19–23; these themewords will recur in 2 S 15, in which David returns to the passive, "giving" mode of his wilderness days[7]) is reinforced by what the narrator tells us of his inner life: "David . . . was very much afraid of King Achish" (21:12); "David learned that Saul was plotting evil against him" (23:9); "he learned that Saul had come out to seek his life" (23:15).

Given that David also engages in courageous, even brash (two hundred Philistine foreskins) actions, we may ask why our insights are limited to his fear and perception of persecution. Two responses come immediately to mind. First, these feelings and thoughts explain actions (deserting Saul, lying to a priest, running to the Philistines, gathering a band of disreputable fighters) which might otherwise be interpreted in terms of calculating ambition; the fear does not, however, rule out calculating ambition. Second, they elicit our sympathy; most of us identify far more easily with a fearful David than with the cocksure hero of the Goliath story (1 S 17). Nor do we criticize David for timidity: the narrator forestalls that by providing other data (notably insights into Saul's inner life, such as 1 S 18:17 and 25) that show the accuracy of David's assessments.

Yet David's fear and focus on persecution serve to weaken our image of a man whose confidence (in himself, his divinely declared destiny, and the God who will bring it about) never wavers. "The LORD, who saved me from the paw of the lion and from the paw of the bear, will save me from the hand of this Philistine," David says before going to meet Goliath (1 S 17:37). He seems less confident that God will save him from Achish or Saul. However, this lack of confidence may be justified: we know, if David does not, that it is God who incites Saul's attempts at murder (1 S 18:10; 19:8).

Our next glimpse of David's heart comes when Saul wanders into the very cave where David hides with his men. David snips off the corner of Saul's cloak. "Afterward David was stricken to the heart because he had cut off a corner of Saul's cloak" (1 S 24:5 in the English text whose numbering we follow).

What does it mean to say that "David's heart smote him" (KJV/RSV, closely following the Hebrew)? Unfortunately, the expression occurs only twice in the Bible—both times with reference to David. (The other occurrence is in 2 S 24:10.) Klein translates, "David's conscience bothered him."[8] This may be a little too weak; the verb in question ordinarily designates blows that do substantial damage. Fokkelman describes the heart-blows as "palpitations," which preserves the physical force of the image.

Fokkelman offers a structural analysis (his favorite interpretive tool) of the cave sequence in 1 S 24:[9]

A Saul informed, goes with his army after David et al.   2a–3b
B into the cave: Saul searching, David hidden in the rear   4a–d
C speech (3 lines): the men tempt David   5a–d
X unique deed + body language: David cuts the corner of
   Saul's cloak and gets palpitations   5e–6b
C' speech (3 lines): David rejects the temptation   7a–d+8b
B' out of the cave: Saul goes on, David after him   8cd, 9ab
A' David calls after Saul: looking behind Saul sees David   9c–f

Fokkelman then translates and arranges the central element (X above):

5e   David rose and cut the corner from Saul's cloak unnoticed.

6a   It then happened

6b   that David's heart palpitated because he had cut off the corner of Saul('s cloak).[10]

David does not chide his men until *after* he cuts off the cloak and is heart-smitten. Also, Fokkelman argues, "it then happened" ordinarily appears as the opening phrase of a scene. Its position here at the center of an "X" is unusual and implies a different meaning than the phrase ordinarily carries. Fokkelman suggests that at this early date Israel does not have firm rules for dealing with God's anointed. David's cloak cutting is an experimental probe. "Then it happened" marks God's response (identified as such by Abigail in 25:26). David decides after the palpitations that he must go no further. "LORD forbid! I must not do this thing . . ." (1 S 24:6, my translation). David thus formulates the rule of the anointed one's inviolability—a rule stressed repeatedly in this chapter and its parallel, 1 S 26.[11] Incidentally, if David's statements correctly interpret God's wishes regarding the anointed, then his men's exclamation, "Here is the day of which the LORD said to you, 'I will give your enemy into your hand' " (1 S 24:4, the first we have heard about any such prediction) would appear to be mistaken.

Polzin regards David's respect for the anointed with a more jaundiced eye: "nothing is emphasized more in this chapter than that David refused to kill Saul because he was 'the LORD's anointed' (vv. 7, 11; see also 26:9, 11, 16, 23): the reader cannot help realizing that the speaker of these words is *also* the LORD's anointed. And so it turns out that David perhaps is shown not wanting to do anything himself that could also provide a precedent for his own murder later."[12] David himself soon explicitly states such reasoning: "As your life was precious today in my sight, so may my life be precious in the sight of the LORD" (1 S 26:24).

Did God cause David's heart to smite him? Was David stricken by conscience? Or did David suddenly realize that his own fate as anointed one was bound with Saul's? In the very moment of insight, we know less than we might wish.

1 Samuel 27:1 again reports the apprehension which leads David to flee to the Philistines. But after being sponsored by Achish to raid Judah, did David really never carry out any such raids? That's right, says the narrator; he only raided Judah's enemies, and he left none alive to tell the tale (27:8–9). But now, perhaps, we shudder at the wanton slaughter, so the narrator offers a

second insight into David's thoughts: "They might tell about us, and say, 'David has done so and so'" (27:11). This reassures us that David has engaged in such violence only as a matter of necessity. But it also proves to us that David plays duplicitous games in support of his own self-interest, and he will kill—kill foreigners, at least—to forestall discovery.

David's double game finally goes sour when he and his men return from the Philistine muster at Aphek, where they have narrowly escaped being ordered into battle against Saul. An ugly surprise awaits at Ziklag: "Look! burned down, and their wives and sons and daughters taken captive!" (1 S 30:3, my translation). David's men threaten to stone him. "But David," the text tells us, "strengthened himself in the LORD his God" (30:6).

The expression "strengthened himself" has both psychological (he plucked up his courage) and practical (he prepared for action) implications. The fact that he does so "in the LORD" may point forward to his next action: he summons priest with ephod (probably a reassuring move in the eyes of his men) and asks for tactical advice and reassurance. God cooperates by providing the requested answers, in striking contrast to the silence Saul suffers.

1 Samuel 30:5 is our first glimpse of God in David's thoughts. It suggests—without proving, for we don't know what he has been thinking through most of 1 Samuel—that David prays most when things look worst. The dynamics of the incident place God and David on one side and "all the people" on the other, a pattern reminiscent of the one between Samuel and God vis-à-vis the people.

Our inquiry into David's heart next takes us to 2 Samuel and the story of Abner's assassination. Joab takes David to task for allowing Abner (his opposing commander in the war between Saul's house and David's) to visit and depart in peace. Joab then sends messengers to fetch Abner, "but David did not know" (2 S 3:26).

Readers not infrequently feel that the narrator protests David's innocence too much at this point. Insistence that "David did not know" implies someone's suspicion that David *did* know. But even if we accept the narrator's assurance on this point, a question remains: *Should* David have known?

Joab already had a blood-claim against Abner, who had killed Joab's brother Asahel. Abner himself had anticipated the trouble this blood-debt would cause (see his plea to Asahel in 2 S 2:22). Now David has negotiated for Abner's help. Joab surely speculated (as modern interpreters do) that Abner had been promised Joab's job. David knows Joab's dismay over Abner's peaceful departure (3:24–25). David surely knows Joab's decisiveness (recall the interchange with Joab's brother Abishai in 1 S 26 and see the comment in 2 S 2:39). David himself has exclaimed that Abner deserves to die (1 S 26:16). *Should* not David know what Joab will do? No wonder David expresses no surprise when he hears of the murder. No wonder he exhibits such anxiety about his own culpability (3:28–29). "David did not know" is a defensive technicality.

The narrator's subsequent note that David "pleased all the people" (3:36) is hardly comforting; it rings too strongly of the people's pleasure in the book of Judges. Then, there was no king and people did "what was right in their own eyes" (Jdg 21:25 and elsewhere). Now we have a king whose every deed is "good in the eyes of all the people" (3:36, my translation). We also find ourselves skeptical of David's self-alleged powerlessness vis-à-vis Joab (3:39). If the anointed—responsible for justice and civil order—cannot restrain his own officers from violence, what use is it to have a king?

But if David is *not* powerless against Joab (who exerts considerable effort in David's behalf), then he is playing a callous public relations game: he reaps the benefit of Joab's realpolitik while Joab bears popular and sacred blame for it. Does David care no more for Joab than for the slaughtered witnesses in the towns David raided?

In short order David secures his position over all the tribes, captures Jerusalem, and moves into a palace. "David then perceived that the LORD had established him king over Israel, and that he had exalted his kingdom for the sake of his people Israel" (2 S 5:12; the verb translated "perceived" is more commonly rendered "know"). Is his perception accurate? To a first approximation, yes, for the narrator has told us just two verses prior to this that "David became greater and greater, for the LORD, the God of hosts, was with him." This information casts a light of hidden Providence on the seemingly mundane events of David's rise.

But why does the narrator separately and specifically state David's perception of God's involvement? If we know that David attributes his establishment to God, we can ask whether his subsequent actions are appropriate to God's support of David *for the sake of Israel*. We can also ask why David arrives at this perception just after—at least narratively just after—a Phoenician king builds him a palace. Does David reach his conclusion for the wrong reasons? Can he tell the difference between Hiram's action and God's? Can we? Within the universe of biblical thought, one might argue either that (1) the foreign king's favor is a visible symbol of God's support or (2) palaces built by foreign kings are not the form of "establishment" God favors.

Our uncertainty is not resolved by the following verse. David takes "more concubines and wives." This is positive, insofar as abundance of children suggests divine blessing, but it recalls Dt 17:17's warning that the king "must not acquire many wives for himself." Is David now trying to exalt his own kingdom?

Leo Perdue has suggested that the consistently "double" portrait of David in Samuel—a portrait in which incident after incident can be read in either complimentary or troubling terms—reflects ambivalence about monarchy itself.[13] Our uncertainty over the meanings of David's palace, wives, and offspring is a good example; they could be signs of divine favor or evidence of abused royal privilege. Do David's acquisitions climax his ascent or foreshadow his coming fall? The question refuses resolution.

The following sequence (2 S 5:17–6:23) resonates powerfully with the ark stories of 1 S 4–7. Similarities and differences may most easily be seen by means of a chart:

1 Samuel 4–7	2 Samuel 5–6
Fighting with Philistines	Fighting with Philistines
No consultation with God reported	God consulted before battle
Two brothers accompany ark	Two brothers accompany ark
God's role in battle unstated	God's role in battle explicit
Philistines capture Israelite symbol	Israelites capture Philistine symbols
Woman gives birth and dies	Woman bears no more children
Ark wreaks havoc among Philistines	Blessing comes to Philistine house
Philistines: To whom will it go?[14]	David: How can it come to me?
Ark travels on new cart	Ark travels on new cart
Israelites rejoice, sacrifice	Israelites rejoice, sacrifice
Unexpected deaths associated with ark	Unexpected death associated with ark
Ark sent to someone's house	Ark sent to someone's house
Ark remains twenty years, Israel laments	Ark remains three months, blessing
Samuel makes offerings, judges Israel	David makes offerings, rules Israel[15]

Uzzah's death early in 1 S 6 leaves most readers uncomfortable. He meant well; why must he die? Interpreters sometimes appeal to 1 C 15:2 in explaining that Uzzah died because proper protocol had not been observed. But given the circumstances in which the ark came to Abinadab's house (1 S 6:19–7:1), one can scarcely imagine that members of the household would be careless in its handling. On David's part too the transfer appears to have been arranged with considerable care (escort of thirty thousand, songs and music, "new cart" which was, after all, acceptable transport last time). David's surprise and anger confirm that he has no notion of any problem with the arrangements.

Interpreting at the level of improper ritual procedure also fails to make sense of some other interesting features in the sequence. What about its ties to 1 Samuel's ark stories? And what should we make of connections between ark moving and the preceding battles with Philistines? 2 Samuel 6:8 and 5:20 play on words from the *prṣ* family, and Fokkelman points out that the "marching" (*ṣĕʿādâ*) of 5:24 presages the going (*ṣāʿădû*) six paces (*ṣĕʿādîm*) of the ark bearers in 6:13.[16] Finally, 2 S 6:8–10 gives more intense and extensive insight into David's inner life than any other passage in the primary history, suggesting that Uzzah's death has more to do (narratively speaking) with David than Uzzah.

The ark incident teaches David the same lesson that Israel and the Philistines learned in 1 S 4–7: God's support may not be taken for granted.[17] In 2 S 5:12 David perceives divine support. Later in that chapter, he takes advantage of that support, after due consultation, to strike down the Philistines. In 2 S 6 he decides, with no reported consultation, that the ark, an ancient and awesome symbol of divine power, should reside in the capital with him (except when it goes out to fight his battles, 2 S 11:11). Its presence may help the anointed counter those who might protest, along the lines of Samuel's speech in 1 S 12, that Israel's proper king is God, whose leadership through wilderness and in battle has been symbolized by the ark.

Then Uzzah dies. David's first reported emotion is anger, only then followed by fear. Why anger? The text, as usual, fails to explicate underlying psychodynamics. I suggest that David is angry because he had interpreted kingship, fertility, and victory over Philistines as evidence of God's unconditional support. The outburst against Uzzah seems, to David, like a violation of God's contract with him. Anger turns to fear as David realizes that he was mistaken in his assumption about God's support. The man who set out so confidently with thirty thousand men to fetch the ark now asks, "how can LORD's ark come to me?" (6:9, my translation[18]). We learn his answer to this rhetorical question from statements about both feeling and action. He is not willing for the ark to come to him; he leaves it at Obed-Edom's house.

The "ritual procedure" explanation of Uzzah's death is often presented in a fashion which suggests that we *can* count on God's blessing so long as we observe proper protocol, but the explanation presumes a rational God acting according to clear rules. Here I believe we see something different—the warning of a mysterious, even dangerous quality to God's presence, a power which must always be approached tentatively and never presumed upon.

But we have not yet exhausted the possible explanations of Uzzah's death. Another very simple possibility presents itself. What has the ark's history been? It has brought terror in battle (Josh 6), plague (1 S 5–6), and sudden death (1 S 6:19; 2 S 6:7). Maybe the thing is just dangerous, charged with purely destructive power. This may be David's thought as he abandons the ark at Obed-Edom's house. But subsequent blessing rules out this explanation. The ark can, after all, bring well-being—on a Philistine household at that.[19]

Hearing of the blessing, David sets out once again to bring the ark into his city. This time, determined to stay in step—ṣʿd—with the ark's touchy deity, David offers copious sacrifices. But the second procession has its own dark moment—a sharp exchange between David and Michal (pointedly referred to as "Saul's daughter"). We will explore that altercation further in Chapter 6.

In 2 S 5–6 the narrator refers to David primarily by his proper name, as an individual person.[20] Kingship language enters only via the people's point of view and Michal's (6:12, 16, 20). Jerusalem appears as the "city of David" (6:16). David's language to and about God brims with first person *singular* (me) expressions rather than first person plural (us). "Will you give them [the Philistines] into *my* hand?" "The LORD has burst forth against *my* enemies before *me*." "How can the ark . . . come *to me*?" "The LORD . . . chose . . . *me* as prince over Israel." (2 S 5:19, 20; 6:9—my translation—and 21; emphases added.) Despite David's earlier perception (5:12) that his kingdom was exalted for Israel's sake, he now speaks as if everything happens for his own sake. Will God correct the king's vision?

Immediately following the disconcerting news about Michal's lack of children comes God's famous dynastic pledge to David (2 S 7). David plans to build a temple—another standard activity of ancient Near Eastern kings. But Uzzah's death has taught him caution: this time, David consults a prophet before launching into his project. Nathan appears as confident as most readers of the harmony between David's heart (the traditional translation of the word which NRSV renders "mind" in 7:3) and God.[21] He endorses the project, only to be corrected by God sometime later that night. (Note once again that not all a prophet's words reflect God's opinions.)

The rest of the chapter turns upon various meanings of the word house. David thinks to build God a house; God disclaims any desire for such. Instead, God will build David a house. What this accomplishes, as Eslinger argues at length in *House of God or House of David*, is that God avoids being put in David's debt and instead keeps David in the subordinate, receiving position. Yet God at the same time avoids any open break with David.

The play on "house" links the conversation back to David's insight in 5:12. There, juxtaposition raised the question of differentiation between David's "house of cedar" from a Phoenician lord (7:2; 5:11) and the establishment of his kingship by Israel's God. If David is indeed confused about the source and significance of his own cedar house, God's correction sets him straight: "you are mistaken about which kind of house really matters and who can provide it—not only with respect to my house, but also with respect to your own."

God's speech (which Nathan faithfully reports to David, according to 7:17) again refers to the people's place in God's plans. It also clarifies the limits of divine support: when the king commits iniquity, God will punish (7:14). God will not cast off: a thrice-repeated "forever" (7:13 and twice in 16) emphasizes this. Yet the very language of the guarantee contains a disquieting reminder that God has been known to withdraw loyalty: "I will not take my steadfast love from him, *as I took it from Saul*" (7:15, emphasis added). The speech gives with one hand and takes with the other; even as it offers "forever," it reminds us that promises can be broken.

David's flowery response is even longer (one hundred ninety-eight words) than God's announcement (one hundred ninety-one). Conspicuous by its absence is narratorial confirmation of David's feelings or understandings. The next chapter, however, tells us that "LORD gave victory to David wherever he went" (8:6 and 14) and "David administered justice and equity to all his people" (8:15). For the moment, their agreement appears to be working out.

In 2 S 10:5 David intercepts returning couriers who have been shaven and partially disrobed, "for the men were greatly ashamed." This phrase is apparently an insight into David's reasoning, but it tells us less than we might think. Is David concerned about their feelings? Or is David worried about the reflection of their shame on his own public image? Once again, ambiguity surrounds David's heart.

Our next major sequence of glimpses into David's inner life comes in connection with his affair with Bathsheba and its aftermath. As David walks on the roof of the "king's house" (a familiar motif!) he sees "a woman bathing" (2 S 11:2). I am inclined to view the subsequent comment on her beauty as a continuation of David's perception. According to NRSV's translation, David then sends someone else who inquires about the woman and receives an anonymous answer (11:3). In Hebrew, however, we have three consecutive verbs with no indication of a change in subject,[22] followed by a rhetorical question: "David sent . . . and inquired . . . and said . . . 'Isn't this Bathsheba, Eliam's daughter, wife of Uriah the Hittite?'" (11:3, my translation). Apparently David knows from the very outset that the woman is married to one of his soldiers.

As Meir Sternberg has shown with such force, there is a great deal we do not know about subsequent events: How did Bathsheba feel? Did her husband know why David wanted him to go home? Did Uriah know what was in the letter? Did Joab know why Uriah must die? Did Joab's messenger understand the special significance of Uriah's death?[23] But two facts emerge clearly: David gets Bathsheba pregnant, and David arranges Uriah's death.

We then receive something even rarer than an insight into David—an insight into God. "The thing that David had done displeased the LORD"

(11:27). At last we verify our suspicion: however positive God's regard for David, it is not unconditional.

When Nathan tells David the famous parable of the ewe lamb, David's anger is "greatly kindled against the man" (2 S 12:5). As we saw in Chapter 2, "the man" is an ambiguous designation, but to a first approximation it refers to the rich man in the parable. Most interpreters praise David's anger as a sign that his heart is still in the right place, but Fokkelman questions its appropriateness: "David at once reacts as a judge, but without exercising the sobriety and patient discrimination prerequisite for the practice of such an eminent profession. A good judge does not explode with anger at a mere theft, nor need he employ the forceful terms of an oath. The quickness, severity and intense indignation on David's part all constitute signs of his lack of equilibrium and too great an involvement."[24]

David now receives an explanation of the parable. Polzin points out that God's own words (marked as such by the oracular formula "thus says the LORD") in 12:7–8 put God in the role of rich man. "Before ever the ewe lamb represents the one wife David took from Uriah, it represents the many wives God took from Saul and gave to David."[25] God here assumes the role celebrated in Hannah's song: "The LORD makes poor and makes rich; he brings low, he also exalts" (1 S 2:7). The oracle views David's receipt of wives and power as, in and of itself, nonproblematic: "if that had been too little, I would have added as much more" (2 S 12:8). We recall our earlier observation that perhaps Hannah, representing Israel, should have been more careful what she prayed for.

But now David has usurped God's role, *taking* (a key word throughout 2 S 11–12, recalling the warning of 1 S 8:11–18) in his own behalf and even making decisions about life and death (2 S 12:9–10). We see a parallel to the previous section, where God willingly supported David when asked (2 S 5), but "burst forth" when David manipulated the ark without asking (2 S 6). Is it easier to get forgiveness than permission? Not here.

In the oracle's denouement (12:11–12), Polzin observes, "God is once again the rich man, but David is now the poor king whose beloved lamb is to be taken from him and given to 'the one who comes,' first to Absalom for a time, then to Jeroboam, Assyria and finally Babylon." Israel is caught between God and David—first suffering the king's predation, then trapped in the king's punishment. "The fate of the house of David and that of the house of Israel are so intertwined that Nathan's parable, as interpreted by God and Nathan, may very well explain not only the complex history of David, but even that of Israel itself."[26]

If we are right in supposing that God objects less to David's maltreatment of the people than David's hubris vis-à-vis God self, we begin to understand why David confesses "I have sinned against the LORD" rather than "I have sinned against Uriah and Bathsheba." God's response (as reported by Nathan) deserves our attention. Most English translations of 12:13 suggest that David is forgiven (for example, NRSV: "the LORD has put away your sin"). We are then a little confused to hear that punishment will still occur: "You shall not die. Nevertheless . . . the child that is born to you shall die" (12:14). Does this mean that God has forgiven—but not quite?

The verb translated "put away" means, etymologically, "to make something pass over/across," or more simply "to transfer." In most of its appearances, it has this meaning in a simple physical sense—for example, in 2 S 19:15 where the people of Judah come "to meet the king and to *bring* him *over* the Jordan" (emphasis added). In only a handful of places does it refer to forgiveness (an example would be Zech 3:4, "I have *taken* your guilt *away*," emphasis added).

In the present instance (2 S 12:13), does the verb mean that the sin/guilt is taken away? Or does it retain its sense of "made to pass across"? In the latter case, Nathan says (my translation), "LORD has transferred your sin: *you* will not die . . . rather the child that will be born to you must die." This suits our picture of a David who, like Samuel before him, enjoys more than reasonable favor from God. Even when God does punish David, others (Uzzah, the baby, the concubines of 2 S 15:16, 16:22; 20:3) bear the brunt of punishment.[27]

The possibility that the verb may have this meaning is increased when we look ahead to the only other Samuel passage which uses this verb in connection with sin/forgiveness. The context is David's military census, which presumably violated the Israelite ideal of a volunteer militia (although it was ordered by God). "David was stricken to the heart because he had numbered the people. David said to the LORD, 'I have sinned greatly in what I have done. But now, O LORD, I pray you, *take away* the guilt of your servant; for I have done very foolishly'" (2 S 24:10, emphasis added). The result? A plague which kills seventy thousand people. Has the guilt been "taken away," or has it been "transferred" to a great many other people?

In 2 S 12, God strikes David's child. David pleads with God, fasts, and lies all night on the ground. Does he genuinely believe God's mind will change? Does he regret that the child must bear his sin? Is he worried that the child's death will be read for what it is, a judgment against David? We are not given the answers to these questions; our only glimpse into David comes as he sees the servants whispering and concludes that the child is dead (12:19). At this point he puts aside his mourning, to the great confusion of his staff.

Once again affairs of war and rulership go well (although we may be a little uneasy when David, like Pharaoh, sets his foreign slaves to brickmaking in

2 S 12:31). But sexual misdeeds continue to trouble the royal family. David's eldest son Amnon rapes David's daughter Tamar; her brother Absalom counsels her to swallow her grief. David hears and becomes "very angry"; this is all the traditional Hebrew text tells us. The Qumran copies and Greek versions (followed by NRSV) add, "but he would not distress the spirit of his son Amnon, because he loved him, for he was his firstborn" (2 S 13:21 Greek, my translation).

The traditional Hebrew leaves us a little unclear as to the precise causes and targets of David's anger. Is he more upset about the rape, or Tamar's response, or Absalom's? The longer Greek text suggests Amnon as target of David's anger and gives the reason for David's failure to act upon his anger: "he loved him, for he was his firstborn." If we accept this as part of our Samuel text, it is the one (and only) case in which David is clearly said to love someone.[28] In any case, David remains passive. Years later, Amnon dies at the hand of Absalom's servants. Absalom flees to his grandfather, King Talmai of Geshur.

We now encounter two extremely confusing statements about David's feelings. Immediately after the news of Absalom's flight, we hear that "he mourned after his son all the days" (13:37, my translation). "He" appears to be David. (Ancient translations clarify this by specifying "the king" or "David.") The verb translated "mourned" is used, a few verses later, for an artificial appearance of grief ("*Pretend to be a mourner*; put on mourning garments, do not anoint yourself with oil . . . ," 2 S 14:2, emphasis added; however, the pretense component is not obvious here[29]). And for which son does David mourn—Amnon who is dead or Absalom who has fled to Geshur with bloodguilt on his head?

The final verse of the chapter only increases our confusion. The traditional Hebrew text tells us that "King David (or the king's spirit[30]) *tkl* ('longed' or 'ceased') to 'go out' to Absalom because he was *nḥm* ('grieved' or 'consoled') about Amnon, because he was dead" (2 S 13:39, my nontranslation). This might mean that: (1) David got over his grief for Amnon—who was dead—and longed to go see his living son Absalom, or (2) David got over his grief for Amnon—who was dead—and therefore quit wanting to march out with his army (a common meaning of "go out") against Absalom, or (3) David was still so upset about Amnon—who was dead—that he longed to march out with his army against Absalom.[31]

The confusion persists into 2 S 14:1, which gives us Joab's perception that "the king's heart[32] was [set] *'al* ('upon' or 'against') Absalom" (my translation).

NRSV (like most other standard English translations) suggests option 1: David yearning for reconciliation with Absalom. Commentators in the prestigious Anchor Bible and Word Biblical Commentary series both settle on option 2,[33] noting that Joab's resort to subterfuge and the woman's anxiety in 2 S 14 suggest that David is *not* inclined toward reconciliation. (His refusal to see Absalom after the prince returns points in the same direction.) I am most inclined to agree with Fokkelman, who chooses option 3, arguing that "all the days" in 13:37 precludes an end to David's mourning for Amnon.[34]

Following this reading, we find David—who was angry about the rape but did nothing—unable to reconcile himself to the rapist's death and therefore also unable to reconcile with the surviving son who did do something about it. His paralysis continues even after Joab and the Tekoite woman maneuver him into bringing Absalom home. For two years he refuses to see the returned Absalom (14:28). Even when Joab (himself evidently reluctant to speak to Absalom) finally arranges an audience, we do not hear father and son speak with one another.

We next encounter David's feelings[35] some chapters later, as he receives news of Absalom's death. "The king was deeply moved," we hear in 18:33. The verb in question is a strong one, associated with events such as earthquake. Possibly it is an external rather than internal description—he trembled—but David's subsequent words and actions suggest genuine disturbance.

Fokkelman proposes that David shows more disturbance than the situation merits. "The lamentation in 19:1 [18:33 in most English translations] is moving, nay heart-rending, but . . . it does not merit a sentimental approach offering an ode to paternal love. . . . From a father who suddenly loses a son due to an accident, war, or for whatever cause, the exclamation 'had *I* but died in your place!' is moving, understandable, and sound, but in the mouth of this father who has not the courage required for drastic remedies in connection with such an incorrigible spoiled son, the same exclamation is quite different, a sign of pure self-torment."[36]

Oddly enough, in David's supreme moment of personal grief the narrator refers to him as "the king." This suggests narratorial agreement with the assessments of the messengers (18:28, 31–32) and clear-sighted general Joab (19:5–7): Absalom's defeat comes as part of God's defense of David, and David's people deserve something other than his self-indulgent collapse.

2 Samuel's final glimpses into David's heart come in the final chapters (2 S 21–24), a section sometimes referred to as the book's "appendix" (or appendices). This terminology originated with source critics, but it arises from features that remain quite visible in the final form of the text. David Gunn and Walter Brueggemann have each developed, in different ways, the notion that these "appendix" chapters further problematize an already problematic picture of David, and I will draw on their work both here and in Chapter 6.[37]

We should note here that the stories, poems, and lists of 2 S 21–24 stand in an uncertain temporal relationship to the preceding narrative. For instance, 2 S 21 reports events that may be presupposed by a question much earlier in the book: "Is there still anyone left of the house of Saul?" (2 S 9:1). The narrator even gives us a "tracer" to connect the two stories: each is preceded by a list of David's officials (2 S 8:16–18 and 20:23–26). These lists perform a sort of asterisk function in directing our attention from one story to the other. 2 Samuel 21 also appears to underlie Shimei's reference to "the blood of the house of Saul" in 2 S 16:8.

The story in 21:1–14 is a troubling one in many respects. When David asks God about a three-year famine, God replies that bloodguilt lies on Saul's house for an otherwise unknown action undertaken "in his zeal for the people of Israel and Judah." David, after consultation with the offended parties, extradites seven surviving offspring of Saul. They are impaled "before the LORD" in a ceremony that smacks heavily of human sacrifice and fertility magic.[38] Only a long vigil by Saul's former concubine Rizpah (whose two sons are among the slain) saves the bodies from further desecration by beasts and carrion birds. The story ends on a somewhat happier note: the report of Rizpah's vigil prompts David to gather the bones of these seven and also Saul and Jonathan to an honorable burial in the family tomb. When all this is done, "God heeded supplications for the land" (21:14).

A first reading suggests that in this tale, God approves of or even requires human sacrifice (of Israelites by non-Israelites, no less). Alternatively, we may insist that the only reliable information about God involves the statement of Saul's bloodguilt and the closing response to supplication: intervening actions involve human initiative rather than narratorially certified instructions from God. If we thus excuse God, however, David is left using the Gibeonites' religious customs to accomplish a politically expedient cleanup.

I discuss the story here because it includes one direct insight into David's heart and thought: "The king spared Mephibosheth, the son of Saul's son Jonathan, because of the oath of the LORD that was between them, between David and Jonathan son of Saul" (21:7). Once again insight raises further questions. Does David's restraint stem from respect for the sacred nature of his oath? Or does he spare Mephibosheth out of a more personal loyalty to Jonathan? The wording of the sentence ("the king," "oath of the LORD") points to the power of the oath, whereas the fact that David ignores a similar oath to Saul (1 S 24:21–22) suggests a personal motivation. Mephibosheth was a nonthreatening exemption, for his lameness would probably disqualify him (both ritually and militarily) for kingship.

The language and themes of this story in 2 S 21 tie it closely to the closing chapter of the book; but before moving on we note an intervening pair of insights into David. In 2 S 23:15 David speaks longingly (first insight) of water from his hometown well. Three of his men break through Philistine lines to fetch it for him. David pours the water out as a libation and is unwilling (second insight) to drink it (23:17). This unwillingness to satisfy desire at the expense of others stands in marked contrast to David's "taking" in the Bathsheba story.

Brueggemann correctly notes the contrast between the David of this story, a hero "among brothers" all of whom owe their success to God, and the David who delivers Saul's descendants to sacrifice, "a political killer who hides his actions in religious justification." This contrast, he suggests, counterbalances the rhetoric of royal theology by calling our attention to power's corruption. Gunn finds dissonance even within the unit, pointing out that the theme of blood and the names in surrounding verses remind us of the great quantity of blood which has been spilled in David's rise to power.[39]

The final chapter of 2 Samuel presents another disturbing story which closely parallels the human-sacrifice tale of 2 S 21. God becomes angry with Israel, for unspecified reasons. Given what we have seen about God's anger elsewhere in the books of Samuel, we may or may not want to conclude that Israel has merited this anger by some sin (such as turning away from God). "God was angry" occasionally seems a simple equivalent for "disaster happened," as if all disaster is attributed to God without any assumption of tight moral causality.

In any event, God "incited David against them"—a phrase recalling our earlier question about whether kingship is granted to Israel as a punishment. God instructs David to take a census—an action probably objectionable because it provides data for taxation and conscription purposes ("able to draw the sword," 24:9). Even the militia commander Joab is puzzled by David's command.

David is then "stricken to the heart" (24:10, same phrase as 1 S 24:5) and prays that God will make the guilt pass over (24:10, using the same verb we discussed in connection with 2 S 12:13). God responds with a choice of punishments: famine, persecution, or plague. David chooses plague, expressing hope that God's hand is more merciful than human hands. Seventy thousand people die.

Again God's role is problematic: God commands a census, then punishes David for taking it. If such behavior strikes us as bordering on demonic, we are not alone: the Chronicler, retelling the story, will assign its initial prompt to *śāṭān*, the heavenly prosecutor or at least "an adversary" (1 C 21:1). But the Samuel narrator grants us no such intermediary figure. Responsibility rests squarely on God.

What about David's role in the story? As usual, a first reading shows him very faithful. He obeys the divine command. Then he has conscience (or palpitations) enough to see his error and beg forgiveness. He chooses a punishment on the basis of his confidence in God's mercy (24:14). His reasoning here reminds me of his explanation for his behavior vis-à-vis Bathsheba's sick child: David seems ever-willing to leave the door open for grace from God, although the hoped-for respites do not always materialize. When he realizes what this punishment costs his people, he repents again: "What have they done? Let your hand . . . be against me" (24:17).

Yet it was David who chose the punishment of plague, rather than a period of fleeing before his own enemies (24:13–14). The story's subsequent insight into David's perception is also telling: watch the timing. In 24:16 God relents and tells the angel of destruction, "stay your hand." In 24:17 *David sees the angel*. Only then—when the destruction has already been halted, if we take the narrative sequence seriously—does David offer himself in behalf of the people. As in his exclamation at Absalom's death (2 S 18:33), the wish to die in another's (or many others') behalf comes at a safely late moment, when the damage is already over.

David then follows prophetic instructions for purchase of what will become the temple site, and he offers sacrifices there. The book closes on a positive note: "LORD answered his supplication for the land, and the plague was averted from Israel." Israel has a king to intercede with God on its behalf; but just how much is that worth for Israel, when it is the king's action which brings plague to begin with, and seventy thousand die in the interim?

Thus ends David's story in the books of Samuel. David's brief appearance in Kings contains no glimpses of his inner life beyond the fact that he can be warmed neither by bedclothes nor the lovely girl who shares his couch.

Looking back over our insights into David from his youth through the maturity of his kingship, we see some interesting patterns. Seven times (all in 1 Samuel) our insights concern David's fear or perception of persecution and danger; these incidents are preceded by a glimpse of his ambition (1 S 18:26). Four times (all in 2 Samuel) we see David angry: over Uzzah's death (6:8), Nathan's story (12:5), the rape incident (13:21), and Absalom's murder of Amnon (13:39). In all four of these cases, David bears some responsibility for the incident which angers him. Thrice we hear of grief: 2 S 13:37 and 39 (Amnon) and 18:33 (Absalom). In each case, David grieves for a son with whom he had been angry but whom he did not discipline.

In two very interesting cases (1 S 24:5; 2 S 24:10) David's heart "smites" him: one leads to the principle of sanctity for God's anointed, the other to a

69

place where the anointed makes offerings on behalf of Israel. Only twice do we encounter God in David's inner thoughts: in 1 S 30:5 when his men threaten to stone him; and in 2 S 5:12 when he perceives, perhaps from the wrong evidence, that God has established him.

Several insights tell us less than we might think. For instance, does David's "not knowing" about Joab's recall of Abner (2 S 3:26) really leave David clear of responsibility? Does his message to the envoys (2 S 10:5) convey concern for their reputation or his own?

With the possible exception of 2 S 13:21 (in the Greek version, which speaks of David's love for Amnon as firstborn), David is never said to love either God or another human person. Love for Jonathan may (or may not) underlie David's sparing of Mephibosheth in 2 S 21:7.

Our glimpses of David's heart have shown us a man more worldly-wise, more fallible, and considerably less pious than our first overview of Samuel led us to expect. What has been lost in admirability, however, has been gained in believability. David's heart looks remarkably like anyone else's.

CHAPTER 6

TROUBLING DETAILS:
DAVID'S WORDS AND DEEDS

Our reading of David's heart (Chapter 5) has raised serious questions about the "good David" scenario presented in Chapter 4. In light of these questions, we drop our initial assumption that David's words and deeds are all (or nearly all) "after God's own heart." In this chapter I undertake a more suspicious reading of other details of Samuel's David story. The format will be simple: I quote a problematic statement (in italics), explain the problem—which will sometimes take us across a series of passages—then move on to the next "starter verse." We will skip over problems which have already been discussed.

"*. . . a son of Jesse the Bethlehemite who is skillful in playing, a man of valor, a warrior . . .*" (1 S 16:18). Jesse sends gifts to court with his eighth son (16:20) as well as gifts to the commanders of the three sons he can afford to equip as warriors (17:13 and 17–18). These observations do not necessarily shadow David's character, but they require us to rethink our fairy-tale romanticism about David's age and background. He does not enter court as a young child from a poor family.

"*What have I done?*" (1 S 17:29; 20:1; 26:18; 29:8). As a younger brother's retort to an older brother's criticism in 1 S 17:9, this question from David sounds amusingly familiar. But when it recurs in David's mouth three more times, we must ask what role it plays in characterizing him.

What has David done? When he responds to Eliab, who has already been established as a kind of Saul-figure in 1 S 16:6–7, David has done nothing except reveal his interest in the reward for killing Goliath (David's first words, 1 S 17:26). But by the time he asks Jonathan, "What have I done? . . . And what is my sin against your father?" (1 S 20:1), David has accepted the heir apparent's robe and sword (18:4), married into the royal family, developed popular support (including particularly the army), and publicly flaunted his relationship with the kingmaker Samuel (19:18), who declared Saul's downfall. David's *intentions* may only have been hinted at, but his *actions* point steadily toward the throne.

In 1 S 26:18 David asks Saul directly: "Why does my lord pursue his servant? For what have I done?" David has now had multiple secret meetings with Saul's son, gathered a fighting force, gotten a corner on priestly support, developed contacts in neighboring kingdoms (see especially 22:3), demanded support from landowners (25:8), married into riches (25:42), and possibly run off with Saul's wife (25:43). The Philistines speak of him as king already (21:11).

Yet in another sense, David is correct in suggesting that he is not responsible for the persecution from Saul. The reason for Saul's persecution is clearly stated in the text: "an evil spirit from the LORD tormented him" (16:14; see also 18:10–11 and 19:9–10). What has David done? Please the God who now provokes Saul to persecute David.[1]

In 1 S 29:8 David's "what have I done?" is directed to Achish of Gath. David asks why he should not fight "the enemies of my lord the king." Achish, assuming that he himself is David's lord, hears the question as assurance of David's eagerness to fight against Saul. But David has deceived Achish twice already (21:13 and 27:10). Perhaps "my lord the king" is Saul, and David plans to betray his Philistine protector. (His earlier assurance to Achish—"you shall know what your servant can do," 28:2—exhibits similar ambiguity.) Or perhaps Achish is right, and David has less respect than he declares for God's anointed. Each time David has asked his rhetorical question, the possible answers have become more problematic. Now David betrays someone no matter which possibility we choose.

David prevailed over the Philistine with a sling and a stone . . . there was no sword in David's hand (1 S 17:50). This is ideologically important: it underscores God's ability to save independent of human might (see David's own remark on this in 17:47). David's victory *sans* sword establishes him as a classic underdog hero. And his next action? "He [David] grasped his [Goliath's] sword, drew it out of its sheath" (17:51). Goliath's sword reappears in 1 S 21:9 to accompany David in his departure from Saul's court. Evidently David no longer eschews the trappings of worldly military might.

"Who am I . . . that I should be son-in-law to the king?" (1 S 18:18). Saul has just offered his eldest daughter Merab to David as wife. One condition is attached to the offer: "only be valiant for me and fight the LORD's battles," for Saul hopes that the Philistines will do away with David (18:17). David demurs with the line quoted above. Does this mean that he refused to fight the Philistines? Everything else we hear about David celebrates his activities in battle during this period, but if he were going to fight the Philistines anyway, why not accept Saul's offer? The narrator reports Merab's marriage to somebody else as if it were a violation of contract on Saul's part—"at the time

when Saul's daughter Merab should have been given to David (18:19)—but did not David refuse the offer?

Ironically, Saul's plan—"I will not raise a hand against him [David]; let the Philistines deal with him" (18:17)—is exactly how David finally disposes of Saul.

Saul's daughter Michal loved David (1 S 18:20). This brief statement, immediately following the announcement of Merab's marriage, initiates a long relationship with a bitter end. *Telling Queen Michal's Story*, a collection of essays and articles edited by Clines and Eskenazi, shows just how rich and varied the interpretations of Michal's story can be. Michal's name is mentioned in 1 S 14:49, but reader interest in her normally begins with 1 S 18, "the only instance in all biblical narrative in which we are explicitly told that a woman loves a man."[2] For Saul, the love represents another opportunity to lure David to death by Philistine hands (18:21). This time David agrees to the marriage, because "he was well pleased to be the king's son-in-law" (18:26). Michal soon finds herself deceiving her father in order to send David to safety (19:11–17).

We later hear, following announcements of David's marriages to Abigail and Ahinoam (1 S 25:42–44; we asked in Chapter 2 about the connection between this Ahinoam and the one to whom Saul is wedded), that Saul gives Michal to a new husband (1 S 25:44; NRSV's "had given" is interpretive). She reenters the story in 2 S 3:13 as a pawn in negotiations between David and Abner. We have only one clue as to the nature of her second marriage and her probable feelings about its forced dissolution: "Ishbaal sent and took her from her husband Paltiel the son of Laish. But her husband went with her, weeping as he walked behind her all the way to Bahurim" (2 S 3:15–16).

A few chapters later (2 S 6:16) we find Michal looking down at David as he dances and sacrifices in a garb, apparently skimpy, associated elsewhere with priestly service (1 S 2:18 and 22:18). Some scholars see parallels between this procession and other ancient Near Eastern celebrations which culminated in a "sacred marriage"—a sexual act by the king which was thought to invoke fertility for land and people.[3] Contributing motifs would include the scantiness of David's dress, the woman waiting at his final destination, the "blessings" David offers (for the fertility connotations of this word, see Gen 1 and Deuteronomy) and the detail of raisin cakes (a term appearing elsewhere only in the Chronicles parallel, Hos 3:1, and Cant 2:5). If this association is correct, Michal has good reason to despise David.

But even if David's conduct does not imply a fertility ritual, Michal has cause for concern. Her father's initial rejection was associated with offering sacrifice (1 S 13), and he also suffered from religious frenzy (1 S 10:10–13 and

19:23–24, which includes a nakedness motif).[4] No wonder "Saul's daughter" finds it alarming for a king to behave thus.

All the more bitter, then, is David's retort. Not only has he been chosen over Michal's father and his house, and not only does he get away with behavior which brought Saul condemnation and disgrace, but David preens himself for his piety! Nor does he deign to deny Michal's accusation of sexual display: "by the maids of whom you have spoken, by them I shall be held in honor" (2 S 6:22). Clines comments, "David finds religious ecstasy a good way of impressing women, and it matters very much to him whether they admire him or not. Michal has announced that she doesn't admire him, but David can get along quite happily with those 'maidservants,' if that is what she likes to call them, who do admire him."[5]

We then hear that "Michal the daughter of Saul had no child to the day of her death" (2 S 6:23). The "good David" interpretation sees this as God's judgment upon Saul's daughter and her views. More skeptical readers interpret it as her punishment from *David*—or, as Clines and Exum both suggest, her refusal *of* David.[6] But because her barrenness deprives David of an heir who might unite the kingdom's disparate political factions, we might also consider it God's action against David.

David's relationship with Michal acquires a final dark footnote in the Hebrew text of 2 S 21:8–9: "The king took the two sons of Rizpah . . . and the five sons of Michal, daughter of Saul, whom she bore to Adriel, son of Barzillai the Meholathite; he gave them into the hands of the Gibeonites, and they impaled them" (my translation). However, Adriel was not Michal's husband but her older sister Merab's. This is why the NRSV translator follows those ancient translations (see the textual note), which say "Merab."[7] The Hebrew text raises the haunting possibility that David hands over five of Michal's earlier children for execution in addition to giving her no more, or at least it reminds us, as it narrates the bereavement of her sister, that this is not David's only offense against Saul's daughters. Is David taking revenge for the interchange reported in 1 S 18:17–19?

Jonathan made David swear again (1 S 20:17). At least three times Jonathan and David enter into covenant: 1 S 18:3; 20:16–17; 23:18. In two of the three chapters Jonathan is clearly the initiator.[8] Why this repeated swearing? Does Jonathan at some level question David's reliability, particularly whether David's word will hold once David comes to power? If so the suspicions may be justified: in 2 Samuel David's oath to Jonathan will be recalled; but a very similar oath to Saul, sworn only once (1 S 24:21–22), goes subsequently unmentioned.

David said to the priest Ahimelech, "The king has charged me with a matter" (1 S 21:2). David is not on a mission from the king; he is fleeing from court and will soon arrive in Philistia, Goliath's sword in hand. But that is not all. Later he says, "I knew on that day, when Doeg the Edomite was there, that he would surely tell Saul. I am responsible for the lives of all your father's house" (1 S 22:22 referring to 22:9–19). In our admiration for David's willingness to apologize, and in the midst of asking ourselves whether Saul does not also bear some responsibility, we sometimes fail to note that by not squaring with Ahimelech David really did contribute to the massacre at Nob.

Everyone who was in distress, and everyone who was in debt, and everyone who was discontented gathered to him (1 S 22:2). Our "good David" scenario described these as "men dispossessed by Saul's harmful policies." An alternative explanation is that David keeps bad company, in contrast to Saul, who was followed by "warriors whose hearts God had touched" (1 S 10:26; the next verse dismisses Saul's opponents as "worthless fellows").

"Will the men of Keilah surrender me and my men into the hand of Saul?" The Lord *said, "They will surrender you"* (1 S 23:12). This is remarkable in view of the fact that David has just liberated this city from Philistine harassment. Does that "liberation" require quotation marks? A neighboring people, the Ziphites, show even greater eagerness to aid Saul's capture of David (23:19, 26:1). Why do they want to be rid of David?

"Your shepherds have been with us, and we did them no harm, and they missed nothing . . . Therefore . . . please give whatever you have at hand" (1 S 25:7–8). Is this a protection racket? Perhaps this is why the local people want to be rid of David.

"Evil shall not be found in you so long as you live" (1 S 25:28). Abigail has a great deal to say about David and God's support of David. She knows a rising star when she sees one and she knows how to ingratiate herself with him. (In this regard, the narrator's contrast between Abigail and her husband in 25:3 is absolutely justified.) Commentators regard her anticipation of David's "sure house" (28) as "prophetic." Yet this loquacious flattery comes from a wealthy woman attempting to forestall an attack on her household—a woman who dislikes her husband (25), asks to be remembered by the handsome young man she speaks to (31), and rushes to accept that young man's marriage proposal (41–42). Surely the narrator does not quote her in tones of simple and solemn approval.

Abigail, like Samuel, has an investment in the ideology she presents. Like Samuel, she raises valid concerns. Like Samuel, she neglects valid counter-concerns. The verse cited above is our surest clue that Abigail presents a slanted version of the truth, for it is patently *not* true that David will be free of evil throughout his life.

Abigail got up hurriedly and . . . became his wife (1 S 25:42). Levenson and Halpern identify Abigail with the Abigal of 2 S 17:25, "daughter of Nahash, sister of Zeruiah, Joab's mother."[9] ("Ithra the Ishmaelite" would then be the real name of the man our story refers to only by the nickname *nābāl*, "Churl.") According to 1 C 2:16, Zeruiah and Abigal/Abigail were David's sisters. Ordinarily I hesitate to import information from Chronicles into Samuel, but the Samuel narrative assumes that we know who Zeruiah is, and an identity as "David's sister" fits that assumption and would explain why Joab and his brothers are identified by their mother's name rather than their father's.

If Abigail is David's half-sister, then 1 S 25 foreshadows not only 2 S 11 (death of David's opponent by indirect means, David takes the wife—a parallel reinforced by continued reference to Abigail as "Nabal's wife"[10]) but also 2 S 13 (intercourse between brother and sister). Note Tamar's suggestion in 2 S 13:13 that David would consent to a brother/sister marriage. These parallels put an even more problematic light on Abigail's already-questionable words.

"You are as blameless in my sight as an angel of God" (1 S 29:9).[11] This statement comes from Achish, whom David has been deceiving with respect to his raiding habits and whom David has probably deceived with respect to his plans for the coming battle. David will again be told, twice, that he is "like the angel of God" as the wise woman of Tekoa manipulates him into forgoing vengeance (2 S 14:17, 20). He will hear the phrase a fourth time from his crippled house guest/prisoner Mephibosheth, whose possessions David has given to the deceitful steward Ziba (2 S 19:27). The flattering phrase has an ironic ring, especially because the only other "angel of God" referred to in 1 and 2 Samuel is the plague-angel of 2 S 24.

"This is David's spoil." . . . *When David came to Ziklag, he sent part of the spoil to his friends, the elders of Judah* (1 S 30:20, 26). Two points are interesting. First, this is Amalekite spoil—the same stuff which Saul was so bitterly punished for reserving in 1 S 15. Second, this is no "Robin Hood" operation. David sends presents not to the peasantry but to the elders of walled cities in the region which will shortly crown him king.

"Your blood be on your head; for your own mouth has testified against you, saying, 'I have killed the LORD's *anointed'* " (2 S 1:16). If David had a stake in the sanctity of God's anointed before Saul's death, how much more now that Saul has died! In addition, his outrage against the messenger helps cover the fact that David was enriching himself with Amalekite plunder, whereas Saul died fighting Israel's battles.

Ishbaal, Saul's son, . . . reigned two years. . . . The time that David was king in Hebron over the house of Judah was seven years and six months (2 S 2:10–11). These verses and 2 S 5:5 both seem to suggest that David reigned from Hebron over Judah only and that he moved to Jerusalem very shortly after being recognized king of the northern tribes at the time of Ishbaal's death. If Ishbaal's two-year kingship began within five years of Saul's death (as seems to be suggested by 2:8), then David must already, contrary to the implications of the narrative sequencing, have been king over Judah at Hebron when Saul died.

"And now shall I not require his [Ishbaal's] blood at your hand, and destroy you from the earth?" (2 S 4:11). David's addressees, Rechab and Baanah, clearly thought David would be pleased by their action and probably expected a reward. David's indignation, like his mourning for Abner, helps quell suspicion that he arranged the murder. The executions, like the similar killing of the Amalekite messenger in 2 S 1—underscore the principle of a king's sanctity (the only king remaining now is David). If David did arrange the murder—a point on which we have no information—killing the two men saves him from having to pay a reward and removes any possibility that they will "squeal."

We learn earlier in the chapter that the assassins Rechab and Baanah are Beerothites. The energy with which the narrator explains that they were considered Benjaminites (4:2–3) alerts us to the fact that there must have been some question about their status. This may in turn point us to Josh 9:17, which claims that the Beerothites were natives who tricked the incoming Israelites into a peace treaty. If so, this may be another instance of David killing foreigners to cover his tracks.

He also defeated the Moabites and, making them lie down on the ground . . . he measured two lengths of cord for those who were to be put to death, and one length for those who were to be spared (2 S 8:2). It was Moab that sheltered David's family in 1 S 22:3–4. According to the book of Ruth, which may be working from 1 S 22, David's great-grandmother was Moabite. David's conquest of Moab also infringes on God's grant to Lot's descendants (Dt 2:9).

David's sons were priests (2 S 8:18). This does not sit well with insistence elsewhere upon proper lineage for priests. It echoes unpleasantly with the story in Jdg 17–18 involving a young Judahite from Bethlehem who acts as Levite.

"Is there anyone remaining of the house of Saul to whom I may show the kindness of God?" (2 S 9:3). As many interpreters have noted, this question seems to presuppose David's handover of seven of Saul's descendants for human sacrifice in 2 S 21:1–14 (in that story he has no trouble locating the remnant of the house of Saul). Having located Jonathan's crippled son, David instructs the son's steward Ziba: "Bring in the produce, so that your master's grandson may have food to eat; but your master's grandson Mephibosheth shall always eat at my table" (2 S 9:10). Does David's understanding of "the kindness of God" include asking a house guest (or prisoner) to provide his own food?

So David sent messengers to get her, and she came to him, and he lay with her (2 S 11:4). Whereas not a word about Bathsheba's feelings. For centuries interpreters have argued about whether she led him on. Our "good David" scenario follows a long tradition of trying to mitigate David's guilt by saying he was "seduced by a beautiful woman."

Why was she bathing where David could see her? So far as we know, outdoor baths were common custom. (Scripture's only other outdoor bather, Susanna, is explicitly attested as virtuous and innocent, but her story is set a good many centuries later than Bathsheba's.[12]) The fact that no one mentions a death penalty for Bathsheba (against the instruction of Dt 22:22–24) suggests that she was not considered at fault. But we simply do not know how she felt or acted. We do not need to know: her attitude does not affect the central question of *David's* guilt. The Hebrew Bible demands that a man leave other men's wives alone, regardless of whether they beckon him on.

Could we term David's action "sexual harassment," in the modern sense? Yes, insofar as his sexual misconduct involves abuse of power. The triple use of the term *king's* house ("palace" in some translations) points in this direction, as does the key word "take." But although we would tend to see Bathsheba as the injured party, the narrator treats David's action as an offense against Uriah (and, eventually, God). In fact, one sometimes hears that in biblical thought adultery and rape are offenses *only* against other men/God. To me, the sympathetic treatment of Tamar in 2 S 13 suggests otherwise. 2 Samuel 11 involves issues like those of sexual harassment but does not approaching them in the same way we would.

"Who killed Abimelech son of Jerubbaal?" (2 S 11:21). Joab introduces Abimelech (Jdg 9) as an example of the dangers of coming too near a city wall, but two other features make this a cutting allusion: (1) Abimelech is Judges' parade example of what happens when you make someone king; and (2) a woman brings about his downfall. Possibly the messenger omits this part of his assigned report (2 S 1:23–24) because he is afraid of David's reaction to the implied rebuke. After all, David has executed messengers before; see 2 S 1:15 and 2:12. (In the Greek version of Samuel, followed by some English translations, the messenger sticks exactly to Joab's script.)

He took the crown of Milcom from his head . . . and it was placed on David's head (2 S 12:30). If we follow the Greek reading, as NRSV does, David takes and wears the crown from an idol (Milcom—*mlkm*—is the god of the Ammonites, mentioned in 1 K 11:5 and 33). Medieval Jewish tradition understood that what David took was the crown of "their king" (*mlkm*) and inserted the vowels of this less incriminating reading. But the Greek translators would not have attributed such an objectionable act to David unless there were a strong tradition to that effect, while it is quite likely that later generations might have cleaned up the story. This reasoning points to "Milcom" as the correct interpretation.

David's treatment of the Ammonites in the following verse has unpleasant echoes of Pharaoh's policies in Moses' time. As with Moab, we may ask whether this war violates an earlier divine grant (Dt 2:19).

Then Absalom said, "If not, please let my brother Amnon go with us." The king said to him, "Why should he go with you?" (2 S 13:26). David, who knows Absalom shelters the sister that Amnon raped (13:21), shows culpable negligence in acceding to Absalom's request.

The king said, "Let him go to his own house; he is not to come into my presence" (2 S 14:24). Fokkelman comments, "David has not executed the spirit of the oath [to bring Absalom home], merely its letter."[13]

Absalom would say, ". . . there is no one deputed by the king to hear you." . . . so Absalom stole the hearts of the people of Israel (2 S 15:3–6). We know how poorly David handled judgments with respect to his own children. Did he do any better for the people at large? Upon what reservoir of public dissatisfaction does Absalom draw?

"You are a man of blood" (2 S 16:8). At first glance Shimei's accusation may seem unjustified. At least twice David has had Saul in his power and refused to harm him (1 S 24 and 26), and David has also protested his innocence of Abner's and Ishbosheth's blood (2 S 3 and 4). But at this point in the story David may already have handed over seven of Saul's descendants for sacrifice (2 S 21:1–14; see the discussion of 9:3). Gunn reminds us that Shimei's statement also points backward to the massacre at Nob.[14]

Now Absalom and all the Israelites came to Jerusalem; Ahithophel was with him (2 S 16:15).[15] Who stays loyal to David? His foreign mercenaries (15:18,22), palace bureaucrats (15:15, 32; Hushai's epithet "the king's friend" in 16:16–17 appears to be an official title), priests in royal employ (15:24–29), Mephibosheth's opportunistic steward Ziba (16:4), bloodthirsty Abishai (16:9, recall 1 S 26:8), and well-to-do trans-Jordanian lords (17:27). Who sides with Absalom? "All the Israelites" and Ahithophel, whose counsel "was as if one consulted the oracle of God" (16:23). This tells us a great deal about who benefits from David's policies and who does not.

By the way, if 2 S 23:34's Eliam is the same as 11:3's, then Ahithophel is Bathsheba's grandfather. Delekat suggests that the author leaves this connection unmentioned in order not to muddy the contrast between a weak, indecisive David and his clear-sighted opponent.[16]

"Say to Amasa, 'Are you not my bone and my flesh? So may God do to me, and more, if you are not the commander of my army from now on, in place of Joab' " (2 S 19:13). Three implications trouble this innocent-seeming statement. First, if Levenson and Halpern's speculations about Abigail/Abigal (1 S 25:42; 2 S 17:25) are correct, "my bone and my flesh" is not mere patriotic rhetoric; Amasa's mother may be both sister and wife to David.[17] Second, Joab has just

saved David's throne (first by killing Absalom, then by insisting that David thank his troops). David, however, remains mired in resentment over a killing ultimately necessitated by David's irresolute dealings with his sons. Third, David knows how Joab responds to potential rivals (2 S 23:27). Amasa will not long survive this ostensible favor (2 S 20:8–10).

The king said to Shimei, "You shall not die." And the king gave him his oath (2 S 19:23). But David will instruct Solomon, "do not hold him guiltless . . . you must bring his gray head down with blood to Sheol" (1 K 2:9). Earlier we asked why Jonathan required David's oath so many times. Now we get confirmation that David's oaths do not promise all they seem to.

"I have decided: you and Ziba shall divide the land" (2 S 19:29). No matter which of the men involved is telling the truth (most interpreters, including myself, feel that the evidence points toward Mephibosheth's innocence and Ziba's guilt), David's non-Solomonic decision rewards the guilty party with half of Saul's estate. Again we see his failure to establish justice. David's division of the estate foreshadows the eventual division of David's own realm.

So all the people of Israel withdrew from David and followed Sheba son of Bichri (2 S 20:2). Here is more evidence of David's "popularity." This time, however, the people of Judah stay with David, whose post-Absalom politicking seems to have exacerbated sectional rivalries between Judah and Israel.[18]

Elhanan son of Jaare-oregim, the Bethlehemite, killed Goliath the Gittite (2 S 21:19). In Chapter 2 we looked at this verse in connection with historical uncertainties in the books of Samuel. However, as Gunn points out in "Reading Right," the verse creates problems even within a literary reading, for it raises the question of whether we can trust the narrator. All this time we have been allowed to suppose that David killed Goliath. Only now do we discover that someone else is also credited with the feat. What else may turn out to be uncertain before the story is over?

I will have more to say about "unreliable narration" in Chapter 8. For now, the verse reminds us we are dealing with the work of a human storyteller rather than a reporter of unmediated and unquestionable "facts."

"I was blameless before him, / and I kept myself from guilt" (2 S 22:24). David's psalm reprises themes from the song of Hannah in 1 S 2: "my" God, God as a rock, victory, deliverance of the humble and bringing low of the arrogant, God's dominion over the foundations of the world, God's care for the faithful and cutting-off of the wicked, thunder, and giving strength to the king. However, 2 S 22 explores these themes more exuberantly than does the earlier psalm. The psalmist describes his own distress as "torrents of perdition" and "cords of Sheol" (22:5–6). He recalls God's journey to assist: "the earth reeled and rocked," "he bowed the heavens, and came down," "he rode on a cherub, and flew," "the foundations of the world were laid bare" (22:8, 10, 11, 16).

We have spent many chapters with David, but never did God fly down on a cherub (a winged bull or lion); the closest we came was "the sound of marching in the tops of the balsam trees" in 2 S 5:24. David's struggles with Saul, referred to in the introductory verse of the psalm, were played out in the dusty reality of wilderness caves and ravines. "I pursued my enemies and destroyed them, / and did not turn back until they were consumed" (22:38). Is this the same person who claimed to be "a dead dog, a single flea" (1 S 24:14)? For the psalmist God is a "lamp," enabling him to "crush a troop" (22:29–39). Yet David agreed in the preceding chapter to avoid battle, lest Israel's "lamp" be quenched (21:17)!

If the disjunction between narrative and concluding poem concerned only such matters of imagery, we might say that David's psalm pierces through mundane reality to the mythic truth behind it. Unfortunately, we also sense a moral disjunction. How can David say "I was blameless before him" (22:24)? If God's eyes "are upon the haughty to bring them down" (22:28), does not this psalmist have something to worry about? What does it mean to call God "a shield for all who take refuge in him," then assert that one's enemies "cried to the LORD, but he did not answer them" (22:31, 42)? The effect, Gunn correctly observes, "is to proclaim not righteousness but self-righteousness, not piety but hypocrisy."[19]

"One who rules over people justly, / ruling in the fear of God, / is like the light of morning, / . . . Is not my house like this with God?" (23:3–5). This shorter psalm, with its lovely images of sunrise and glistening raindrops, creates problems similar to those of the preceding poem—perhaps worse. It emphasizes rulerly responsibility to maintain justice, but we have seen far less of this than success in battle. The psalm is called an "oracle," as if David were a prophet. But prophets have not fared entirely well in the books of Samuel; we saw both Samuel and Nathan speaking inaccurately of God. Likewise David's vision seems blurred when he asks, "Is not my house like this with God?" No, not after Uriah, Tamar, Amnon and Absalom. And certainly not—if these are really his "last words"—after the ugly business of Solomon's accession.

"Uriah the Hittite" (2 S 23:39). Today's readers generally find it difficult to pronounce the names in 23:18–39, let alone remember who these people are. But as both Gunn and Brueggemann remind us, the names recall the story of David's adultery and murder: Joab, Nathan, the Ammonites, Eliam (Bathsheba's father), and Uriah himself (23:18, 24, 34, 37).[20] Many of the names will also recur in the succession story at the beginning of 1 Kings.

"Did you not, my lord the king, swear to your servant, saying: Your son Solomon shall succeed me . . ." (1 K 1:13). We have no other record of this promise, and a number of people seem to have expected Adonijah to take the throne. Do Nathan and Bathsheba really recall the king to his promise, or do they sim-

ply insinuate one into an old man's failing memory? The story brings unsettling memories of Rebekah's trickery which led Isaac to bless a different son (Jacob) than he had intended (Gen 27). Although we were told at the time of Solomon's birth that "LORD loved him" (2 S 12:24), this did not necessarily make him the legitimate successor. It is also—in view of our experience with David—no guarantee of Solomon's moral excellence. Conspicuous by its absence is any narratorial confirmation of Solomon as God's choice; the closest we come is a blessing pronounced by Solomon's hatchet man Benaiah (1 K 1:36–37).[21]

"Moreover you know also what Joab son of Zeruiah did to me . . . do not let his gray head go down to Sheol in peace" (1 K 2:5–6). David's final instructions regarding Joab are even more disturbing than those regarding Shimei, because Joab was not an enemy but a major power upholding David's throne. The condemnation recollects 2 S 3:29, where David lays guilt for Abner's death on Joab's house. We have already asked whether David's "not knowing" about that murder was a self-protective technicality. His continued concern more than three decades later confirms that David felt more responsibility than he wanted to admit.

Joab's hands indeed have blood on them, but the killings of Abner, Absalom, and Amasa (2 S 3, 18, 20) can be defended as necessary acts which redound to David's advantage. Twice (2 S 2:28 and 20:21) Joab forgoes mass armed encounter in favor of a single party's death. His killing of Absalom could also be seen in such a light. The most problematic blood on Joab's hands is Uriah's—blood shed at David's command, which is never mentioned in David's deathbed condemnation of Joab. David has at best a double standard when it comes to the deeds of this loyal commander.

SUMMARY

The details of David's words and actions reinforce the impression we gained from our insights into David's heart: David is a complex person whose motives are often suspect. Nor is he an unmixed blessing for his people, as we see in his treatment of women, the bloody denouement of his failed fathering, the seventy thousand plague deaths of 2 S 24, and the assassinations he orders on his deathbed. With these details in mind, we will take a second look at the grid comparing David to Saul (Chapter 7) and trace the continuation of the story in Kings (Chapter 8).

CHAPTER 7

SAUL, DAVID, AND GOD

SAUL AND DAVID REVISITED

In Chapter 4 we examined a grid of commonly assumed contrasts between David and Saul. We have since noted many troubling details in 1 and 2 Samuel's portrait of David. We now take another look at the parallels and contrasts between Israel's founding kings. We begin with points on which both kings receive the same evaluation:

1. *Of wealthy family.* Saul, 1 S 9:1. David, 1 S 16:20 and 17:14–18.

2. *Physically impressive.* Saul, 1 S 9:2. David, 1 S 16:18. (Judging by Goliath's reaction, 1 S 16:12 and 17:42 describe a somewhat boyish charm.)

3. *Chosen by God.* Saul, 1 S 9:15–17 and 10:20–24. David, 1 S 16:1, 12.

4. *A good (ṭôb) man.* Saul, 1 S 9:2 (narrator says "no one more ṭôb"). David, 1 S 15:28 (Samuel mentions one "more ṭôb" than Saul).

5. *Anointed by Samuel.* Saul, 1 S 10:1. David, 1 S 16:13.

6. *Early victory reminiscent of judges' stories.* Saul, 1 S 11:5–11. David, 1 S 17.

7. *Opposers described as "worthless fellows."* Saul, 1 S 10:27. David, 1 S 25:17, 25; 2 S 20:1 (all using similar expressions in Hebrew).

8. *Touched by God's spirit.* Saul, 1 S 10:10; 11:6; 19:23. David, 1 S 16:13.

9. *Should anyone be killed this day?* Saul, 1 S 11:3. David, 2 S 19:23.

83

10. *Says enemy should not be put to death, but later reneges.* Saul, 1 S 19:6. David, 2 S 19:23 and 1 K 2:8–9.

More interesting, perhaps, are items which apply to both kings but with different evaluations: Saul is criticized about things for which David is praised or at least receives no censure.

11. *Offers sacrifices.* Saul, 1 S 13:8–14. David, 2 S 6:13, 17; 24:25.

12. *Takes booty from Amalekites.* Saul, 1 S 15. David, 1 S 27:9; 30:19–20, 26–31. Saul intends to offer his booty in sacrifice (15:15, which we will discuss shortly). David uses his booty for political bribes.

13. *Sparing/having pity.*"[1] Saul, 1 S 15:9. David, 1 S 23:21; 2 S 21:7. David's 2 S 21 example involves a royal figure (Jonathan's son Mephibosheth) against whom there is a divine claim—a very similar situation to Saul's with Agag.

14. *Involved in prophecy.* Saul, 1 S 10:10–11; 18:10; 19:23–24. David, 2 S 23:2. NRSV translates Saul's activity in 18:10 with the word "raved," but it is the same Hebrew verb as we find in 10:5, 6, 10, 13 and 19:20–24. The verb for prophesying is not used of David in 2 S 23, but the term "oracle" is firmly associated with prophetic utterance. We discussed problems with this "oracle" in Chapter 6.

15. *Self-deprecating.* Saul, 1 S 9:2; 10:22 (Samuel's comment in 1 S 15:17 may also suggest humbleness). David, 1 S 18:23; 24:14; 26:20; 2 S 7:18.

16. *Leaves enemy to hand of Philistines.* Saul, 1 S 18:17, 25. David, 1 S 29:11. (Saul is certainly the more honest about his intention.)

17. *Flaunts self in religious frenzy.* Saul, 1 S 19:24. David, 2 S 6.

Finally, we note some interesting points of difference between the two kings. Even though most of the "no" evaluations are arguments from silence, they reflect the situation as given to us by the narrator.

18. *Acquiring horses* (Dt 17:16). Saul, no. David, yes (2 S 8:4). Three of David's sons (Absalom, Adonijah, and—above all—Solomon) are also

mentioned as having horses, although more commonly we hear of them riding mules. David's personal mount was evidently a mule (1 K 1:33). The closest Saul comes to horses or chariotry (other than being attacked by them on the battlefield) is the introductory scene where he searches for his father's lost donkeys.

19. *Multiplying wives* (Dt 17:17). Saul, no. So far as we know, he had one wife (Ahinoam) and one concubine (Rizpah: 2 S 3:7; 21:8–11). David, yes. He has six women in 2 S 3:2–5 plus "more concubines and wives" (5:13) and eventually Bathsheba. He leaves ten concubines behind when he runs from Absalom (15:16).

20. *"Taking" (taxes, conscription, major public work projects)*—not to mention other men's wives. Saul, no. David, yes.

21. *Copy of law* (Dt 17:18). Saul, yes, if the "rights and duties" written up by Samuel are the "law" of Dt 17, and if Saul is apprised of them along with his people. (Samuel directs the process.) No written materials are mentioned in conjunction with David.

22. *Quality of supporters.* Saul, "warriors whose hearts God had touched" (1 S 10:26). David, "everyone who was in distress, and everyone who was in debt, and everyone who was discontented" (1 S 22:2).

23. *Corrupt children.* Saul, no. David (and Eli and Samuel), yes.

24. *Sexual misconduct.* Saul, no. David, yes.

These lists offer little support for the common perception that Saul is a miserable sinner who deserves his fate, whereas David is an innocent and virtuous hero with just enough peccadilloes to verify his humanity. Where did Saul sin? Even casual readers sense the lack of proportion in 1 S 13's condemnation. As Gunn has argued at length, their discomfort is justified.[2] Did Saul sin in failing to wait for Samuel? Saul *did* wait "the time appointed by Samuel" (13:8). Did Saul sin by presuming to offer sacrifice? If a general prohibition existed against sacrifice by the king, David broke it too, with none of the bitter rebuke Saul suffers. Or did Samuel's "wait seven days" really mean "wait until I come"? In that case, the issue is one of interpretation, with most readers on Saul's side of the argument. We sense a "frame" on the part of grudging Samuel rather than high-handed sin on the part of Saul. However, in the subsequent chapter, Saul's rash vows and anxiety about knowing God's will suggest that his clash with Samuel has shaken his confidence.

Gunn argues that in 1 S 15 the issue is again one of interpretation rather than egregious disobedience.[3] God has commanded that the spoil be ḥrm (15:3). This clearly requires that none of it be kept by human parties—thus NRSV's "utterly destroy." But must destruction take place immediately, at the battle site? Samuel and God apparently consider this to be the case. Saul, on the other hand, has brought captured livestock and his prisoner to an official sanctuary, Gilgal—quite in line with his explanation that he means to sacrifice them there, and hardly, as Gunn points out, where one would stash personal booty taken against God's command. Saul appears to be acting in good faith, but neither Samuel nor God shows any interest in hearing Saul's side of the case or ameliorating the verdict.

When Saul finally accedes to Samuel's argument and asks pardon, Samuel rebuffs him with the statement that God "is not a mortal, that he should change his mind [nḥm]" (1 S 15:29). Yet the whole condemnation began when God said to Samuel, "I regret [nḥm] that I made Saul king" (15:11). The narrator confirms at the end of the chapter that "LORD was sorry [nḥm] that he had made Saul king" (15:35). The Hebrew text shows us what NRSV's varying translations (all reasonable, in and of themselves) obscure: Samuel is wrong. God can and does nḥm, and Samuel knows it because such a change of mind was very recently announced to him. Given Saul's contrition, Samuel might at least ask God to hear an appeal. Instead he cuts Saul off. We do not know what might have happened had Samuel not been so intransigent.[4] Not surprisingly, Saul thereafter speaks, like the Israelites of 12:19, of God as "your [Samuel's] God." Surprisingly, Saul still desires to worship (15:30–31).

In the next chapter (1 S 16) Samuel anoints David. The narrator tells us that "the spirit of the LORD came mightily upon David from that day forward" (1 S 16:13). Meanwhile "the spirit of the LORD departed from Saul, and an evil spirit from the LORD tormented him" (16:14). But Saul remains king. Bereft of divine support—indeed, beset by an evil spirit—he must still govern and protect the people. If it was ever true that God's rejection was caused by Saul's sins, it is true no longer. From 1 S 16 forward, it is the other way around: God's rejection seems to *cause* Saul's sins. Although we hear repeatedly that God has turned from Saul, we are never told that Saul turns from God. Even on that last desperate night when Saul appeals to the medium in Endor (1 S 28), the spirit he asks for is God's prophet Samuel.[5]

86

"LORD WAS WITH DAVID"

We come now to a crucial question: What does the statement that "LORD was with David" tell us about David's character? The question usually elicits a logic something like this: (1) God punishes sinners and rewards good people. (2) God helps David succeed. (3) Therefore David must be a good person.

Does the narrative support these propositions? Of the three, the middle receives the clearest affirmation: God helps David succeed. David says so, most prominently in the psalm of 2 S 22. People around David, such as Saul's courtier (1 S 16:18) and Abigail (1 S 25), say so. God says so (note especially 2 S 7 and 12). And most important of all (in narrative terms), the narrator says so. When Samuel anointed David, "the spirit of the LORD came mightily upon David from that day forward" (1 S 16:13). Thereafter "David had success in all his undertakings, for the LORD was with him" (1 S 18:14). "David became greater and greater, for the LORD, the God of hosts, was with him" (2 S 5:10). Divine support continues even after Uriah's death, in God's intervention against Absalom (2 S 17:14), and in response to supplication after the plague (2 S 24:25).

We get a few hints of the ways in which this divine support for David functions. God speaks to David directly ("God said") and via prophetic oracles ("thus says the LORD") more frequently than to any other character in 1 and 2 Samuel, even Samuel himself. Contrast the statements in 1 S 14:37 and 28:6 about God's refusal to answer Saul. Many of God's communications to David involve tactical information or instructions, for example, God's counsel about Keilah in 1 S 23:2–4, 11–12, encouragement to pursue the Amalekites in 1 S 30:8, instructions to go to Hebron in 2 S 2:1, and advice about fighting Philistines in 2 S 5:19, 23–24. (Which "he," David or God, then strikes down the Philistines in 5:25—or does it matter?) In 2 S 17:14 we are informed, without knowing the exact mechanism, that God has arranged for Absalom to follow Hushai's counsel rather than Ahithophel's.

These are not, especially in the Absalom/Hushai instance, flashy miracles. Instead we gain the impression of God's action as a "more constant, much more widely embracing factor concealed in the whole breadth of secular affairs, and pervading every single sphere of human life."[6] In our day, we might call David talented, well-positioned, and lucky. For the Samuel narratives, such success demonstrates divine support.

Does David deserve it? Is he as good as he is successful?

After our discussions in Chapters 5 and 6 we have reason to doubt this. With regard to Uriah and Bathsheba, we *know* David was not good. Substantial doubt exists about his "goodness" vis-à-vis Saul, Achish, Nabal and Abi-

87

gail, Abner and Joab, Uzzah, Michal, the Ammonites and Moabites, Tamar, Amnon, Absalom, Mephibosheth, Amasa, Rizpah's two sons and Merab's (or Michal's?) five who were handed over for human sacrifice, and the seventy thousand Israelites who die of plague after David's census. I do not argue that David is unrelievedly "bad"; rather, I see a very human mix of good, bad, and indeterminate features. But Eli and his entire line were disowned for sins that Eli himself did not commit (God having influenced Eli's sons in order "to kill them," just as God subverted Ahithophel's advice to Absalom—1 S 2:25 and 2 S 17:14). Saul and his entire line were disowned over what seem to have been disagreements in interpretation. Why, in David's case, do we see such an extraordinary degree of divine support?

One possible answer is that God supports David not for David's sake, but Israel's. But how convincing would this be to the Israelites who fell at Gilboa (1 S 31:1), or the victims of the ensuing civil war (2 S 2:30–31; 3:1), or the twenty thousand killed by the sword and the even greater number claimed by the forest in the next civil war (2 S 18:8)—presumably because of the sword over David's house (2 S 12:10)—or the concubines publicly dishonored and then "shut up until the day of their death" (2 S 12:11; 16:22; 20:3), not to mention the seventy thousand people killed by plague (2 S 24:15)?

If God helps David to achieve extraordinary success, but David shows far less than extraordinary goodness, there may be a problem in the starting premise of our logic. Is it true that God punishes sinners and rewards good people?

We certainly find statements to that effect. Before we ever arrive at the books of Samuel, Moses says, "I am setting before you today a blessing and a curse: the blessing, if you obey the commandments of the LORD your God . . . and the curse, if you do not obey the commandments of the LORD your God" (Dt 11:26–28). Closer to home, Hannah proclaims, "He will guard the feet of his faithful ones, / but the wicked shall be cut off in darkness" (1 S 2:9). Samuel warns, "if both you and the king who reigns over you will follow the LORD your God, it will be well; but if you will not heed the voice of the LORD . . . then the hand of the LORD will be against you and your king" (1 S 12:14–15). David himself says, "with the pure you show yourself pure, / and with the crooked you show yourself perverse" (2 S 22:27).

Notice, however, that these statements come from characters in the narrative world. We have seen enough by now to know that not everything a biblical character says is necessarily true, even when the character is a prophet. Samuel makes several incorrect or misleading statements, and Nathan fluffs his first response to David's temple proposal, 2 S 7:3. Even God misleads on several occasions. God asserts that Eli did not restrain his sons (1 S 3:13), but Eli's attempt to do so is on record in 1 S 2:23–25, with God's intervention given as the reason why Eli's attempt fails. In 1 S 16:2 God instructs Samuel to mislead Bethlehem's elders about his purpose, and in 16:7 manages to insinuate that the choice of Saul was a human mistake. In 1 S 2:30 God dismantles a promise "forever," and by the end of the primary history the promise of 2 S 7:16 has turned out to be revocable as well. If we look ahead to 1 K 22:22–23 we find a case of deception termed "lying" even by the spirit who does it.

Uncomfortable as it may be, especially for those schooled in the dogmatic interpretive tradition, it seems that the narrator of the Samuel books—and more largely the narrative voice of the primary history—offers us reason to question divine consistency and justice. And although we might be happy to trade consistency for benevolence, God's benevolence seems highly questionable as well. The narrative does not force us to understand God as inconsistent, unjust, and malevolent. Centuries of interpretation show that such understandings can be, and usually have been, avoided. But the narrative does give us ground to raise such questions.

For more on the possibility that the narrator of 1 and 2 Samuel offers grounds for a negative evaluation of God, I refer the reader especially to Eslinger's *Kingship of God in Crisis* and my own essay on "The Problematic God of Samuel." David Gunn's *Fate of King Saul* and the discussions of Samuel texts in Gunn and Fewell's *Narrative in the Hebrew Bible* also suggest this possibility. Here, however, our most central concern is David. How do the shadows around God's character in Samuel affect our understanding of David?

God's justice and David's virtue are interdependent interpretive constructs. Both were fully at play in Chapter 4's "good David" reading. But as soon as either of them begins to slip, which both are now doing, the other begins to crumble as well. If David is not good, God may not be fair. If God is not fair, we have far less reason to suppose that David is good, because so much of David's "goodness" is back-calculated from God's support for him.

If God is not fair, perhaps God supports David simply because God likes him; we have certainly seen a lot of other characters (including Saul and Jonathan) react to David in that way. This would not be the only part of the primary history which shows God favoring a problematic character. In particular, the book of Genesis contains many stories in which God leads Abraham or Jacob to success in spite of questionable behavior from the human protagonist. An example is the tale in which Abraham (still named Abram at this point in the story) allows Pharaoh to take Sarai into the palace harem (Gen 12:10–20). Some claim that Abram simply trusts in God's protection for his wife. But if he has such trust in God, why mislead Pharaoh to begin with? God finally intervenes, and an irritated Pharaoh drives Abram away—Abram, who takes with him Sarai and a host of animals and servants given to him by

Pharaoh. We have absolutely no evidence that Abram's initial concern—that Pharaoh would kill him and take his wife—was justified. In the entire Hebrew Bible there is only one king who actually does kill a man and take his wife— David.[7]

This is only one of many thematic ties between stories of David in Samuel and Kings and those of the ancestors in Genesis. Other links include promises about offspring and ruling over enemies, special connections to Hebron and Salem/Jerusalem, confusion about whether wives are also sisters, a wife maneuvering her aged and infirm husband to declare a younger son the heir, and a younger daughter who involves household gods (*terāpim*, Gen 31:19, 34–35; 1 S 19:13, 16) when she sides with her husband against her father. In Genesis as in Samuel, we occasionally wonder about the justice of God's favoritism; examples would be the treatment of Pharaoh in Gen 12 and the slaughter of Shechemites in Genesis 34. (This incident, like Absalom's rebellion, begins with a rape. Jacob's interchange with his sons in 34:30–31 sounds nearly as indecisive as David's handling of Amnon and Absalom.) We even wonder occasionally, as we did while reading Eli's story and Saul's, whether one would want to be chosen by such a God (Gen 22). Overall, however, the tone might be described as one of meditation on the mystery of chosenness. Genesis ends, as does Kings, with the chosen family in a foreign land.

Although God puts up with an amazing amount of double-dealing from the ancestors in Genesis, we also find stories that stress the need for virtue and obedience (again Gen 22 comes to mind). With David, too, God retains some sense of standards; 2 S 12 leaves no doubt of this. But the dominant note is God's freedom to flex. David knows this. Where retributive justice may benefit him, he occasionally appeals to it (for example, 1 S 26:23 and 2 S 3:39), but for the most part he emphasizes God's freedom to repent and return good for evil. "Who knows? The LORD may be gracious to me" (2 S 12:22). "Let him curse, for the LORD has bidden him. It may be . . . that the LORD will repay me with good for this cursing" (2 S 16:11–12). "Let us fall into the hand of the LORD, for his mercy is great" (2 S 24:14). Sometimes David receives the hoped-for clemency and sometimes he does not, but he leaves the door open.

We see this relationship between God and David clearly in the keynote speech of 2 S 7. God begins by rehearsing divine favors for David, never mentioning any qualifying goodness or merit on David's part. Then, as with Abraham, God extends the promise to future generations. God does not abandon all demands for obedience. "When he commits iniquity, I will punish him" (2 S 7:14). But beneath and around the promise of discipline stands a pledge of faithfulness: "I will not take my steadfast love from him" (2 S

7:15). Although I disagree with some details of Eslinger's book-length study of this speech (*House of God or House of David*), I do concur with his opinion that David's proposed temple would put God "in a box." God's response squelches that initiative, but God remains eager to find a way forward with David. David's subsequent prayer presses for all that God has offered and more, but in carefully courteous language.

As we meet David in 1 and 2 Samuel, he is hardly a model of Sunday-school virtue, but neither does the story read like heavy-handed anti-Davidic propaganda; its problematic details are too subtle. (Some of the prophet Samuel's speeches do sound like heavy-handed antimonarchic propaganda, but Samuel is not the narrator.) Most readers like David, and our imaginations latch onto him as an image of divinely favored success. Yet the dark undertones of his story haunt us. Our questions about David reflect back onto the God who supports him. How wonderful that God would so embrace a fallible human! How terrifying that divine power might flow in such a flawed channel!

CHAPTER 8

DAVID'S LEGACY

The books of Samuel present David's relationship with God in strikingly personal terms. For instance, 2 S 7:1 speaks of God's giving *David* (not Israel) rest from *his* (not its) enemies. Yet David entered the story as part of the larger tale of Israel's desire for a king, and that king's relationship with God has major import for the people's welfare. With David, we saw in Chapter 7, that the impact has been a mixed one. He enjoys major military success, and 2 S 8:15 tells us that he "administered justice and equity to all his people." Yet they have also suffered civil war and plague. Their ready accession to Absalom's blandishments in 2 S 15:2–6 suggests some justice problems as well.

We have been given to understand in the course of the story that God's pleasure (2 S 7) and displeasure (2 S 12) with David will have permanent influence on the nation's history. How does all this play out in the books of Kings?

DAVID IN KINGS

The first two chapters of Kings are much like 2 S 9–20 in style and theme, which is why they have so often been considered part of the succession narrative. Bathsheba and Solomon appear for the first time since 2 S 12, and we hear again about David's ineffectual fathering (1 K 1:6). God's involvement is discussed much by characters and little by the narrator.

David is by now an old man, sexually impotent and perhaps blind (1 K 1:4, 22–23). We do not know if he actually made the vow of which Nathan and Bathsheba speak (1:13–17). Does an aging king ensure that the son whom God loves will take his place, or is a decrepit old man maneuvered by a wife's ambitions for her son? Here, as throughout 1 and 2 Samuel, David can be read optimistically or cynically.

David's "last words" in 1 K 2 (different from the ones in 2 S 23) also point in two directions. First, he exhorts Solomon to follow the "law of Moses" (a name we have not heard since Samuel's farewell speech in 1 S 12:6–8). He quotes God's promise: *"If your heirs take heed to their way,* to walk before me in faithfulness with all their heart and with all their soul, there shall not fail you a successor on the throne of Israel" (1 K 2:4, emphasis added; this language is far more openly conditional than what we heard in 2 S 7). David's words encourage readers to think of David, Solomon, and indeed God as rule abiding.

But David also has instructions regarding Joab, Shimei, and Barzillai (1 K 2:5–9). The narrator reports Solomon's liquidations of Joab and Shimei (along with the rival prince Adonijah) in grisly detail—*after* noting that "his [Solomon's] kingdom was firmly established" (2:12), implying that the bloodbath was politically unnecessary. We hear nothing about Barzillai's reward. The Solomon we see here seems likely to perpetuate the least savory aspects of his father's reign, but God does not send Nathan to chide him.

After David's death, Solomon and God play a rhetorical game around his name. Solomon emphasizes David's virtue, God's promise to David, and Solomon's own status as David's replacement (1 K 3:6–7; 8:15–20, 24–26). God remains noncommittal, using David's name to warn Solomon that he must walk in God's ways (3:14; 6:12; 9:4–5). The narrator tells us at the outset that Solomon does not quite measure up ("he sacrificed and offered incense at the high places," 3:3). A later passage confirms that "his heart was not true to the LORD his God, as was the heart of his father David" (11:4–6). Toward the end of Solomon's life God reacts: "I will surely tear the kingdom from you. . . . Yet for the sake of your father David I will not do it in your lifetime" (1 K 11:11–12). Thus we continue the pattern of displaced punishment foreshadowed by the "passing over" of David's death penalty to Bathsheba's child. Against Solomon himself God raises adversaries with grudges dating back to David's time (1 K 11:14–15, 23–24, compare 2 S 8:3–8 and 10:15–19).

The northern tribes break away from Solomon's son with the same rallying cry Sheba used against David (2 S 20:1; 1 K 12:16). God promises the breakaway leader, *"If* you will listen . . . I will . . . build you an enduring house, as I built for David" (1 K 11:38, emphasis added). But Jeroboam does not walk in David's ways (1 K 14:8). David henceforth ceases to function as a point of reference for the northern kings. When God preserves Israel in spite of its kings (2 K 13:23), it happens for the sake of Abraham, Isaac, and Jacob, rather than David.

From 1 K 15 forward references to David (leaving aside phrases such as "city of David") become less frequent and more formulaic. Most appear in summary assessments of Judean kings.

1 K 15:3–5	Abijam	heart not true like David's, but lamp left and son set up for David's sake
I K 15:11	Asa	did right in God's sight as David did, but high places remain
2 K 8:19	Jehoram	did evil, but Judah preserved for David's sake
2 K 14:3	Amaziah	does right, but not like David
2 K 16:2	Ahaz	does not do right as David did
2 K 18:3	Hezekiah	did right "just as" David did, kept Moses' commandments
2 K 21:7	Manasseh	desecrates the house of which God said to David . . .
2 K 22:2	Josiah	walks in "all the way" of his father David

David's name also occurs in two prophecies of deliverance (one national, one personal) delivered to Hezekiah by the prophet Isaiah (2 K 19:34; 20:1).

After all we have seen in Samuel and even the opening chapters of Kings, it jolts us to find David held up as a model of perfect obedience, creator of a reservoir of divine goodwill. How, after the shenanigans reported in 1 and 2 Samuel, can the narrator offer such a rosy summary of David's life? This is not just a question of fact (like the uncertainty over who killed Goliath) but one of moral consistency. We have a range of options for understanding the disjunction between the David of 1 S 16 through 1 K 2 and the David spoken of in 1 K 3 forward:

We could (1) dismiss the narrator (and hence the narrative) as incoherent, concluding that the parts only make sense separately. This has been the tactic of some historical critics. Or we could (2) return to the "good David" reading of Chapter 4, as many dogmatic and not a few historical critics have done.

Alternatively, we might (3) suppose that the narrator suffers from selective memory, so that as the story draws further away from David it remembers him in optimistic outline rather than troubling detail. Or we could (4) follow the lead of 1 K 15:3–5 ("did not turn aside . . . except in the matter of Uriah") and assume that "followed all the way of the LORD as David did" is shorthand for "followed all the way of the LORD as David did sometimes."

These options lead toward alternative (5), an ironic reading. David Gunn proposes this for 1 K 3:3 in "Reading Right " (a tongue-in-cheek title, for the essay attacks the hypothesis of a single right reading). We can extend it to other comments. If Ahaz failed to "do what was right . . . as his ancester David had done" (2 K 16:2), then he must *really* have failed.

Finally (6), we might ask what these successors did (or did not do) "as David did." We discover that Judah's kings are judged almost entirely by their cultic policies—their attitudes toward high places, Baals and Asherahs, sacrifices to Molech, and unorthodox temple arrangements. When "following all the commandments" pertains specifically to religious practice, most of David's dubious behaviors drop out of sight.

IRONIC NARRATION?

Occasionally, we have seen the primary history's narrator slip into a character's point of view, for instance, when David assesses Bathsheba's beauty in 2 S 11:2. In such cases the narrator may also adopt a character's language. So, for instance, when the narrator tells us that Michal sees "King David" leaping and dancing (2 S 6:16), the word "king" reflects Michal's own way of talking about David (see her words in 6:20). Such mimicry of a character's phrasing can have an ironic edge, as when David's "last words"—which claim "the spirit of the LORD speaks through me" (2 S 23:2)—are introduced as "the oracle of David" (23:1).

The narrator's evaluative statements in Kings sound so similar to prophetic speeches in the narrative that some historical critics have understood them as a single voice, that of "deuteronomistic historians" or their prophetically oriented predecessors. What does it mean for the narrator to speak with a prophetlike accent, when his or her presentation of prophets has had such an unsympathetic edge?[1]

Eslinger says the Israelites ask for a king in 1 S 8 because they don't want to be slaughtered (by God) for the misdeeds of their judges and priests. But we've seen that kingship doesn't solve the problem; thousands of people also die when God rejects Saul and disciplines David. In 1 and 2 Kings all of Israel and Judah are finally cast off for the sins of their divinely appointed kings. Further, in 1 Samuel God reacts violently to the cultic sins of Eli's sons but remains silent when Samuel's sons pervert justice. Evaluation of later kings in terms of their worship practices continues to suggest a God driven more by touchy ego than concern for the people's welfare. But the people are locked in relationship to this God and must make the best they can of it.[2]

When the narrator, whose overall approach seems sympathetic to the people, begins to echo the judgment language of prophets and God, we may well suspect irony.[3] God supports or rejects kings according to whether they do right "as David did"? Just what kind of God is this?

And yet—and yet—"David had success in all his undertakings; for the LORD was with him. . . . all Israel and Judah loved David" (1 S 18:14, 16). Even if we feel uneasy about the God to whom "our" people (imagining ourselves, in accord with the narrative horizon, as Judean deportees) is yoked—

perhaps *especially* if we feel uneasy about that God—can we resist fascination with this David who fascinated God?

In the final paragraph of 2 Kings, a Davidic descendant dines at the table of the Babylonian king, a picture reminiscent of Mephibosheth at David's table (2 S 9:13). Have the Davidic kings been cast off as surely as Saul was? Indeed, is Babylon's king now God's chosen? Or does the scene show that credit yet remains in David's account? "Who knows?" asks David, "the LORD may be gracious" (2 S 12:22). "It may be that the LORD . . . will repay me with good for this cursing" (2 S 16:11–12). "Let us fall into the hand of the LORD, for his mercy is great" (2 S 24:14).

PART 3

THE POWER OF A CONGREGATION
David in Chronicles

CHAPTER 9

CHRONICLES: AN OVERVIEW

In Chapter 1, I compared Chronicles to a stained-glass window. The center of this window features famous scenes from the days of the kings. Many of the scenes in which David appears, but not all, involve events familiar from Samuel. Some, indeed, are so similarly outlined that they could be tracings. But whereas Samuel casts complex shadows across David, Chronicles stylizes him in bright clear colors.

At the bottom of the window and in scattered panels higher up we find another kind of content—names, *lots* of names, mostly of the congregation's founding families and original staff members. Lists also appear across the room, in a companion window, Ezra-Nehemiah, which depicts construction of the building in which the windows are installed. What is this building; where do we stand, when, and with whom?

This chapter will address such questions through a preliminary survey of the context of Chronicles' portrayal of David, with specific attention to the Ezra-Nehemiah window, what the paired windows tell us about where we stand, whether they presuppose our acquaintance with the Samuel books, and how their lists of names function. In Chapter 10 we will narrow our focus to Chronicles, and to David as he appears in its narrative plot. In Chapter 11 we will narrow the focus still further to key speeches given by this David, and will then back away to ask about the relationship between Chronicles' David and the Second Temple congregation.

EZRA-NEHEMIAH AND ITS RELATIONSHIP TO CHRONICLES

1 and 2 Chronicles (once a single book) appear just before Ezra and Nehemiah (also once a single book) in most English-language Bibles. This placement reflects the ancient Greek arrangement that put historical books together and in order. Ezra-Nehemiah quite literally begins where Chronicles leaves off: Ezra 1:2 quotes 2 C 36:23. Most Hebrew Bibles also pair Chronicles with Ezra-Nehemiah but put Chronicles *last*, so the matching verses bracket the sequence at its beginning and end rather than hinging it in

the middle. There is another ancient tradition which puts Chronicles at the beginning of the Writings[1] and Ezra-Nehemiah at the end, using them as bookends for this division of the canon.

Both Chronicles and Ezra-Nehemiah emphasize joyful worship supported by willing offerings. Many motifs run between the books, such as the fact that Chronicles depicts exile as a time when the land makes up for lost sabbaths (2 C 26:21), and Nehemiah insists that in the time of return such sabbaths must be observed (Neh 10:31). Both contain lists enough to cross the eyes of modern readers. Indeed, 1 C 9 and Neh 11 give us variants of the same list. These verbal and thematic features link the books so strongly that they have often been attributed to a common author.

However, recent work, especially by Sara Japhet and H. G. M. Williamson, points to other features—beyond the different historical periods they describe—that separate Chronicles and Ezra-Nehemiah.[2] Ezra-Nehemiah speaks of the Persian period as a time of slavery (Ezra 9:8–9; Neh 9:36) and complains of the Second Temple's inadequacy (Ezra 3:12); whereas Chronicles, by locating its list of returnees in the same section as lists pertaining to periods before Jerusalem's fall, suggests that the Second Temple community stands in essential continuity with the monarchic one. The works differ in their attitude toward the Levites (in whom they both show a strong interest). We will also come to see that they take different positions on the boundaries of "all Israel." Because of the similarities of the books, I describe them as companion windows. Because of their differences, I put them on opposite sides of the room.

Following the Hebrew sequence, let's scan Ezra-Nehemiah before we turn to Chronicles. We see a variety of materials: Persian imperial decrees, lists of families, bits of diplomatic correspondence, and first-person accounts from two Jewish leaders, Ezra and Nehemiah. The relationship between these leaders is not entirely clear. Are we to understand that Ezra, who appears first in the book, was commissioned by Artaxerxes I in 458 BCE, some years before Nehemiah's appointment in 445? Or was Ezra commissioned by Artaxerxes II decades later in 398, thus explaining why we see so little interaction between him and Nehemiah?[3] Fortunately, for our study of David we do not need to resolve this question. We do need to notice some concerns which Ezra and Nehemiah share.

Ezra-Nehemiah opens by recalling the Persian emperor Cyrus's decree that Judeans living in exile might return to their homeland and rebuild its temple.[4] "The heads of the families of Judah and Benjamin, and the priests and the Levites" (Ezra 1:5)—who are descendants of "those captive exiles whom King Nebuchadnezzar had carried captive to Babylonia" (2:1)—respond enthusiastically to the emperor's invitation. Ezra 2:2 refers to these

Judahites and Benjaminites as simply "the Israelite people." When they arrive in what is now the Persian province of Yehud, the returnees lay a foundation for a new temple.

But opposition emerges. "Adversaries of Judah and Benjamin" (Ezra 4:1) ask to participate in the temple building (!). When returnee leaders spurn their offer, these "people of the land" turn against the project (4:3–5), delaying its completion until the reign of Darius (6:15).

In Ezra 7 we meet the priest Ezra himself, sent to Jerusalem by the Persian emperor Artaxerxes to oversee judicial and religious matters. In first person, Ezra reports his horrifying discovery that "the people of Israel, the priests, and the Levites" (that is, the returnee families) "have not separated themselves from the peoples of the lands" (9:1)—in fact, the groups have intermarried! Ezra makes the offenders swear to divorce their foreign wives (10:5). The remainder of the book of Ezra details fulfillment of this vow.

The book of Nehemiah introduces a new first-person narrator. Nehemiah, a Jewish official high in the Persian court, receives permission to oversee the building/repair of Jerusalem's walls (Neh 1:1–2:8). Foreigners criticize his project (2:19, 4:1–3, 7–8; 6:5–7), but Nehemiah and other influential leaders successfully complete the rebuilding. Nehemiah also struggles against problems related to usury (5:1–13) and against market activity on the sabbath (13:15–22).

Nehemiah, like Ezra, defines "the Israelite people" as those "who came up out of the captivity" in Babylon (Neh 7:6–7). A historical review in the middle of the book emphasizes conflict and separation between Israel and foreigners even in ancient times (Neh 9).[5] Nehemiah and other returnee leaders covenant with one another to support the temple, observe the land's sabbaths, and separate themselves from the "peoples of the land" (10:28, 30). In the final chapter Nehemiah recounts his eviction of foreigners and their Jewish collaborators from the temple and priesthood (13:7–8, 28, 30).

Ezra-Nehemiah shows a deep interest in the temple and mentions David several times as an organizer of temple worship (Ezra 3:10, 8:20; Neh 12:24, 36, 45–46; elsewhere Ezra-Nehemiah mentions David only in geographical phrases—Neh 3:15–16 and 12:37—and a genealogical list, Ezra 8:2). We also see commitment to observe God's commandments as taught by Moses. But it is evident from the book that not everyone agrees how the temple should be financed, who may serve in it, or whether Mosaic law should bind economic activity. Above all we see continuing tension over the distinction between Israelite returnees and foreign "people(s) of the land." Both Ezra and Nehemiah spend much time trying to ensure the separation of those two groups, whereas some of their cohorts, including a high priest's grandson (Neh 13:28), intermarry with people of the land.

101

THE ROOM FROM WHICH WE VIEW THE WINDOWS

Ezra-Nehemiah imaginatively places its readers in the Persian province of Yehud, more than a century and a half after Jerusalem's fall. At first glance, Chronicles, which begins (literally) with Adam and ends with Cyrus's proclamation, may seem to work within an earlier framework. But its returnee list overlaps with Nehemiah's list of contemporaries (1 C 9 and Neh 11), and 1 C 3:22–24 tracks David's family two generations beyond that of Hattuph, who returns with Ezra (Ezra 8:2). Thus Chronicles, just as surely as Ezra-Nehemiah, has us viewing events from a standpoint at least midway through the Persian period. This standpoint prompts us to seek continuity between the monarchic period being narrated and the Second Temple time from which we view it.

ARTISTIC ANTECEDENTS

I commented in the opening paragraph of this chapter that Chronicles repeats a number of scenes from Samuel. In making that comment, I implicitly suggested that the story in 1 and 2 Samuel came first and that Chronicles' audience would be aware of the earlier story. But are the Samuel books indeed within Chronicles' literary horizon? To put the question another way, are we meant to read Chronicles with the primary history and especially the books of Samuel in mind? Or should we "bracket out" the other story and read Chronicles as if it were our only source of information? The answer depends in part upon our historical-critical understanding of the relationship between Samuel-Kings and Chronicles. If Samuel and Kings did not yet exist when Chronicles was produced, then surely Chronicles does not suppose our acquaintance with them. But if they did exist, we face the further *literary* question of whether Chronicles acknowledges that existence. Does Chronicles play on Samuel in the same way that contemporary movies often draw upon other films, so that a watcher who has not seen the earlier works has a feeling of missing something? Or does Chronicles offer itself as an independent history for the period in question, playing upon the reader as upon a blank slate?

Chronicles does point explicitly to written sources (for example, 1 C 9:1 and 29:29), although the relationship between titles cited by the "Chronicler" (the imagined author of the finished book) and material in our present Bible remains unclear. We may also note that Chronicles takes its audience's knowledge of Abraham and Moses for granted. It launches into the story of Saul's final battle (1 C 10) without bothering to explain that he was king. Later it alludes to Saul's consultation with the medium (1 C 10:13; see 1 S 28), David's service under Saul (1 C 11:2), and Samuel's identification of David as God's anointed (1 C 11:3), in apparent confidence that we will understand—although these matters are not otherwise explained in Chronicles. These allusions are indications that Chronicles, like most stained-glass windows, depicts figures with which the observers are assumed to be familiar.

In today's Bible, our prior exposure to the Chronicler's characters occurs in the primary history (Genesis through 2 Kings). But we saw in Chapter 2 that differences between today's Hebrew text of those books and ancient Greek translations suggest that the primary history may have reached final form fairly late, especially in Samuel. If so, the narrative presupposed by Chronicles may not have contained all the material we looked at in our study of the primary history's David. In particular, the stories of the succession narrative—David's affair with Bathsheba and murder of Uriah, the problems with David's children, and the scheming around Solomon's succession—are identified by some scholars as late additions to the history.[6] Did the Chronicler excise these from the narrative, or did they simply not exist within the Chronicler's horizon?

Because the present Hebrew canon does present all this material, and prior to Chronicles at that, in one sense we cannot exclude our knowledge of it. However, we can be sensitive to the difference between the "strong" background presence of stories to which Chronicles openly alludes, such as David's troubles with Saul, and those about which the Chronicler says nothing, such as David's misdeeds in connection with Bathsheba and Uriah.

I also note that even where allusions are present, the Chronicler probably does not expect us to compare accounts on a word-by-word basis. The expense of writing materials and the difficulty of hand copying books in the Chronicler's day meant that few readers would have access to manuscripts which could be compared at leisure. So far as we know, books tended to be read/recited aloud to audiences (see, for instance, Ezra 4:23; Neh 8:1–3; 9:3; 13:1) rather than perused by individual readers. Thus we should think of having the earlier narrative "in mind" rather than "at hand."[7] We have, as it were, seen the primary history paintings elsewhere in this building, but not in the same room as the stained-glass windows. Chronicles also cites Psalms (1 C 16:6–36 and 2 C 6:41–42) and refers to Jeremiah (2 C 35:25 and 36:12, 21–22), although again perhaps knowing these traditions in different form than we do.

LISTS OF NAMES IN CHRONICLES

Most modern readers skip or at best skim the first nine chapters of Chronicles, along with later chapters which list temple personnel. We feel alienated by the strange (to us) names, correctly concluding that these chapters must be addressed to someone other than ourselves. But think of the quite different feeling when we encounter our own and neighbor families' names in local histories and newspaper stories. The names jump out at us; our attention rises. This is how we might feel as Yehudite readers; the lists give names we might recognize, inviting us to locate ourselves in the text, whether by family, geographical connection, or stories like that of Jabez (1 C 4:9–10), who does not branch from the genealogical tree but attaches himself to it by his prayer. Staff rosters such as those in 1 C 23–27 tell how we or our contemporaries came to hold present positions, further increasing the sense of connection. The story becomes in effect (although not grammatically) a second-person ("you") narrative that includes us and our own times.

Unlike the lists of Ezra-Nehemiah, with which they overlap, Chronicles' lists are not confined to returnee families. The first chapter establishes Israel's kinship to other nations. Chapters 4–5 and 7 cover tribes not included in Ezra-Nehemiah's "Israel." The Judah genealogies show mixed marriages—so deplored by Ezra and Nehemiah—even in the royal lineage: Judah marries the Canaanite Bath-shua (1 C 2:3); David's sister Abigail's son is fathered by an Ishmaelite (1 C 2:17); and David marries a Jezreelite, a Carmelite, and a Geshurite (1 C 3:1–2).[8] Thus already in the lists we encounter a possible ideological difference between Chronicles and Ezra-Nehemiah.

When I call these chapters "lists" I use the term in a very loose and nontechnical sense. Scholars who study the various genres of lists note that a genealogy intended to legitimate or glorify a leader normally traces only his particular line (for example, the lineages of Jesus in Mt 1 and Lk 3:23–38).[9] But the opening chapters of Chronicles cast David (along with other worthies such as Moses, Aaron, and Samuel) as simply one twig on the bountiful bush of "all Israel." To be sure, his ancestry launches the specifically Israelite section of the genealogies (1 C 2:1–15). But each level includes siblings (1 C 2:15, by the way, makes David a seventh son rather than an eighth). The next forty verses deal with collateral lines (2:16–55). The Davidic thread resumes in 2 C 3, then gives way to another set of collaterals going all the way back to the tribal ancestor Judah (1 C 4:1–23). Among David's offspring, kings occupy just seven verses (3:10–16). David's own royal status receives only passing mention (1 C 3:4; 4:31). His establishment of Levitical duties (6:31; 9:22)—a task which touches the Yehudite reader's time—figures as prominently as his kingship.

Osborne has pointed out that the genealogies of 1 C 1–9 also give us, in small insets of narrative and editorial comment, rules which will govern the history to come.[10] For instance: "Er . . . was wicked in the sight of the LORD, and he put him to death" (1 C 2:3); and "Jabez called on the God of Israel. . . . And God granted what he asked" (4:10). The Reubenites "cried to God in the battle, and he granted their entreaty because they trusted in him" (5:20). But "Judah was taken into exile in Babylon because of their unfaithfulness" (9:1). These comments suggest key dynamics (sin brings punishment, but crying out to God results in deliverance) for the narrative which follows.

The lists tell us that in Chronicles, David is one among many Israelites—indeed, among many humans—and God's action applies to obscure as well as famous characters. The reader and David stand side by side, in a narrative universe controlled by God's protection of all who trust—an option as open to the reader as to David.

CHAPTER 10

DAVID'S DEEDS IN CHRONICLES

Chronicles and Ezra-Nehemiah suggest a Second Temple context in which the ideal of a restored Israel—giving generously to sustain joyful united worship—contains undertones of conflict. Who may participate in worship life? How shall social transactions—including marriage, trade, and financing—be conducted? Chronicles' opening chapters of lists and genealogies, so strange to us, serve to establish continuity between the Yehudite community and its monarchic past and to probe the boundaries of that community. What now about the narrative which focuses on David?

We will begin with a survey comparison between Chronicles and the primary history (Genesis through Kings) in order to see how different Chronicles is, even in its basic plot line. We will then move sequentially through the David story of 1 Chronicles, watching how David is characterized by actions and events. In Chapter 11 we will attend more closely to the major speeches given by David in Chronicles.

CHRONICLES AND THE PRIMARY HISTORY

In my NRSV Bible, the primary history moves from Adam to exile in 394 pages, 51 of which tell David's story. Chronicles covers the same period in 65 pages, with David's story occupying 18. Relatively speaking, then, David's story is more than twice as prominent in Chronicles (27 percent of the pages) as it is in the primary history (13 percent). But in actual number of pages, Chronicles' David story is only about a third the length of the one in Samuel and Kings. If Samuel's presentation is more memorable to most readers, that may in part be because there is so much more of it.

Let's now compare the events of the stories (in broad terms, not verse-by-verse detail):

Samuel/Kings	*Chronicles*
David anointed by Samuel (1 S 16)	———
David and Goliath (1 S 17)	———
David and Saul's children (1 S 18–20)	———
David flees from Saul (1 S 21–24, 26)	———
David and Abigail (1 S 25)	———
David as a Philistine vassal (1 S 27, 29–30)	———
Saul and the medium at Endor (1 S 28)	———
Saul's death (1 S 31)	Saul's death (1 C 10)
David and Saul's house (2 S 1–4, 9, 21)	———
David "established" (2 S 5)	David "established" (1 C 11, 14)
David brings up the ark (2 S 6)	David brings up the ark (1 C 13, 15)
———	David's worship arrangements (1 C 16)
God's promise to David (2 S 7)	God's promise to David (1 C 17)
David's wars (2 S 8, 10)	David's wars (1 C 18–20)
David and Bathsheba (2 S 11–12)	———
Problems with David's children (2 S 13–18)	———
Consolidating after rebellion (2 S 19–20)	———
David's poems about God (2 S 22, 23)	———
David's heroes (2 S 23)	David's heros (1 C 11–12)
Census/plague/altar (2 S 24)	Census/plague/altar (1 C 21)
———	Speeches about temple (1 C 22, 28–29)
———	More arrangements and appointments (1 C 23–27)
Adonijah's bid for succession (1 K 1)	———

Present in Samuel but not Chronicles are whole sets of stories: David's relations to Saul's house, his service to the Philistines, his interactions with women, Uriah's murder, rebellions in David's house and at large, the slaughter of Saul's descendants, and scheming over succession. The two narratives share stories of establishment: David's establishment *by* God (personally, militarily, and dynastically) and David's establishment *of* Jerusalem (militarily, politically, and above all religiously). Present in Chronicles but not Samuel are David's staffing arrangements and speeches pertaining to the temple.

Chronicles has often been seen as a "cleanup job," scrubbing away David's troubled relationship with Saul, marital misadventures, and children gone wrong. But Chronicles also lacks more positive stories, such as David's battle with Goliath and friendship with Jonathan. Rather than presenting Chronicles as a cleanup job, one might say that it offers us a public David—representative of the nation, a leader against whom no one even thinks of rebelling—whereas Samuel concentrates on David as a human individual involved in particular personal relationships with their attendant mixed motives and complications.

Chronicles' emphasis on David as Israelite par excellence helps Yehudite readers imagine themselves shoulder-to-shoulder with David. It presents him as an ideal to which they can aspire rather than a historical problem for them to ponder. His role in temple arrangements supplies a concrete point of contact with his activities. An untarnished David also provides an archetypal example of the blessing which follows right conduct, rather than prompting questions about the justice of God's ways with humankind.

THE STORY IN SEQUENCE

Chronicles collapses the history of Genesis through Joshua to names in genealogies and a few brief later allusions. The major figures of Judges—Deborah, Gideon, Abimelech, Jephthah, and Samson—do not appear even in genealogies. Chronicles' narrative proper begins with Saul's death and Israel's defeat at Gilboa (1 C 10). Only after Saul and his sons have been buried does David appear in an unsuspenseful succession: "the LORD put him [Saul] to death and turned the kingdom over to David son of Jesse" (1 C 10:14). "All Israel" promptly gathers to David at Hebron and anoints him king (11:1–3). As Chronicles presents this event, "all Israel" means all the tribes, with no undertones of tension between Judah and an "Israel" comprised of northern tribes, nor any hint that David was already acknowledged king by Judah. The "word of the LORD by Samuel" (11:3) seems to speak in unison with the elders, in contrast to 1 S 16 where it set off a long period of tension between God's plan and the existing government.

David immediately assumes residence in Jerusalem. Joab gets credit for the city's capture (11:6). This detail, absent in Samuel, is characteristic of Chronicles, which cares deeply about the worthies who surround David.

In Chronicles' telling, David's comrades *are* "worthies," not questionable companions sharing a precarious wilderness existence. Around David gather "chiefs" (11:10), "mighty warriors" (11:11, 12:1), "mighty and experienced warriors, expert with shield and spear" (12:8), "a great army, like an army of

God" (12:22), and "warriors arrayed in battle order" (12:38).[1] No ruddy-cheeked shepherd here, no refugee with spittle in his beard, nor any local residents eager to turn him in as a bandit. Chronicles' David is no underdog, and his supporters are the elite of Israel.

For some, like Shammoth in 11:27, we get nothing but names. For others, like Eleazar in 11:12–14, we get brief stories. Odd little touches show the narrator's Second Temple consciousness. An example is the name Jashobeam (possibly for two different people, 11:11 and 12:6). This name, which does not occur outside 1 Chronicles, means "the people will return" (or "the people will repent").[2] It would be an odd name in the tenth century, but from a Yehudite standpoint it is ripe with meaning.

We saw in Chapter 9 that Chronicles' genealogies frame David as a brother among the men of Israel. The same idea is emphasized by the narrative: "We are your bone and flesh," say the Israelites in 1 C 11:1, with no hint of the irony we heard in 2 S 5:1. In Chronicles' telling, David has support from non-Judean tribes (Benjamin, Gad, Manasseh, 12:1–22) even during Saul's days. By the time we finish meeting the mighty men and return to the coronation at Hebron, twelve tribes have turned out en masse to support David (12:23–40).

Following the pattern of camaraderie suggested in 1 C 11–12, David consults with "every leader" before proposing to "the whole assembly of Israel" that "if it seems good" to them, and if it is the will of God, everyone (including those not present) should come together to fetch the ark (13:1–3). The "whole assembly" agrees, for it pleases "all the people." Moving the ark to Jerusalem is now a national enterprise, not a personal attempt to consolidate power.

Uzzah's death, however, interrupts the parade. Because David has in this book shown no symptoms of presumptuousness and because he enlisted both God and people as supporters of his project, nothing prompts us to see the death as a rebuke or warning. For the moment, it remains unexplained. In Chronicles, David's palace from Hiram, his acquisition of more wives and children, and his divinely assisted victories against the Philistines (1 C 14, paralleling 2 S 5) *follow* the ark parade, almost as if they are part of the same blessing that falls on Obed-Edom's household (13:14). These blessings dispel any sense that God has been offended by the ark project.

Fortified by success, David prepares for his second ark parade with two full chapters of ritual, musical, and staffing arrangements (1 C 15–16). Here the NRSV translation misleads us slightly: it has David "commanding" (15:2, 16) worship protocols just as Moses did (15:15). The Hebrew text is more cautious; in these verses it speaks of Moses "commanding," whereas for David's statements it employs the more ordinary verb "said." Nonetheless David's role parallels that of Moses. Chronicles' David may be a comrade among brothers politically and militarily, but with regard to worship he is a founding legislator of great authority.

David's restriction of ark bearing to Levites receives special emphasis (15:2, 12–15, 26) and retroactively explains Uzzah's death (15:13, which is, however, less straightforward in Hebrew than in English translation). If this explanation had come in 1 C 13, we might have blamed David for causing the problem by not making proper arrangements. By delaying the explanation to 1 C 15, the Chronicler portrays David as author of the cure: his orders ensure that the tragedy will not be repeated. Note, by the way, how David speaks of the ark's outburst against "us" (15:13). Suspiciously one could regard this as an attempt to spread the blame for an error which was really his. Given what surrounds it in Chronicles, however, it sounds more like a king's expression of solidarity with his subjects.

Lists of "mighty warriors" expressed public support for David's kingship. Now lists of Levites and other functionaries show that he is not alone in his desire for correct worship. The lists also underscore continuity between David's time and the narrator's, for the groups named (Asaph's kin in 16:7, 37, the sons of Jeduthun in 16:42, and so forth) probably held office in the Yehudite temple.[3] The praises these Levites sing (16:8–36) may well have been hymns from the narrator's own time. (Some of the same lyrics surface in Pss 96, 105, and 106, although we don't know if Chronicles draws on these psalms or vice versa.)

Once again, then, familiar names and structures draw the audience into the story alongside a David who is leader but also fellow in the praise. The form of the psalm in 1 C 16—addressed to the assembly and calling them to praise, with a first person plural appeal for blessing at the end—offers generous space for reader participation. Contrast the poems in 2 S 1; 3:33–34; 22; and 23: the first two speak of very particular events in David's time, the second two express David's own position in the first person, and all four leave the audience as observers rather than participants. Whereas most of the Chronicles psalm speaks in generic terms equally appropriate to David's or the readers' day, the final appeal ("gather and rescue us from among the nations" 16:35) has little or nothing to do with David's time and everything to do with a later era's exilic history, diaspora population, and sense of vulnerability to national enemies (visible across the room in Nehemiah's struggle to rebuild Jerusalem's wall).

The second attempt at ark bringing in Chronicles contains one dark note—Michal's despising in 15:29. The Chronicler assumes that we know who Michal is, otherwise we would require a note that she was David's wife as well as Saul's daughter. But stories which might prompt us to view her with sympathy have been left aside. We see only a mean-spirited queen who serves, like her father, as dark counterpoint to the bright and shining David.

We now arrive at God's interaction with David on the subject of house building (1 C 17). Although the chapter generally coincides with 2 S 7, differences in setting sharply affect its impact. Samuel emphasized David's unique standing with God, but Chronicles has made him bone and flesh with "all Israel." Samuel gave us an opaque and sometimes disquieting David, but in Chronicles we have little reason to question his motives and piety. Samuel meditated darkly on the blindnesses and failures of prophets as well as kings, but Chronicles has mentioned prophets only in passing and there positively. Where Samuel raised questions about God's own promise keeping (with respect to Eli and Saul), Chronicles reduces these questions to negligibility. Eli's rejection has not been mentioned at all; Saul's was dealt with in passing in a manner which assumed its deservedness. Chronicles further dissipates any lingering discomfort about Saul's rejection by omitting his name from 17:13. (It appears in the parallel, 2 S 7:15.) Instead Chronicles emphasizes that those who call on God will find salvation. It underscores the point by prefacing the covenant interchange with a hymn proclaiming God's steadfastness (1 C 16:34; see also 16:41).

Our reading of Nathan's oracle is also affected by what follows it. In Samuel it precedes the adultery and murder which drive the remainder of David's life downhill. In Chronicles, David will spend most of the rest of his life (narratively speaking) preparing for the project discussed in the oracle. The temple-builder Solomon himself will be a very mixed character in Kings, whereas in Chronicles he models piety as well as wealth. Lifting our eyes to the narrative horizon, we recall that the primary history shows us nothing beyond a temple (a mistaken project to begin with?) in ashes, whereas Chronicles tells the story from a post-return standpoint which celebrates the temple as the heart of community life in God's presence.

Chronicles thus nullifies some of the questions which troubled our reading of 2 S 7. God's promise comes as generous reward to a king who has, alongside his people, served God well. Solidarity between king and people mutes questions about whether David's elevation comes at the people's expense. Because the preceding chapters have already laid such stress on worship and the arrangements for it, the house which David's son *will* build (17:12) stands out as the important part of the prophecy, in contrast to the house which David will *not* build (17:3) or the house to be built *for* David (17:10). The words of the oracle have changed in only a few places, but by changing the setting Chronicles suggests that God's answer is finally "yes" rather than "no" to David's proposal.

As if in reward for David's offer, God grants David victory against a host of foreign kings and their lands (1 C 18–20). Once again, small nuances show that the story is sifted through the consciousness of a Second Temple narrator. For example, 18:8 contains a note (not present in 2 S 8:8) that the bronze taken from Hadadezer's cities will be used by Solomon for temple equipment. In 1 C 18:17 we hear that David's sons were "chief officials in the service of the king" (avoiding the question raised by 2 S 8:18 about the propriety of his sons' serving as priests).

The fact that Chronicles credits Elhanan with killing Goliath's *brother* (1 C 20:5, contrast 2 S 21:19) probably signals that the Chronicler is aware of 1 S 17, which credits Goliath's death to David. However, David's own victory goes unmentioned. Once again, Chronicles shifts focus from David's personal prowess to David as leader in solidarity with his capable, worthy subjects.

1 Chronicles 20:1 begins with words from 2 S 11:1 and ends with words from 2 S 12:26. It displays no awareness of Samuel's intervening story about David, Bathsheba, Uriah, Nathan, and the nameless baby, except possibly in the phrase "David remained at Jerusalem."[4] Gone are the adultery and murder, gone is the curse on David's house. Not only does this leave us with a much cleaner David, but the troubles of later Davidic kings must now be explained on grounds of their own behavior (rather than a curse on the house). Removing Nathan's oracle is one part of Chronicles' larger attack on the notion that punishments and rewards may be diverted from one generation to the next.

If the Chronicler knows of the stories in 2 S 13–21 (the rape of Tamar, Amnon's death, Absalom's rebellion, Sheba's rebellion, and the sacrifice of Saul's descendants), that knowledge enters the book only in the naming of Tamar (1 C 3:9). The story of census, plague, and David's purchase of a certain threshing floor (1 C 21) thus comes as David's first real experience with sin and divine displeasure. In 2 S 24 this story began with God ordering a census and then punishing David for obeying that order, but Chronicles reports that Satan—or more likely "a *śāṭān*" ("an adversary," not necessarily a supernatural one[5])—provokes David to take the census. God's wrath responds to the census (21:7), rather than prompting the order for it.

"Let me fall into the hand of the LORD, for his mercy is very great," says David when asked to select a punishment for his sin, "but let me not fall into human hands" (1 C 21:13). His statement resonates with a series of other assertions and examples of God's responsiveness to those who seek.[6] It belongs here in the story of the temple site's selection, for the temple symbolizes divine willingness to grant mercy. This theme will be reemphasized in

Solomon's dedicatory prayer (2 C 6:22–42) and God's response to it (2 C 7:12–14).

Chronicles expands slightly upon the angel's appearance and actions in a way which highlights the importance of David's altar building. God's initial sending of the angel against Jerusalem appears as a separate event from (rather than a continuation of) the plague which afflicts the rest of Israel. This underlines Jerusalem's special significance. The angel stands, as in Samuel, "by the threshing floor" of a certain Jebusite, but Chronicles tells us in addition that David saw the angel "standing between earth and heaven" (1 C 21:15–16). If the threshing floor is "between earth and heaven," no wonder it makes a good temple site! Israel is deeply indebted to David for this discernment of the site's mytho-geographic significance.

When David sees the angel, it still holds "a drawn sword stretched out over Jerusalem," a clear suggestion that God's order has only temporarily halted the plague rather than bringing it to a decisive end. David bows in sackcloth as he prays, "these sheep, what have they done? Let your hand, I pray . . . be against me and against my father's house" (1 C 21:16–17). "The elders" bow with him, yet again setting Chronicles' David in fellowship with his people's leaders.

The angel himself gives Gad instructions for David. In Samuel the threshing floor's Jebusite owner sees only David approaching. Here he sees the angel also. The reactions of his four sons (they hide) and the Jebusite himself (who continues to thresh until David arrives) contrast with the more appropriate actions of the elders and David.

David brushes aside the Jebusite's offered donations with enhanced insistence on paying a dramatically higher price than in Samuel (50 silver shekels in 2 S 24:24, 600 gold shekels in 1 C 21:25). God responds spectacularly with "fire from heaven" (21:26). We then receive a specific report that at God's command the angel sheaths its sword (21:27).

Samuel closes simply, "LORD answered his supplication for the land, and the plague was averted from Israel" (2 S 24:25). Chronicles moves from the threshing-floor story into one of the book's central concerns, the temple. "Here shall be the house of the LORD God," announces David, "and here the altar of burnt offering for Israel" (1 C 22:1). Not only does this underscore the connection between the threshing floor and the temple, but it subtly suggests that the altar will be able to perform the same role as a king's supplication—an important assertion for the claim of continuity between Davidic monarchy and Second Temple times.

1 Chronicles 22–29 covers the same time span as 1 K 1–2: the period from the census/plague[7] event to David's death, with special emphasis on David's appointment of Solomon as his successor. But we can see at a glance that

Kings and Chronicles offer drastically different outlooks on this period of David's life.

1 K 1–2	*1 C 22–29*
Frail, ailing, impotent David	A good old age, full of days, riches, and honor
David lies abed	David actively gathers temple materials
Court split over succession	Adonijah's ambitions unmentioned
Nathan and Bathsheba manipulate David	Initiative entirely with David
Last instructions concern retribution[8]	Last instructions concern temple
Solomon begins reign with executions	All pledge to Solomon who prospers

In Kings, David ends his career as a frail man surrounded by manipulative underlings and obsessed by old grudges (1 K 1–2). Chronicles presents a quite different picture. It reports in 1 C 23:1 that when David was "full of days" he made Solomon king. We might expect this to precede a report on Solomon's actions in assuming kingship. Instead, we get seven more chapters on *David's* arrangements for the temple and its staffing. An active and commanding David makes all arrangements for the crowning achievement of Solomon's reign (1 C 22–29). Solomon meekly cooperates.

Five of these final chapters involve personnel arrangements parallel to those of the reader's own day (1 C 23–27), once again building a bridge between David and Yehud. Under David, the Levites have continued the role assigned by Moses of carrying the tabernacle (23:26). Under Solomon—*but by David's direction*—they will assume new duties assisting Aaron's descendants. This detail casts David parallel to Moses.

Alongside the temple staffing reports we find a section on military and civic officials (1 C 27) in which "mighty men" of previous sections take positions in the new bureaucracy. We find characters here such as Benaiah (the mercenary commander who murders Adonijah and Joab in 1 K 2:25, 34), Asahel (Joab's younger brother, who in 2 Samuel dies before David becomes king), Ahithophel (who in 2 S 17:23 committed suicide when Absalom refused his advice), and Joab himself. We also find newer-sounding names such as that of Jashobeam (27:2) and Hashabiah (27:17), a proper name that occurs sixteen times in Chronicles and Ezra-Nehemiah but nowhere else in the Hebrew canon. By placing the names of familiar heroes in lists parallel to those naming singers and other temple functionaries, chapters 23–27 rhetorically link the institutions of monarchic and Persian eras.

The chapters about David's staffing arrangements are bracketed by major speeches in 1 C 22 and 28–29. We will examine these speeches in detail in Chapter 13. For now, however, we skip over them and move on to the retrospective treatment of David in 2 Chronicles.

David appears already in the book's first verse, which says of Solomon not only that he was firmly established in his kingdom (an observation shared with 1 K 2:12) but that God was "with him." Acting remarkably like the Chronicles' version of his father David, Solomon immediately summons "all Israel, the commanders of the thousands and of the hundreds, the judges, and all the leaders of all Israel, the heads of families" (1:2) to worship. A retrospective note (1:4) reminds us that although the tent of meeting is at Gibeon, David has already brought the ark to Jerusalem. This is the first of 2 Chronicles' eighteen references to David's preparations for temple worship.[9]

Solomon's subsequent references to David in prayer (1:8–9) are less flowery and obsequious than their Kings parallels (1 K 3:6–7), matter-of-factly presenting Solomon the temple builder as a man like David rather than a slick-tongued courtier. (Solomon even takes a census "after the census that his father David had taken"—2 C 2:17—but a negative divine reaction is not recorded.) Solomon's later prayer of dedication (6:6) quotes God as choosing Jerusalem in parallel with choosing David, yet another piece of the chain by which the Chronicler claims monarchic tradition for a later day (Jerusalem is not mentioned in the parallel, 1 K 8:16). Later Solomon mentions Torah (NRSV "law")—another motif precious to the Second Temple's priests—in connection with the dynastic promise (2 C 6:16 paralleling 1 K 8:25, which speaks more generally of walking before God).

Ultimately, 2 Chronicles mentions the promise to David fourteen times, ten of them in the chapters concerning Solomon's reign.[10] (Some of these verses use the words "promise" or "covenant"; others speak of "choice" or "steadfast love.") Among these verses, 6:42 (which has no Kings parallel) is particularly striking, for it pleads against rejection of the "anointed one" in terms like those of Ps 132. We will see later that this psalm not only reclaims royal theology in the Second Temple context of the Psalter's final division, but does so in a way which allows transference of the royal promise to priestly leaders.

David also figures in 2 Chronicles as a model of obedience, a consideration raised in five verses (four of them post-Solomonic).[11] In Chronicles, of course, citations of David's obedience require no qualification (contrast 1 K 15:5). Only one of the kings compared to David receives a negative evaluation (Ahaz in 2 C 28:1). One evaluation (2 C 11:17) pertains not to a king but to Levites who "walked . . . in the way of David and Solomon." In Chronicles, then, comparison with David is used primarily to praise rather than condemn. However, no king receives a rating higher than David (contrast 2 K 18:5 and 23:25).

One significant category of retrospective references in Kings does not occur in Chronicles—passages in which God ameliorates or delays punishment for love of David. God preserves the *dynasty* for David's sake ("yet the LORD would not destroy the house of David because of the covenant that he had made with David," 2 C 21:7), but each individual king within it suffers or prospers according to his own vice or virtue. For instance, the long and prosperous reign of the wicked king Manasseh is now explained by a dramatic repentance on his part (2 C 33:10–17). Good King Uzziah's[12] leprosy is attributed to a cultic misdeed (2 C 26:16–20). Chronicles interprets the untimely death of King Josiah, the greatest reformer of all, not as an overflow of God's wrath against Manasseh (compare 2 K 23:26–27) but as punishment for Josiah's own refusal to "listen to the words of Neco [a pharaoh!] from the mouth of God" (2 C 35:22). In each case, God warns before punishing. To those who repent and return, God offers forgiveness and renewed well-being.

This dynamic of punishment (following warning) and reward (for those who repent or did not err to begin with) does not apply only to monarchs. In Chronicles, the people are active players rather than passive followers. This pattern, set in the narration of David's reign, continues in the Chronicler's depiction of subsequent Judean history. When Shishak attacks Rehoboam, for instance, "the prophet Shemaiah came to Rehoboam *and to the officers of Judah*," all of whom then "humbled themselves and said, 'The LORD is in the right' " (2 C 12:5–6, emphasis added).[13] In particular, the Chronicler speaks repeatedly of individuals and groups from the north who give their allegiance to Jerusalem's king and temple and thereby receive blessing.[14] These, like Jabez who cried to the God in 1 C 4:9–10, find full acceptance in the Chronicler's "all Israel."

In sum, Chronicles gives far more emphasis than Samuel to the heroes and leaders who surround the king and to their solidarity with him. We see David in association with the military (chapters 11–12, 14, 18–20, and 27), but even greater space goes to his religious activity (chapters 13, 15–17, 22–26, and 28–29). Religious activity also dominates retrospective references to David's reign. The David of Chronicles seems to have no enemies aside from Philistines, Ammonites, and some Arameans. His problems with Saul are alluded to only passingly (primarily in 1 C 12:1, 19) and in retrospect, after it has already been established that there will be no problem with David's accession. No one within Israel subsequently rebels against him, with the possible exception of the "adversary" in 21:1—who, if human, is downplayed by anonymity. Chapter 21 likewise provides our only serious episode of problems *within* David, as he follows the tempter's advice. His misjudgment leads, as in Samuel, to a sobering number of deaths. But it culminates with assurance of God's care for Jerusalem and willingness to hear prayer—and an anticipation of the altar by which supplication can be made in the Chronicler's own day. In the Chronicler's narrative universe, sins redound only to the generation which commits them. Yehudites need no longer fear that the misdeeds of bygone generations will be visited upon them.

CHAPTER 11

DAVID'S MESSAGE TO YEHUD

From David's appearance in the opening genealogies of 1 Chronicles to 2 Chronicles' retrospective glances at him—and of course in the narrative between—we have seen solidarity between David and his people, and strong suggestions of continuity between monarchic Israel and the Second Temple community. The Chronicler's David has a direct message for Yehud, and nowhere does it become more apparent than in David's speeches toward the end of 1 Chronicles. These speeches recall and remodel the promise oracle in 1 C 17 (parallel to 2 S 7), so we will begin this chapter with another brief look at that oracle. Next we turn to the speeches themselves, with special attention to their use of key words. This will prepare us for our summary reflection on the significance of David in Chronicles.

THE PROMISE ORACLE (1 C 17)

When we compare the promise chapter of Chronicles with its parallel in 2 S 7, we notice in the very first verse that Samuel's David proposes a temple after God gives him "rest from all his enemies around him" (7:1). "Rest" (the Hebrew verb *nûaḥ* and its associated nouns[1]) designates both the peace which God's people enjoy when established in their land (for instance, 2 S 7:11 and 1 K 8:56) and a special quality associated with the temple. 1 C 6:31, for instance, speaks of David's preparations for the day when the ark will "rest" in the "house of the LORD." (This verse connects in interesting ways to Ps 132, which twice speaks of Zion or the temple as God's "resting place" and which we saw quoted by Solomon in his dedicatory prayer, 2 C 6:41–42.) In 1 C 23:25 David grounds Levitical assignments in the fact that God "has given rest to his people." 2 Chronicles associates the divine gift of rest with the reigns of good kings (2 C 14:6–7; 15:15; 20:30).

"Rest" is absent in the opening verse of 1 C 17 for two reasons. First, Chronicles holds that David himself could not build the temple because he was a man of war (we will look at this shortly). Second, rest for Chronicles results from—as well as being a precondition for—temple building. Again, rest at this point would be premature.

God responds to David's proposal with a statement: "*You* shall not build a house . . ." (1 C 17:5, my translation) rather than 2 S 7:5's sarcastic question, "shall *you* build *me* a house?" (my translation). The question in Samuel contrasts David—who proposes to build a house for God—and God, who will build a house for David. Chronicles' phrasing shifts the contrast to one between David—who will not build—and his son, who will.

Japhet's fine commentary on this passage points out how Chronicles emphasizes the son's role with puns that link God's building (*yibneh*, 10) with the seed from "among your sons" (*mibbanêkā*, 11) who will in turn build (*yibneh*, 12) the house for God.[2] Chronicles' oracle climaxes with God's promise to confirm "him" (Solomon, 14) and "his throne" rather than David's house and throne (2 S 7:16). Chronicles also promises confirmation of David's offspring in *God's* house, whereas in Samuel we heard that *David's* house would be made sure. Again Chronicles chooses phrasing which strengthens the links between dynastic theology and temple.

Japhet also notes that 2 S 7:14's line about punishment of Davidic kings' sins is missing in Chronicles. Without that line, steadfast love "forever" (1 C 17:14) contrasts not with God's reserved right to punish the king, but more simply with God's rejection of "him who was before you" (1 C 17:13; the verse refuses even to mention Saul's name.) This reinforces Chronicles' pro-David, anti-Saul contrast.

What is the significance of such small modifications, in light of our comment in Chapter 9 that Chronicles probably expects us to have the Samuel story "in mind" rather than "at hand"? Most audiences do not hear each subtle change; rather, they notice the overall similarity (verbatim at many points) between the two versions of the oracle. This echo effect lends authenticity to the Chronicler's retelling; the reader or hearer has an impression of history faithfully retold rather than history rewritten. Yet the retelling shifts and changes meanings in ways which serve the Chronicler's own agendas.[3]

DAVID'S FIRST SPEECH TO SOLOMON AND THE LEADERS (1 C 22)

Although God has said that David's son, not David himself, will build the house, David responds to his experience at the threshing floor (1 C 21) by assembling temple materials (22:1–4). He explains his action in 22:5: "Solomon is young and inexperienced." He then "charges" Solomon, using a verb recalling David's Moses-like quality, to do the actual building (22:6).

"I had it in my heart to build," says David, ". . . but the word of LORD came to me, saying" (22:7–8, my translation). We expect to hear a recounting of the oracle in 1 C 17. Instead, David cites words we have never heard before. He tells us he was forbidden to build a temple because of his bloodshed (22:8). We know David has shed blood, for chapters 18–20 concern his military successes. But, reports David, his son will be a "man of rest" to whom God "will give rest" (22:9, my translation; the passage uses two words from the *nûaḥ*—"rest"—family). The son will thus be qualified to build the temple, and to Solomon (*šĕlōmōh*) God will give "peace and quiet" (*šālôm wāšeqeṭ*, a nice alliteration with his name).

This explanation of David's nonbuilding is stronger than Solomon's allegation in 1 K 5:3 that war kept David too busy to build, although Chronicles' idea may have been prompted by the phrasing in Kings. 1 Chronicles 22 presents war as a religious rather than merely practical disqualification. It rationalizes David's failure to build without casting doubt upon the project's worthiness (as 2 S 7 tends to do). It also helps Yehudites justify compliance with Persian restrictions on military activity; after all, temple building is the really important thing, and it cannot be done by warriors. From David himself as a report of God's own words, the reasoning carries authority.

David's next words (22:10) return to the language of the oracle, encouraging us to meld the new explanation—David couldn't build because of bloodshed—with our memory of 1 C 17, which didn't provide such an explanation. (I have even heard readers retroject the "man of peace" reasoning into 2 S 7.)

We now arrive at the moment of bestowal. "LORD be with you," David says to Solomon in 1 C 22:11 and 16. As if linguistically to enact the wish, David—who spoke in 22:7 of "my God"—speaks in 22:11 and 12 of "your [Solomon's] God." He requests discretion and understanding for Solomon. (Solomon's request for wisdom in 2 C 1:10 is thus a reprise of David's prayer, not a fresh initiative.) David reminds Solomon, in terms highly reminiscent of 1 K 2:2–3, that prosperity depends on careful observance of the laws of Moses.

In 22:13 David gives Solomon a fourfold charge: "Be strong and of good courage. Do not be afraid or dismayed." These are exactly the words with which Moses encourages Joshua in Dt 31:7–8, another hint of a David/Moses parallel.[4] But we also find this command directed at the people—from Moses and Joshua in Dt 31:6 and Josh 10:25, and from the Davidic king Hezekiah in 2 C 32:7. The juxtaposition of various occurrences of this distinctive phrase suggests that temple building is as courageous and rest bringing an activity as Joshua's campaigns.

When he has finished speaking to Solomon, David turns to Israel's leaders and charges them to "help" in the building (22:17). The word "help" (which in Chronicles has strong military connotations) recalls 1 C 12, where it appeared seven times to define the relationship of Israel's mighty men to the commander who would not drink at the cost of their blood. It supplies yet another link between the warrior heroes of old and the activities of civic leaders who support a sanctuary.

David can expect such help from the leaders because God has now, at the point of Solomon's accession, "given . . . rest [a form of the verb *nûaḥ*] on every side" (22:18, my translation). The same Hebrew phrase describing God's gift of "rest on every side" occurs in Dt 12:10 and 25:9 anticipating possession of the land, Josh 21:44 and 23:1 reporting that possession, 1 C 22:9 reporting God's promise to David about Solomon, and 2 C 14:7, 15:15, and 20:30 describing conditions under good kings. These occurrences suggest a spiritual equivalence between Joshua's conquest, monarchic life at its best, and temple building.

DAVID'S FAREWELL SPEECHES (1 C 28–29)

In 1 C 28–29 David makes his farewell addresses to Solomon and the people. Speaking to the political and military movers and shakers of the country, he underscores his kinship with them by addressing them as "my brothers and my people," telling them it had been "in my heart" (28:2, my translation) to build "a house of rest" for the ark. This language echoes not only 22:18–19 but 6:16 and Ps 132.

As in 22:8, David reports a divine response which disqualifies him from building because of his bloodshed. But, David says, as he himself was chosen by God to rule Israel, so his son Solomon has been chosen *by God* to succeed him (28:6). This is, strikingly, the only place in the Bible where a king subsequent to David is spoken of as "chosen" by God.[5] Solomon is chosen not only for kingship but for building the house and a filial relationship with God, provided that he keeps the commandments. David then segues from Solomon's commandment keeping to an exhortation. The assembled leaders must also observe the commandments, in order that they can possess the land (a theme tightly tied to "rest") and leave it to their children (the Chronicler's Yehudite audience) "forever."

David packs his advice to Solomon with terminology that merges king's and people's callings (28:9–10, 20–21). David himself had been made king by a people of "single mind" (1 C 12:38). He now advises Solomon to seek God with "single mind" (1 C 28:9 and 29:19), but the people too are of "single mind" in their free offerings to God and God's house (29:6–9). The word "single" (*šālēm*) suggests completeness or fulfillment.[6] It employs the same core consonants (*šlm*) as the word "peace" and Solomon's own name.

121

David also assures Solomon that if he seeks, God will be found by him; but "if you forsake him, he will abandon you forever" (28:9). The phrasing here is completely conditional: the "forever" of absolute promise (28:4) gives way to a warning of abandonment "forever" for those who forsake. In verse 10, Solomon's mission as "chosen" is defined entirely in terms of temple building. These verses contain both promise and threat for the Yehudite community, which is also "chosen" but must not forsake its God.

David attributes his plans for the temple, its components, and its staffing directly to God (28:19), then repeats his Moses-like command: "Be strong and of good courage. . . . Do not be afraid or dismayed" (1 C 28:20, compare 22:13 and Dt 31:7–8). After all, "every volunteer . . . also the officers and all the people" will be with Solomon (28:21).

In the next and final chapter of 1 Chronicles, David asks the assembly to verify their willingness to support Solomon and the temple project. Words from the *ndb* family—describing generosity, volunteerism, and freewill giving—begin to appear in 28:21 ("volunteer") and recur seven times in 1 C 29.[7] But God asks more than generosity. The people must observe God's commandments (28:8) just as Solomon must (22:13; 28:7; 29:19). They (22:19; 28:8), like Solomon (28:9), must seek (*drš*) God and God's teachings, for God self searches (*drš*, 28:9) every mind. Seeking God, David now suggests, will bring "joy" (*śmḥ* and its derivates, in 29:9 three times plus verses 17 and 22).

In 29:10–19 David presents the people's freely given gifts to God and commends the givers and Solomon to divine care. He starts out by attributing all glory and power in heaven and earth to God, with special emphasis on the corollary that those who have riches or might have them only as a gift from God.[8] Although David does not spell out all the implications, he wields a theological sword which cuts two ways. On the one hand, the privileged can use it to argue that their privileges are their reward from God and that those who are poor must be so because they are undeserving. Yet David's assertion can also undercut rich donors' claims that God owes them something in return for their gifts.

In 29:15 David follows his observations about riches with a remarkable statement: "we are aliens and transients before you, as were all our ancestors." The term "alien" (*gēr*) denotes someone settled long-term in a foreign land; NRSV sometimes translates it "resident alien." The companion word "transient" (*tôšāb*) sometimes functions as a synonym for *gēr* and at other times denotes, as "transient" suggests, a less permanent visitor.

At one level this language recalls the Bible's insistence that the Israelites were not indigenous to Canaan but were given the land by God. But what would be the point of this for Chronicles' Second Temple audience? One might suppose that folk like Ezra and Nehemiah, who had been born in

Babylon and moved as adults to Yehud, would identify with the sense of being "aliens and transients." This might explain why such returnees told the narratives of the exodus and entrance into the land (remember all the vocabulary links we have observed between Chronicles and Joshua) with such relish, and why writers such as Second Isaiah (the otherwise anonymous composer of Isa 40–55) consistently speak of the return as a new exodus. But at the explicit ideological level, both Chronicles and Ezra-Nehemiah insist that to come to Yehud was to come "home." Ezra-Nehemiah takes the logic a step further: if homecoming returnees are the real "natives," then the folk already in Yehud, the "peoples of the land," must be foreigners.

Where did those people come from? The Bible gives us mixed signals on this matter. Chronicles says that Nebuchadnezzar "took into exile in Babylon those who had escaped from the sword," while the land itself "lay desolate" for seventy years (2 C 36:20–21), as if no one lived there at all. Kings says that when Jehoiachin capitulated to Nebuchadnezzar in 597 BCE, the Babylonian king

> carried away all Jerusalem, all the officials, all the warriors, ten thousand captives, all the artisans and the smiths; no one remained, except the poorest people of the land. He carried away Jehoiachin to Babylon; the king's mother, the king's wives, his officials, and the elite of the land, he took into captivity from Jerusalem to Babylon. The king of Babylon brought captive to Babylon all the men of valor, seven thousand, the artisans and the smiths, one thousand, all of them strong and fit for war. (2 K 24:14–16)

The figures seem unreliable: within this very paragraph we hear first of "ten thousand" deportees, then "seven thousand" plus "one thousand." However, the general message is clear: in 597 Nebuchadnezzar hauled off everybody who was anybody. Yet according to the book of Jeremiah—which in chapter 24 agrees that Jerusalem's cream went to Babylon in this deportation—Jeremiah himself (of a priestly family) was left behind, along with his scribe Baruch and various relatives and officials whose interactions with Jeremiah are described. Those left behind had power enough to withstand a second siege by Nebuchadnezzar for eighteen months (2 K 25:1–8). This second siege ended with the burning of the First Temple in 586 BCE (2 K 25:8–9). Then, the Kings narrator tells us, the Babylonians "carried into exile the rest of the people who were left in the city . . . all the rest of the population" (2 K 25:11).

Notice that this deportation, like the previous one, involved specifically the *Jerusalem* population. And again we are told that the Babylonians "left some of the poorest people of the land to be vinedressers and tillers of the soil" (2 K 25:12). But the writer implies that these dimly remembered peas-

123

ants are of no real importance, and tells us that in any case they eventually fled to Egypt (25:26).

The Hebrew Bible was largely written and compiled by expatriates in Babylon or their descendants. For them, Jerusalem had contained everything and everyone that mattered. For them, the "real" Judah/Israel was their own group—an understanding shared by Ezra-Nehemiah and 2 Kings. Readers today tend to accept this view; hence the common impression that the whole nation was carried off and the land left empty behind.[9]

But the exile was total only in the eyes of those who went to Babylon. The archaeological record suggests that for the majority of Palestine's population, life changed amazingly little.[10] We can understand that the locals may not have been pleased when descendants of the former ruling elite showed up decades later, with Persian imperial backing, to claim control of government, taxation, religious affairs, and prime farmland.

Ezra-Nehemiah (the only book which discusses this problem explicitly) recognizes that the returnees did not find an empty land, but it describes the occupants as foreigners brought to the land by the Assyrian king Esar-haddon (Ezra 4:2), presumably to resettle the territory of the fallen northern kingdom (Esar-haddon's reign ended decades before the fall of Judah). 2 Kings 17:24–41 also alleges that Assyria settled foreigners in northern Is-raelite territory, and that the foreigners "to this day" (17:41) serve God but also other gods. Chronicles, however, says nothing about such foreign settle-ment but recounts Hezekiah's invitation to defeated *Israelites* in the northern region (2 C 30:6–9). The dissonance between various pieces of this picture suggests that the argument about who was truly "Israelite" was an argument about access to power.[11]

The temple stood at the center of this storm, for it was not only a place of worship and symbol of identity, but the provincial treasury and economic center. In Chronicles David speaks of it as "a house of rest for the ark of the covenant of the LORD, for the footstool of our God" (1 C 28:2). In Isa 66:1 an opposition voice expresses a very different attitude:[12]

Thus says the LORD:
Heaven is my throne
   and the earth is my footstool;
what is the house that you would build for me,
   and what is my resting place?"

124

In most respects Chronicles agrees with Ezra-Nehemiah in supporting the temple and the legitimacy of the returnee groups who control it. Its David authorizes the privileges of the Levites and exhorts everyone to contribute, openhandedly and openheartedly, to temple coffers. But on this question of "foreigners," Chronicles seems to offer a different outlook than Ezra-Nehemiah. Its congregation is undivided. It says nothing about Assyrian settlement of pagan peoples in the land. Its genealogies associate such luminaries as Abraham and Judah with foreign and Canaanite women (1 C 1:32, 2:3–4). Its "all Israel" contains twelve tribes, not just Judah, Benjamin, and Levi. Foreign laborers, artisans—one of whom is from a mixed marriage—and kings contribute to its temple-building effort (1 C 22:2; 2 C 2:7, 13–14; 4:11–16). Its Solomon dedicates his temple on behalf of "all the peoples of the earth" and asks that God hear even the prayers of foreigners when directed toward that temple (2 C 6:32–33)—a component also present in the Kings parallel but less striking there because not juxtaposed to Ezra-Nehemiah. Chronicles' Hezekiah, who did "what was right in the sight of the LORD, just as his ancestor David had done," welcomes residents of the fallen northern kingdom to Jerusalem, even when they are "not in accordance with the sanctuary's rules of cleanness" (2 C 29:2 and 30:19). And no one at all opposes the building of the temple.[13]

Returning now to David's statement in 1 C 29:15 that "we are aliens and transients before you," it begins to look like a direct repudiation of the ethnic separation program advocated by Ezra and Nehemiah. If David and all the Israelite ancestors were themselves aliens and transients, what point or even possibility is there of maintaining an Israelite line uncontaminated by the blood of "foreign" wives?

With blessing and celebration, the people respond to David by affirming their commitment to Solomon's rule and to the building project (so that again the meaning of monarchy merges into the temple). On this note we take farewell of David, who "died in a good old age, full of days, riches, and honor" (29:28).

SUMMARY

The Chronicler's David is paradigmatic rather than unique—a quintessential Israelite in solidarity with all worthy Israelite leaders. His Israel is more congregation than nation, defined by its temple preparations rather than transition in political status (contrast Samuel's emphasis on the institution of monarchy). David himself is the preparer par excellence. One of Chronicles' favorite verbs is *kôn*—to prepare or establish. Fifteen of the fifty usages of that verb in Chronicles describe David's preparations for ark and temple.[14] His legacy of worship and music, carried forward especially by the Levites, far outweighs the legacy of his throne.

This emphasis on worship creates a bridge across the discontinuity of Jerusalem's fall, connecting monarchic Judah to Persian Yehud. David in his close association with temple and Levites symbolizes not the part of the national heritage which has been lost (monarchy), but the aspect which has continued (worship). Indeed, Cyrus's exhortation to build a "house at Jerusalem" (2 C 36:23) can be seen as the decree of a new Persian "David."

In Chronicles, David's relationship with God is not a matter of extravagant and inscrutable divine favor but divine response to human service. Chronicles clearly suggests how its audience may—by seeking God, keeping commandments, giving freely, and worshiping joyously—follow the highly accessible lead of David to ensure continued divine favor for their own generation.

Finally, this David of Chronicles is a model accessible even to "aliens and transients," for Chronicles does not sanction the exclusiveness of its companion work Ezra-Nehemiah, in which "all Israel" legitimately includes only certain named Judahite, Benjaminite, priestly, and Levitical families (and these only to the extent that they hold themselves aloof from "the peoples of the land"). Does Chronicles' position *following* Ezra-Nehemiah in some Hebrew arrangements reflect its being written after Ezra-Nehemiah, as a companion piece but also as a corrective on certain points such as this one?

Ezra-Nehemiah mentions David and Moses ten times apiece. David represents the monarchic temple tradition which is so dear to Ezra-Nehemiah. But Moses—born abroad, raised in a foreign court, and bringing his people "home" to an already-occupied territory—provides a natural reference point for returnee leaders like Ezra and Nehemiah, who are born abroad, raised in a foreign court, and bring their people "home" to an already-occupied territory. (Notice that another relatively exclusivist book of the Bible, Deuteronomy, also claims Moses as a central figure.)

Chronicles drastically shifts the Moses/David balance, mentioning Moses twenty-one times and David over two hundred times. One could protest that this is because its narrative tells about David; but why, in a narrative running from Adam to Cyrus, tell so little about Moses and so much about David? Why skip over the capture of land from its occupants to begin with a people at home in their land? Possibly because David represents not only the temple tradition—dear to the Chronicler as to Ezra-Nehemiah—but also unity of the territory's people. It is interesting that the book of Ruth, another pro-inclusion work which may date from about the same period, concerns an ancestress of David.

It would be a mistake to understand Chronicles as homeland Judah's manifesto against the returnees. Its David is no revolutionary. Chronicles is by and large an "establishment" document. Its suggested incorporation of local "foreigners" into the congregation of "all Israel" will bring their donations into that congregation's storerooms. But neither does Chronicles accept Ezra-Nehemiah's program as a full embodiment of God's will for the congregation. For Ezra-Nehemiah, the joy of the present congregation falls short of ideal because political independence is still lacking. For Chronicles it falls short if "all Israel" fails to find inclusion.

I do not think that Chronicles leaves us with "messianic" expectations—that is, hope for a dramatic future fulfillment of God's promises, especially with regard to David's eternal kingship. Nor does it regard those promises as bankrupt. Rather, it displays what theologians call a realized eschatology in which "that day"—God's promised era of blessedness—has already come into effect, though perhaps not full flower.[15] The Chronicler depicts David and Solomon's time as a benchmark for what life should be like, then argues a fundamental continuity between that time and the Levitically led worship of the Second Temple. Fear, tightfistedness, and schism in the community mar but do not destroy the Davidic legacy.

We return to our opening metaphor, imagining ourselves as members of the Second Temple congregation, gazing at the luminescent colors of David in the Chronicles window, our eyes moving occasionally to the companion window which shows Ezra and Nehemiah preaching to their congregations in this very building.[16] The Chronicles window shows scenes from a history well beyond living memory, but the window's designer has chosen not to emphasize its distantness. Instead, the window dresses its ancient characters in the clothing of a contemporary (for the reader) Persian province.

As Ezra and Nehemiah dominate their window, David and Solomon—especially David—dominate the Chronicles panel. Around David "all Israel" gathers, willingly bringing gifts for joyous worship guided by the Levites David has appointed. The similarity of this worship to our Yehudite congregation's own observances reassures us of an essential continuity with our Davidic roots. God's warmly rewarding acceptance of David's overtures assures us that we too shall be established, so long as we continue to seek God. But Ezra's and Nehemiah's "Israel" looks narrow alongside Chronicles' broad congregation, which finds place even for foreigners in the temple's support and prayers.

Chronicles' David (alien though he calls himself!) has made all necessary preparations for God's, and Israel's, "house of rest." The legacy now passes to "all Israel," not just returnee families, of the Chronicler's own time.

"Keep forever such purposes and thoughts in the hearts of your people," David prays to God on our behalf, "and direct their hearts toward you" (1 C 29:18). It remains for us as Yehudite readers to "be strong and of good courage" in seizing the opportunity.

PART 4

THE POWER OF PRAYER
David in the Book of Psalms

CHAPTER 12

THE PSALTER: AN OVERVIEW

We turn now to our giant Picasso mural, the book of Psalms. David appears here in three ways: as someone spoken about *by* certain psalms, as the supposed speaker *of* certain psalms, and more loosely as the voice—imaginatively—of the entire Psalter (book of Psalms). We will devote a chapter to each of these modes of presence (Chapters 13–15). First, however, it behooves us to take a general look at the characteristics of the Psalter, for it is a quite different kind of literature than the narratives in Samuel and Chronicles.

PSALM STYLE

In several ways the Psalter resembles a modern hymnal. It contains poems of various ages and types. Most or all were probably sung (musical instructions accompany many selections). However, we lack precise information on authors and composers, and we find some sentiments that today's hymnal committees would frown upon (for instance, Ps 109:10, "may his children wander about and beg").

At first glance psalmic form is very different from that of English hymn lyrics:

Psalms	*Hymn Lyrics*
Very irregular stanzas	Regular stanzas
Meter based on accented syllables only (usually lost in translation)	Meter includes both accented and unaccented syllables
Meter often varies	Meter strictly observed
Rhymes few and irregular, much alliteration	Strong, regular rhyme pattern

More than English poems, psalms also tend to repeat both ideas (a technique sometimes described as "thought-rhyme") and actual words. In other respects they are much like our poetry. They use dense, elliptical language, packing much into few words and omitting some. Figures of speech flourish.

Table 1: Psalter Overview

Book 1			Book 2			Book 3		
1	none	Torah	42-43	Korah	lament	73	Asaph	wisdom
2	none	royal	44	Korah	LAMENT	74	Asaph	Lament
3	David*	lament	45	Korah	royal	75	Asaph	liturgy
4	David	lament	46	Korah	Zion	76	Asaph	praise
5	David	lament	47	Korah	throne	77	Asaph	LAMENT
6	David	lament	48	Korah	Zion	78	Asaph	praise+
7	David*	lament	49	Korah	wisdom	79	Asaph	LAMENT
8	David	praise	50	Asaph	liturgy	80	Asaph	LAMENT
9-10	David	lament	51	David*	lament	81	Asaph	liturgy
11	David	trust	52	David*	wisdom	82	Asaph	liturgy
12	David	LAMENT	53	David	wisdom	83	Asaph	LAMENT
13	David	lament	54	David*	lament	84	Korah	Zion
14	David	wisdom	55	David	lament	85	Korah	LAMENT
15	David	liturgy	56	David*	lament	86	David	lament
16	David	trust	57	David*	lament	87	Korah	Zion
17	David	lament	58	David	LAMENT	88	Korah	lament
18	David*	royal+	59	David*	lament	89	other	royal+
19	David	Torah	60	David*	LAMENT			
20	David	royal	61	David	royal			
21	David	royal	62	David	trust			
22	David	lament	63	David*	trust	**Book 4**		
23	David	trust	64	David	lament			
24	David	liturgy	65	David	THANKS	90	Moses	LAMENT
25	David	lament	66	other	thanks	91	none	liturgy
26	David	lament	67	other	THANKS	92	other	thanks
27	David	trust	68	David	praise	93	none	throne
28	David	lament	69	David	lament	94	none	LAMENT
29	David	praise	70	David	lament	95	none	liturgy
30	David	thanks	71	none	lament	96	none	throne
31	David	lament	72	Solomon	royal	97	none	throne
32	David	thanks				98	other	throne
33	none	praise	"The prayers of David			99	none	throne
34	David*	thanks	son of Jesse are ended"			100	other	praise
35	David	lament	(Ps 72:20).			101	David	royal
36	David	wisdom				102	other	lament
37	David	wisdom				103	David	praise
38	David	lament				104	praise!	praise
39	David	lament				105	praise!	praise
40	David	lament				106	praise!	LAMENT
41	David	lament						

Book 5			124	David, ascents	THANKS	141	David	lament
						142	David*	lament
107	thank!	THANKS	125	ascents	wisdom	143	David	lament
108	David	LAMENT	126	ascents	LAMENT	144	David	royal+
109	David	lament	127	Solomon, ascents	wisdom	145	David	praise
110	David	royal				146	praise!	praise
111	praise!	praise	128	ascents	wisdom	147	praise!	praise
112	praise!	wisdom	129	ascents	LAMENT	148	praise!	praise
113	praise!	praise	130	ascents	lament	149	praise!	praise
114	none	praise	131	David, ascents	trust	150	praise!	praise
115	praise!	liturgy						
116	praise!	thanks	132	ascents	royal+	*in the second column in-		
117	praise!	praise	133	ascents	wisdom	dicates that the title gives		
118	thank!	liturgy	134	ascents	praise	a Davidic life setting for		
119	none	Torah	135	praise!	praise	the psalm		
120	ascents	lament	136	thank!	THANKS			
121	ascents	liturgy	137	none	LAMENT	+in the third column in-		
122	David, ascents	Zion+	138	David	thanks	dicates that the text of the		
			139	David	lament	psalm mentions David		
123	ascents	LAMENT	140	David	lament			

One finds unusual vocabulary, oft archaic. Such language (in Hebrew or English) may indicate a very old poem or simply an accepted style for religious poetry. Words frequently appear in unusual order (twisted often the syntax), forcing us to think twice about their meaning. The complex syntax and vocabulary make translation difficult, which is why standard English translations tend to differ more from one another in Psalms than in narrative books.

Table 1 presents a sweeping overview of the Psalter, giving selected information about each psalm's heading (middle column) and type (right column). I treat 9–10 (in which each stanza begins with a successive letter of the Hebrew alphabet) and 42–43 (united by a common refrain) as single psalms. Table 1 also shows the Psalter's division into five "books" (separated by blessings with "Amen" in 41:13, 72:18–20, 89:52, 106:48).

HEADINGS

Psalm headings contain several types of information; Table 1 shows only those notations which will figure in our eventual discussions. Most prominent, and most important for us, are the David headings. In the standard Hebrew text, seventy-three psalms contain the notation *lĕdāvid*[1] ("to/for/by/of/about David," abbreviated "David" in the table). However, ancient Aramaic and some Greek manuscripts lack a David heading on Ps 133. Because these translations tend to add David headings, a missing heading probably means that David's name was not attached to the psalm on the Hebrew text they were translating. Thus, with the NRSV translator I omit the David heading on this psalm, leaving seventy-two *lĕdāvid* psalms. Thirteen of these headings, asterisked on the table, not only carry David's name but mention situations in his life. David psalms occur especially in Books 1 and 2, which end with a notation that "the prayers of David, son of Jesse are ended" (72:20). However, David psalms also appear in Books 3–5.

Books 2 and 3 also contain collections ascribed to the Korahites (abbreviated "Korah," eleven psalms) and Asaph (twelve psalms)—names of families or guilds of temple singers. In Book 5, fifteen psalms bear the heading "A Song of Ascents"—perhaps a collection of pilgrimage songs. Two psalms are attributed to Solomon and one to Moses. The middle column of Table 1 also notes psalms which begin or end "Praise the LORD!" (*halĕlû yāh*, marked "praise!") or begin "O give thanks to the LORD, for he is good" (marked "thank!"). These phrases are not, strictly speaking, headings, but research on the final form of the Psalter suggests that they do have a structural role. We will say more about this in Chapter 15.

"Other" in the second column of Table 1 indicates that the psalm does have a heading, but its information is not important to our study of David. An example would be the title line of Ps 67: "To the leader: with stringed instruments. A Psalm. A Song."

TYPES OF PSALMS

The right-hand column in Table 1 gives a type designation for each psalm. (A dagger next to this designation indicates that the psalm's text names David.) Identifying type is an important step in psalm study because our understanding of type influences interpretation. With what emotion, for instance, are the lines "LORD, you have searched me and known me" (139:1) colored? If we take this as a psalm of trust, the words express delight in intimate relationship with God. If we read it as a confession, they express dismay over the same relationship. But if the psalm protests innocence in the face of false accusations, the words present an urgent appeal: not "I know that you love me" or "you know what a sinner I am" but "you know that I am innocent."[2]

As important as type identification is, Psalms experts agree on neither the number and definition of types nor the classification of many individual

134

psalms.[3] In Table 1 my goal is simply to show what "meets the eye" in the book of Psalms, so I work with a simplified list of types, confine each psalm to a single designation, and go with the "most obvious reading." For instance, psalms using "I" are treated as individual psalms, although we will later see that a community may be speaking through some of them. I use the "royal" designation only for the most obviously kingly psalms. We will see in subsequent chapters how complex and flexible individual psalms, and the Psalter, actually are.

The most common psalm type (over a quarter of the total) is the *lament*, an individual's complaint to or appeal for help from God. The designation *LAMENT* (in capitals) marks a similar appeal regarding national troubles. Closely associated with laments are the psalms of *thanks*, in which an individual acknowledges help received from God. Because most laments end with thanks for anticipated deliverance and most thank psalms begin with a recollection of previous trouble, it can be difficult to tell the difference between the two. Capital letters distinguish community psalms of *THANKS*. Also related to the lament are psalms of *trust*, which express confidence in God's help.

Wisdom psalms have a more philosophical tone, reflecting on the general course of human affairs. Characteristic terms (such as "happy are . . .") and motifs (for instance, the contrasting fates of "foolish" and "wise" persons) help identify wisdom psalms. My wisdom category includes some psalms which—like the book of Job—fervently question God's justice. I classify these as wisdom psalms rather than individual laments because they seem to reflect on the character of life rather than to plead for assistance. A special wisdom subset, the *Torah* psalms, celebrate God's teaching.

In some *royal* psalms the king speaks. We also hear other people speak to or about the king. A third of the royal psalms mention David by name.

Zion psalms celebrate the beauty of Jerusalem and its temple and God's protection of them. ("Zion" is a name used for Jerusalem in contexts which emphasize its special religious status.) I include 46 and 122 in this category even though they do not contain the word "Zion," whereas some other psalms which do contain the word bear some other overall designation (for instance, I have called 76 a psalm of praise).

Liturgy designates psalms which (a) do not easily fit in some other category and (b) seemed designed for particular moments in temple service; for instance, Ps 24 was probably used in connection with ark parades and Ps 100 at the opening of worship. I do not mean to suggest that other psalms are non-liturgical. Most liturgy psalms, again 24 is a good example, seem written for several voices. Ones which include first person speeches from God (50, 75, 76, 81, 82, 91, and 95) are sometimes referred to as "prophetic liturgies," on the assumption that a "cult prophet"[4] would deliver the oracular portion on God's behalf.

Finally, a great many psalms especially toward the end of the Psalter enunciate *praise*.[5] They may describe nature—citing its beauty as proof of God's goodness and power or calling upon it to join in the praise—or rehearse Israel's history, especially the events of exodus and wilderness wandering. (Here the line between praise and community thanksgiving blurs.) A special subgroup, the *enthronement psalms* (abbreviated "throne" in Table 1) celebrate God as king of the universe. Be sure not to confuse these with the royal psalms which concern human kingship.

READER POSITION

The imaginative historical horizon of Psalms is both wider and more vague than those suggested by the primary history and Chronicles/Ezra-Nehemiah. At points we think we spot historical connections, but they are allusive rather than solidly determined. Almost any psalm can be applied to a variety of contexts and read with a variety of meanings. This makes sense when we think about it, for such flexibility enhances each psalm's potential usefulness. We can see a similar dynamic in our own hymnals: songs with precise, unambiguous references and theology seldom survive hymnal revision, whereas vague but highly evocative hymns reappear in edition after edition.[6]

The Psalter as a whole knows of Jerusalem's fall, Babylonian exile (see especially Ps 137), and a currently standing temple (for example, Ps 122). Although the Psalter probably crystallized late—in Hellenistic or Roman times[7] —no unambiguous internal reference to leaders such as Alexander demonstrates this dating. In Chapter 15 I will suggest two frameworks for reading the book: as the history of Israel[8] into the Second Temple period and as an exploration of individual relationship to God. Before attempting to interpret the entire Psalter, however, let us see how David appears in more specific focus.

CHAPTER 13

PSALMS SPEAKING ABOUT DAVID

We now turn our attention to the ways in which psalm texts (as opposed to headings) speak about David. A simple perusal of the psalms which mention him (18, 78, 89, 122, 132, 144) shows that David is always mentioned as king—the anointed (18:50), shepherd of the people (78:70–71), recipient of dynastic promises (132:11), and one to whom God gives rescue and victory (144:10). This suggests that to understand the psalmic David, we must also understand how the psalms speak of monarchy. For this we will look to the royal psalms.

Two psalms, 89 and 132, stand out because they mention David four times apiece (no other psalm mentions David more than once in its text body). We will begin with these two particularly David-centered psalms, letting them set the categories for our further exploration. We will then shuffle together the remaining psalms of our overlapping groups (psalms mentioning David and royal psalms) and look at them in numerical order. This will help set the stage for discussion in Chapter 15 of the Psalter's overall layout.

PSALM 89

The opening verses of Psalm 89 introduce three keywords, each of which will appear seven times in the psalm: "steadfast love" (Ḥesed; remember that ḥ denotes a hard "ch" as in "loch"), "faithfulness," and "forever."[1] ḥesed—typically translated as "steadfast love," "loyal love," "lovingkindness," or "mercy"—names the reliability and goodwill which make God's promises trustworthy for tomorrow as well as today.[2] (My own favorite translation for it is "trustworthiness"; "faithfulness" would also be good, were we not already using it for the companion term.) Psalmists frequently cite ḥesed as the reason why God ought to help them. Ḥesed and faithfulness thus go quite naturally with "forever" and "to all generations."

Verses 3–4 (following English verse numbering, which in Psalms often varies from Hebrew numbering by a verse or two) focus the issue more sharply; the psalmist celebrates the ḥesed expressed in God's promise to David. We see verbs—bnh ("established" in 2 and "build" in 4) and kôn ("is firm" in 2 and "establish" in 4)—familiar from the promise narratives of 2 S 7 and 1 C 17, 22, and 28. However, Ps 89 uses them only in connection with dynasty, not mentioning the temple.

Verse 3 calls the promise a "covenant." This would be a covenant of grant—in which an overlord assumes an obligation toward or bestows a gift upon a vassal ("my servant")—rather than a suzerainty covenant, which details what a vassal should do in return for past favors.[3] Both covenants involve mutual obligations, but the suzerainty model used at Sinai stresses the vassal's responsibilities, whereas the Davidic covenant emphasizes God's pledges.

In keeping with the metaphor of God as suzerain (overlord), the psalm now tells of God's cosmic kingship (89:5–14). God dominates the divine council (5, 7) by virtue of victory over chaotic forces embodied in the sea, the primeval dragon (9–10).[4] In other ancient Near Eastern texts, such battle precedes creation of the world and the victor's palace (or temple) building and enthronement.[5] Here too we move on to announcements of creation (11–12) and enthronement (14). God's throne is founded on righteousness and justice. *Hesed* and Faithfulness (not the same Hebrew word for faithfulness as in 89:1–2, but a related one) serve as courtiers to the divine king.

Verses 15–18 provide a bridge from this cosmic scene to a particular people's concerns. "The people who know the festal shout" join the heavens (5), their inhabitants (5), and the world (12) in praising God. Their ongoing praise ("all day long," 16) corresponds on its limited mortal scale to the unlimited faithfulness ("forever") of God. In 17–18 the word "our" identifies the speaker (or speakers) as part of this people, whom God has provided with "strength," a "horn," and a "shield"—that is, a "king"!

Now the poet expands upon God's promises regarding David (19–28) and his dynasty (29–37). Verse 19 refers to "a vision"—vocabulary tied to 1 C 17:15 more than 2 S 7:17—in which God addresses a "faithful one" (*ḥāsîd*). This creates a nice correspondence between God's *ḥesed* and its *ḥāsîd* recipient David.[6]

The Hebrew text of verse 19 reads, "I have set help ('*ēzer*) upon / over a mighty one, I have raised up a chosen one (*bāḥûr*) from the people" (my translation). This is an odd way to use the word "help." NRSV's translator follows a common opinion that the word should really be "crown" (*nēzer*), which looks very similar in Hebrew script. If so, we have a picture like that of Chronicles, which stresses David's strength and the support he receives from every quarter.

But '*zr*—writing the word now as it originally appeared, with consonants only—could be an old-fashioned word for "lad, hero."[7] This yields a nice parallel to *bāḥûr*, which comes from the verb "choose" but usually designates a handsome young fellow in contrast to an older man.[8] If we solve the problem this way (which I prefer), David is not the "mighty" of 89:19, but the "lad" whom God sets *over* the mighty—an "underdog" picture of David very much in line with Samuel's stories of his anointing and victory over Goliath (1 S 16–17).

The psalm develops its theme of divine support for David in a chiastic (V-shaped) pattern:

A God exalts, raises up king (19)
  B David God's servant, anointed (20)
    C God's hand and arm with David (21)
      D David's enemies struck down (22–23)
      D' Faithfulness and *Ḥesed* attend, David exalted (24)
    C' David's hand, right hand on sea/river (25)
  B' David calls God "father and "rock" (26)
A' David will be firstborn, highest of kings (27–28)

The outermost bracketing elements (A and A') tell of God's actions for David, elevating the lad (*'zr, bāḥûr*, 19) to "firstborn" (27). B and B' detail David's relationship to God (servant, anointed) and God's to David (father, rock). Both "servant" and "father" are covenant terms.[9] Note that 2 S 7:14 and 1 C 17:13 say God will be as father to David's *son*, but Ps 89 applies the son relationship to David himself. The "C" elements tell what God's hand does for David and where God sets David's hand. The innermost pair (D and D') contrasts the fate of David's enemies (struck down) with David's own fate (exalted).

This section on David's kingship (19–28) echoes the section on God's kingship (5–18) in striking ways. God who rules the sea (9–10) sets David's hand on sea and rivers (25). God's arm and hand, praised in 13, support David (21) and his hands (25). God's own servants, *Ḥesed* and Faithfulness, also attend David (14, 24).[10] God's throne (14) parallels David's (36). As God's enemies are scattered (10), so David's will be struck down (22–23). God is great and awesome in the heavenly council (5–7); David will be "highest of " earth's kings (27). The NRSV translation obscures the scope of this claim: the Hebrew text asserts that David will be *'elyôn*—"Most High" (a title usually used for God)—over the earth's kings.

God's *ḥesed* for David will last "forever" (28). Verses 29–37 spell out how: God will establish David's line (or more literally, "seed").

Both the primary history and Chronicles expressed uncertainty about the parameters of this promise, introducing it as unconditional, then switching to more conditional language: "*If* your heirs take heed to their way . . ." (1 K 2:4,

139

emphasis added). Ps 89 indulges in no such waffling. Even in the worst-case scenario ("if his children forsake my law," 30), God promises,

> . . . I will punish their transgression with the rod
>   and their iniquity with scourges;
> *but I will not remove from him my steadfast love [ḥesed].*
>   (89:32–33, emphasis added)

God drives at the same point for several more lines: "[will not] be false," "will not violate my covenant, / or alter the word," "once and for all I have sworn," "I will not lie" (89:33–35). If the promise is not kept, God—by God's own witness—will be false, a covenant violator, an oathbreaker, and a liar.

Between verses 37 and 38 lies a rift so deep that some commentators have seen two separate psalms here. Verses 38–51 still focus on David's dynasty but with a dismaying change of tone. The opening verses (38–40) give a sevenfold description of God's actions: "spurned," "rejected," "wrath," "renounced," "defiled," broken," "laid . . . in ruins." Divine rejection allows similar "plunder" and "scorn" by human foes (41). God exalts the enemy's right hand instead of the king's, takes the king's scepter away, hurls his throne to the ground, cuts his days short, and covers him with shame (42–45).

When did this happen? The psalm gives no dates or names. A few scholars suppose a ritual in which the king was ceremonially deposed and humiliated.[11] The majority envision an actual military defeat. The biblical record hints that defeats did occur in Judah's history (see for instance 1 K 14:25–26), but most are downplayed. In the final telling, one defeat overwhelms all the others—Jerusalem's fall to Babylon. In canonical context, Ps 89 surely points to the events of 586.

The psalm's closing stanzas open with insistent questions: "How long, O LORD?" (46). "Where is your ḥesed?" (49). The speaker stands not under god's hand (yād) but under the hand (yād, NRSV "power") of Sheol (48).[12] God is hidden (46). Ḥesed and Faithfulness (entirely missing from the disaster report in 38–45) appear only as qualities "of old" (49). God's promise is drowned by the insults and taunts of God's enemies (51).

Here the psalm stops. In fact, here stops Book 3 of the Psalter, separated from Book 4 by the brief blessing of 89:52. The next move will have to be God's.

This ending troubles readers who believe every prayer must end in thanks and hope.[13] It reflects a psalmic spirituality which prizes honesty above orthodoxy. Two points may help modern readers come to grips with Ps 89's close. First, the psalm is situational. It does not say God's *ḥesed* has been forever disproven, but simply explains how things look at its own moment. Second, it assumes a God who answers back. The attaching of answers to prayers often arises from an unconscious assumption that God will not answer; the person praying assumes that his or her own words will be the end of the conversation. Psalm 89, by contrast, presents a human perception and holds God responsible for disproving it; indeed the psalm seems designed to provoke such a response.

If we imagine the psalm's speaker as a Davidic king (supported by the apparent self-description "your servant" in 89:50), we can understand 1–37 as a king's praise and thanks to his paton God. That praise affirms God's power to keep promises (89:5–18) and gently reminds God to do so. Verses 38–51 less gently assert that God has been remiss and invite God to correct this reversal. In this reading, the verses about human mortality (47–48) intimate that God must help the anointed *soon* while he still lives.

What if we assume a nonroyal speaker for Ps 89? What now do the pleas "remember how short *my* time is" and "... how *I* bear in my bosom the insults" (89:47, 50, emphasis added) have to do with dynastic promises?

One possibility is to suppose that God's *ḥesed* to the speaker is embodied in the monarch. The king is his people's "strength," "horn," and "shield" (89:17–18). God has failed the psalmist by failing to uphold the king who represents justice, security, national pride, and religious confidence.

Another possibility is that God's faithfulness to Davidic kings is a test case for God's general faithfulness. Now the argument runs: "LORD, you are faithful—to me and to David (89:1–37). But you reneged on your promise to David (38–45)! Will wrath be your final word to me, and to all Sheol-bound mortals as well (46–48)? Find for me *ḥesed* like that which you promised David (49)! Make good the Davidic promise, so I can have confidence in your promise to me (50–51)!"

We find yet a third possibility in Isa 55:3: "I [God] will make with you [plural] a covenant forever, my sure *ḥesed* for David" (my translation).[14] This oracle to God's "servants" (54:17) announces that as David witnessed and led (55:4) so the servants will "call" and lead nations (55:5). It uses our keywords "forever" (translated "everlasting" in NRSV) and *ḥesed* as well as a variant ("sure") of Ps 89's keyword "faithfulness." It transfers God's promise of *ḥesed* from the Davidic dynasty to the people at large, or at least to those who consider themselves God's servants (89:50). If we read Ps 89 with the idea that God's promise to David has become a promise to the "servants" in general, then asking God to remember that promise is the same as invoking God's *ḥesed* for oneself, without seeing monarchy as the intermediary of that *ḥesed* or presuming that the speaker is a Davidic king.

I do not mean to argue that the original writer of Ps 89 was acquainted with Isa 55:3 (or the ideas therein); historically, the reverse would be more likely or the connection may involve ideas rather than exact texts. But for the psalm as part of the completed Psalter, the theology of Isa 55:3 is an available mode of interpretation.

Let us summarize the possibilities we have just discussed:

1. Davidic king requests that God be faithful to him by honoring the dynastic promise. (Problem: God has failed to support the king.)

2. A nonroyal Israelite requests that God be faithful to him or her by restoring the Davidic king ("our shield"). (Problem: God has failed other Israelites by not supporting the king.)

3. A nonroyal Israelite requests that God be faithful to him or her as God ought to be faithful to David. (Problem: God's unfaithfulness to David raises questions about God's faithfulness to the speaker.)

4. A nonroyal Israelite requests that God be faithful to him or her by fulfilling the promise which has been transferred from David to the speaker. (Problem: The promise transferred from David still awaits fulfillment.)

Even in the third and fourth options, the speaker's personal problem appears tied up with community welfare ("our" in 89:17–18, "insults of the peoples" in 89:50) rather than being a strictly private matter. The psalmist seems to speak on behalf of the community; if we imagined the psalmist to be the community personified, it would not materially change the meaning of the psalm.

What now does the psalm tell us about David?

1. Psalm 89 remembers David as God's "servant." It speaks of him as vassal in a covenant of grant (also suggested by 89:29's "father" language).

2. It regards the dynastic promise as unconditional. God may punish David's successors (89:32) but nonetheless pledges to maintain the throne forever (36–37). The psalm interprets this promise in concrete military and political terms.

The fact that Ps 89 can be read as the prayer of either a king or a nonroyal Israelite casts further light on David's significance, although nuances vary with our exact interpretation of the situation. Two general models emerge.

3. The psalm anchors the people's safety and well-being directly in God's faithfulness to David, either through the king's function as military defender or through transference of the promise from the royal line to the people at large (as per Isa 55:3).

4. Or the psalm offers God's relationship to David as a model for God's relationship to others.

Finally, we note:

5. The psalm allows David's significance to be read either in terms of national well-being or in terms of an individual's concerns.

With these observations in hand, we turn our attention to the other psalm which mentions David four times.

PSALM 132

Psalm 132 is the only psalm containing the word "ark" (although perhaps not the only one alluding to that object[15]). We naturally connect it with the stories of David's ark parade. "Ephrathah" designates David's home clan or its territory (1 S 17:12), whereas "fields of Jaar" would be Kiriath-Jearim (1 S 6:21–7:2; 1 C 13:6). However, David's oath in 132:3–5 is far stronger than anything reported in the Samuel or Chronicles ark stories (2 S 6; 1 C 13, 15–16). It seems to contradict Samuel's timetable, which had David established in his house prior to fetching the ark (2 S 5:11–16).[16]

Psalm 132 employs a rich vocabulary of dynastic promise: "your servant," "anointed one," "sure," "throne," "forevermore," "horn," "lamp," and "crown." But a thoughtful reading of 132:10 shows the "anointed one" is not David but a later ruler, for a request for someone's sake (in this case "your servant David's sake") is typically made in behalf of someone other than the one for whose sake it is to be granted. A collection of temple-associated terms reinforces the notion of a post-Davidic setting: "place,"[17] "dwelling place," "footstool," "resting place" (*mĕnûḥâ*),[18] "priests," "shout for joy," "habitation," and "Zion."[19]

The psalm contains two parallel sections:

	Distinctive words	Part 1	Part 2
swore	2		11
I will not (*'im*)[20]/if (*'im*)	3, 3, 4		12
place names	6, 6		13
rest (*mĕnûḥâ*)	8		14
priests	9		16
faithful	9		16
shout for joy	9		16, 16
clothe	9		16, 18
anointed one	10		17

Each part mentions David's name at the beginning (132:1, 11) and near the end (10, 17). His name and the words "not turn" (132:10, 11) link the end of Part 1 to the beginning of Part 2.

143

The parts stand in request/response relationship:

Part 1	Part 2
LORD, remember what David swore (1–5)	LORD swore to David (11–12)
I [David] will find a place for LORD (3–5)	I [LORD] will set throne for David (11–12)
Go from Jaar to "resting place" (6–8)	I will rest in and bless Zion (13–15)
Let celebrants rejoice (9)	I will make celebrants rejoice (16)
Don't turn away anointed one (10)	I will look after anointed one (17–18)

Part 2 consists mostly of a first person proclamation by God, probably delivered by a priest or prophet.[21] But who speaks Part 1? The speaker could be a Davidic king (but not David himself, in light of 132:10). 2 Chronicles 6:41–42 shows that an ancient writer thought such prayers appropriate for a Davidic heir.

Whereas Ps 89 grounded its covenantal appeal in what God had done for David, 132 appeals (at least in Part 1) to what David has done for God. The word which NRSV translates "hardships" (132:1) is uncertain: the Hebrew word denotes suffering, whereas ancient Greek and Syriac translations presuppose a similar-looking word meaning "humility."[22] (In this connection it is interesting that this psalm should be preceded by 131, which emphasizes humility and carries a David heading.[23]) Following the general rule that context should guide explanation,[24] we may conclude that whichever word was used, it intended to remind God of David's effort in relocating the ark.

Verses 1–5 recollect David's virtuous commitment to establishing a "place" for God. Verse 6 recalls the excitement of locating the ark. Verse 7's "place" could be Jaar, but more likely introduces the movement to Zion. Verses 7–9 speak simultaneously from David's day and the psalm's own time. Only in verse 10 do we fully enter the post-Davidic moment. Its negative petition ("*do not turn away* the face of your anointed one," emphasis added) may hint that God has seemed to be doing just that, but we get no firm picture.

In Part 2 God responds. Again the opening lines (11–12) flash back to David's time, whereas the middle section (13–16) simultaneously speaks in David's time and the present moment. The last two verses shift attention to the future. "Sprout up" (17) suggests reinstatement after discontinuity, subtly reinforcing verse 10's hint that things have not been going well.

Returning to the question "who speaks?" let's reread Ps 132 as a community's prayer rather than a king's prayer. This suits the psalm's pronouns, which always refer to the post-Davidic king in third person.[25] A community interpretation highlights 6–7's first person plurals and the petitions in 132:9.

Verse 15's promises of provision and bread (which lack a well-defined parallel in Part 1) also suit an oracle to the community. We now interpret the prayer for God's anointed (10) as part of the community's plea for its own well-being. (The psalm assumes interdependence between the community's well-being and the anointed's; the question is, "for whose sake is it requested?")

If the petition and responding oracle primarily concern the community's well-being, the psalm may make sense even when there is no Davidic monarch on the throne—for instance, in a Second Temple setting. Such a setting suits the psalm's location in the "Ascents" collection and explains the ark's disappearance in Part 2, where it is replaced by Zion (a correspondence more striking in Hebrew, where both take feminine pronouns).[26]

A postmonarchic interpretation resonates particularly with the closing promise of a horn to "sprout up" (ṣmḥ) for David. This verb and the related noun ṣemaḥ ("branch") appear repeatedly in prophetic texts such as Jer 23:5, "I will raise up for David a righteous Branch (ṣemaḥ), and he shall reign as king"; 33:15, "I will cause a righteous branch (ṣemaḥ) to spring up (ṣmḥ) for David"; and Ezek 29:21, "I will cause a horn to sprout up (ṣmḥ) for the house of Israel."[27] These statements anticipate a restoration of the Davidic dynasty at some date after Jerusalem's destruction. Our psalm may likewise be read as a promise of such a restoration.

Zechariah offers a different possibility. In Zech 3:8 God promises to "bring my servant [who is] the Branch (ṣmḥ)"; in Zech 6:12–13 God announces, "Here is a man whose name is Branch (ṣemaḥ): for he shall branch out (ṣmḥ) in his place, and he shall build the temple of the LORD . . . he shall bear royal honor, and shall sit and rule on his throne."

These pronouncements—dated early in the reign of the Persian emperor Darius[28]—may originally have pertained to a leader named Zerubbabel, whom the Hebrew Bible calls a descendant of David and whom God promises to make "like a signet ring" in the closing verse of Haggai. But as Zechariah now stands, the "Branch" who receives a gold and silver crown is the high priest Joshua (Zech 6:11–12). (An earlier reference in Zechariah, 4:14, speaks of *two* "anointed ones," evidently the prince and the priest.)

Thus Zechariah transfers the terminology of Davidic promise ("Branch," "anointed one") to the high priest. Psalm 132—which speaks only of an "anointed one," never of "king" per se[29]—makes sense as a prayer for restoration of the political monarchy, but even better sense if the promise is transferred to priests. Its prayers for priests and "faithful ones" and oracles about support for the temple/Zion now cohere neatly with language about the "anointed." The "enemies" of 132:18 could be political and religious as well as military.[30] Against this interpretation, we have "sons of your [David's]

145

body" in 132:11 and the prevailing application of "anointed" language to Davidic rather than high-priestly "branches."

In today's usage, "messiah" connotes not an ancient king but a ruler coming at the close of this age's history. This psalm allows a "messianic" interpretation in that future sense but does not require one. Its petitions and promises also make good sense in terms of a worldview like Chronicles', where God's promises have already come to partial fulfillment.

To summarize our discussion, Ps 132 contains two parts: petition and promise. Each begins with a flashback to David's time, continues in words which might come from David's time or the psalmist's own, and ends with concern for God's anointed in the present and future. The speaker might be a Davidic king or a representative of the community at large. The first choice requires a monarchic setting, but the second could take place even with no king currently in office. In this case, the "anointed one" could be either king or high priest, and the anticipated salvation (132:16) could be either mundane or dramatically eschatological (pertaining to the end time).

This summary with its many options will undoubtedly frustrate those who want to know what the psalm "really means." However, it faithfully reflects Ps 132's indeterminacy. The psalm may once have addressed a particular historical situation, but it probably earned its place in the Psalter by its flexibility and relevance to a variety of situations and concerns.

What does the psalm tell us about David? Like Chronicles, Ps 132 associates David with worship. Also as in Chronicles, David merits the promise he receives from God. God can be counted upon to keep that promise ("a sure oath from which he will not turn back," but only *if* David's offspring "keep my [God's] covenant and my decrees" (132:11–12).

Whether we read it as the petition of a Davidic monarch or of the community, or juxtapose the two possibilities, the Davidic "branch's" fate and the community's intertwine. In the psalm's thought-world, the community's well-being (or hope thereof) flows from God's favor for David.

PSALM 2

Having oriented ourselves to the Psalter's David by careful study of the two psalms most intensively concerned with him, we turn to the other psalms which mention him and to the royal psalms. (We will eventually see that other psalms may have royal overtones, but for now we will stick with the obvious ones.) Some of these psalms play significant roles in the Psalter's overall structure, so taking them in order will help us begin to build up a sense of that structure.

We begin with Ps 2, which dramatizes a conspiracy of the nations "against the LORD and his anointed" (2:2):

Part 1   2:1–3   Earth: the nations plot (their words quoted in 3)
Part 2   2:4–6   Heaven: God laughs (words quoted in 6)
Part 3   2:7–9   Zion: king responds (quotes God's words in 7b-9)
Part 4   2:10–11   Earth: people (or king?) warn the nations

God scoffs (4) at the plotting before thundering an announcement: a king reigns on Zion. That king—we hear from his own mouth—is authorized to shatter[31] the rebellious nations. If they are wise, the other kings will abandon their plots and acknowledge God's sovereignty ("serve," 11).[32]

The relationship between king and God, posited initially by the opponents ("against the LORD and his anointed," 2), is confirmed by God ("my king on . . . my holy hill," 6). The king's quotation of God introduces "son" language (8). We noted the covenant associations of such terminology in our discussion of Ps 89. "This day I have begotten you" (7) suggests that the relationship has just begun, which is why scholars usually describe Ps 2 as a coronation psalm.

As usual, we get no historical particulars—no date or king's name. It is not at all clear that any attack is actually taking place. Rather, the psalm offers a basic worldview: the world is dangerous, and subjects should obey the king because he, enabled by God, can hold back the conspiring nations.[33] We hear nothing of his responsibility for justice within the kingdom.

Although I suspect that this psalm springs from the courts of real kings, its extravagant language can very easily be interpreted in "messianic" (eschatological) terms. The New Testament cites Ps 2 frequently in such a manner.

PSALM 18

This psalm is multiply tied to David by its Davidic heading, the description of context ("on the day when the LORD delivered him from the hand of all his enemies, and from the hand of Saul"), its royal content, specific mention of David in verse 50, and the presence of an almost identical psalm in 2 S 22. The Hebrew seems archaic, and many interpreters feel it could conceivably come from the tenth century BCE—although in our literary approach, we need to take the psalm's Davidic connections seriously, regardless of its date.

Like other psalms we have studied, Ps 18 uses vague language applicable to a variety of occasions. Adversaries remain unnamed (except in the title).

147

The opening description of trouble uses figurative, poetic terms: "the tor-rents of perdition assailed me" (18:4).

The opening stanza (1–3) uses military ("shield") and wilderness ("rock") metaphors for God. Verses 4–15 introduce motifs of the storm god's battle with Sea (chaos personified) and Death.[34] In canonical context, 16–19's talk of victory over sea ("drew me out of mighty waters") delicately resonates with Exodus 15.

The psalmist explains (20–24) that God's help came as reward for right-eousness, clean hands, blamelessness, and observance of God's ordinances. In Samuel these claims clashed with the preceding narrative, but here we have no narratorial counterclaims. Verses 25–30 make reciprocity into a general theological principle: "with the loyal you show yourself loyal."

One might wonder about the implications of verse 27 ("the haughty eyes you bring down") for this king; perhaps it only applies to the king's enemies, just as "a shield for all who take refuge in him" (30) apparently only applies to those who have received promises. We learn in verse 41 that the king's en-emies can expect no such help. As in Samuel, this raises questions about the relationship between God's fairness and support for David. Later in the Psalter this "David's" naive assumption that God will always support him will turn out to be unfounded.

Verses 43–48 and 49–50 again show a tit-for-tat dynamic: God sets David over nations; David then extols God. The psalm's closing covenant refer-ence—"shows steadfast love [ḥesed] to his anointed . . . forever"—speaks only of promise, not conditions.

The closing verse's reference to a king and anointing combined with pre-ceding statements such as "you made me head of nations" (43) and the fact that the opponents seem to be military are the reasons for calling this a royal psalm. The scenario in which Israel's king rules even foreign peoples (43–45) is familiar to us from Ps 2:8–9 and 89:23, 27. Now we get an extended look at that relationship from the king's point of view. The opening verses use in-tensely personal language: "I love you," says the king. He claims God with a series of possessive epithets: *my* strength, *my* rock, *my* fortress, *my* deliverer, *my* God, *my* shield, *my* stronghold. His expectations about the relationship are clear: he will "call upon" God and be saved.

What meaning has such a psalm after the dynasty's fall? We could apply its colorful language to a cosmic battle at the end of time, for an eschatolog-ical messiah is the only king to whom some of these phrases could apply in a literal sense. Alternatively, as we did with Ps 89, we might transfer God's promises to the community at large.

Most readers, however, claim the psalm as a general prayer about God's deliverance of individuals from "the cords of death" and "torrents of perdition" (4). They appropriate for themselves the king's claim upon God as "my rock" and "my shield." The psalm's general statements about God's reciprocity (25–26) and deliverance for the humble (27) and those who take refuge (30) now assume special importance. Use of the psalm by ordinary individuals is facilitated by the fact that the opponents don't assume a clearly military aspect until more than halfway through the psalm (34–42), at which point the military language itself can be read metaphorically. One of my students used Ps 18 for a presentation on homeless persons in downtown Indianapolis. It jolted me, with my scholarly angle on the psalm as a king's prayer, but no one else perceived any dissonance. This illustrates the extent to which even a clearly royal psalm lends itself to other applications.

PSALMS 20 AND 21

Both of these royal psalms contain voices speaking in several directions. Psalm 20 begins with a first person plural voice ("we"—the congregation or an individual speaking on behalf of the congregation) addressing the king (1–5, "you" is masculine singular). In verse 6 an "I" responds—probably the king, although he refers to himself in the third person as "his [LORD's] anointed." Verses 7–8 could be either the king or the congregation asserting the group's trust in God. In the closing verse the congregation prays to God concerning the king.

Psalm 21's opening section (1–7) could be the king speaking to God about himself. More likely someone else addresses God, vouching for the king's faithfulness and giving thanks for God's support of the king. Verses 8–12 then address the king with assurances of success. In verse 13, perhaps a congregational response, "we" speak to God.

What do we learn about the king's role? Like Pss 2 and 18, Ps 20 focuses on God's support for the king in battle, but now primarily from the congregation's point of view. Divine help flows both from Zion (2) and heaven (6), recalling the spatial tension of 1 C 21, where an angel stood simultaneously "by the threshing floor" and "between earth and heaven."[35] As David did in that story, the psalm's king offers a sacrifice (3). "Now I know" (6) suggests that this sacrifice, like David's, elicits a positive response.

"From his holy heaven" (6) recalls the heavenly warrior imagery of 18:7–19. Such help allows this congregation and their king to scoff at peoples who depend upon mere chariots (the heavy tanks of ancient warfare). Yet this nation does experience "days of trouble" (20:1). God's help cannot be assumed, but must be appealed for in sacrifice and prayer.

Psalm 21 reads very smoothly as a thanksgiving for the victory prayed for in Ps 20. In this case "life" (4) denotes survival in battle, and the "enemies" (8) are foreign attackers. But Ps 21 may also offer more general thanks for a king's security, prosperity, and health—"length of days forever and ever" (4). If so, the enemies might be internal. The psalm doesn't mention Zion, but we do note the familiar correspondence of royal trust with God's supporting ḥesed (7).

In each of these psalms the people find well-being and safety in God's support for their king. The degree to which the king's activities embody God's finds expression in the ambiguity of 21:8–12, where "you" could be either the king (primary reading) or God (resonant overtone).

After the monarchy's fall, these psalms could be read "messianically" or through analogy: "we pray for the kind of help you used to give to and through the king." The Hebrew punctuation of Psalms (inserted in the Middle Ages) takes the latter route, attaching 21:9's "LORD" to the preceding phrase as a vocative—"when you appear, O LORD"—rather than to the following phrase as subject (NRSV's decision). The vocative makes the "you" of 21:8–12 God, rendering the psalm more easily appropriable in a diaspora setting. Alternatively, one could follow the lead of the book of Isaiah (see for instance Isa 45:1) in designating a foreign emperor as "anointed."

PSALM 45

This courtly wedding song praises and exhorts a royal groom and his bride. At beginning and end the psalmist comments upon his or her own task: "I address my verses to the king" (1), "I will cause your [king's] name to be celebrated" (17). The king is God's warrior (2–5), whose court's glory demonstrates God's favor (6–9). The queen, who seems to be a foreign princess, must forget her original family (10–12)—a new variation on the theme of foreign royalty bowing to Israel's king. The scribe describes the wedding procession and looks forward to heirs (14–16).

Psalm 45 spells out the wealth and blessings to which Ps 21 alluded. The king is good-looking and well-spoken, a successful warrior, joyous, wears fragrantly scented robes in an ivory-decorated palace filled with fine music and noble ladies. His queen is likewise beautiful, sumptuously bedecked, and recipient of rich gifts. All this wealth comes from God and foreign nations, of course—the psalm says nothing about taxes. Alongside the descriptions of finery we glimpse familiar themes of victory over the peoples and the king as defender of justice (4, 6–7).

The psalm speaks generally of "God" (*ʾĕlōhîm*) rather than specifically of "Lord" (YHWH), and nothing in it identifies the king as Judean or Israelite,[36] although we assume he is because the psalm appears in the Hebrew Bible. It contains nothing that would exclude its use in Tyrian, Moabite, or Syrian courts.

The most striking of the psalm's three mentions of God comes in the middle of the praise section: "Your throne, O God, endures forever and ever" (6). Addressed to God, this sentence would cause no problems. But Psalm 45 addresses it *to the king*. In the psalmody of any other ancient Near Eastern people, we would take this as evidence that the king was considered divine. Because orthodox understandings of Israelite/Judean faith say this could not be, modern translators often work the word "God" into the line in some other way, such as RSV's "your divine throne endures forever."

Pre-exilic thought, however, was almost certainly less orthodox than the later—sometimes *much* later—offshoots from which our definition of orthodoxy derives. After seeing royal titles such as "*ʿelyôn* of the kings of the earth" (89:27, my translation) and "Mighty God" (Isa 9:6),[37] are we sure that a court poet would not address the king as *ʾĕlōhîm*? We should also remember that the Hebrew Bible's writers seem to have understood religious language less literally than some of their modern readers. They knew kings were mortal. The title "God" probably honors the king as embodiment of God's protection and justice rather than simply equating the king with the heavenly warrior. (The same can probably be said about such usages among Israel's neighbors.) Furthermore, the poem's language expresses an ideal reality ("most handsome of men") rather than its imperfect expression at the everyday level.

Like other royal psalms, Ps 45 outlived the kingdom whose monarch it celebrated. As a "love song" (Ps 45, title), it found application to "ordinary" as well as royal weddings (either reflecting or prompting the idea that on their wedding day any couple are king and queen[38]). In this application, the psalm's king becomes any man (or at least any bridegroom).

Both Jews and Christians also understood the psalm in terms of symbolic marriage between a "messianic" ruler—who would perfectly embody God's power and justice—and his people/congregation. Thus an ancient Aramaic translation, the Targum, specifies the psalm's ruler as "king messiah." Alternatively, the bridegroom might be perceived as God self. This identification—different from the identification of king with community that we have seen in postmonarchic applications of some other royal psalms—completely resolves the outrageousness of verse 6.

PSALM 61

This brief little psalm evinces the same flexibility we have seen in much longer royal psalms. "From the end of the earth" (2) could suggest an exiled speaker—or at least one far from the temple[39]—or a near-death situation ("when my heart is faint").[40] We could think of the psalm as a prayer for help (1), an assertion of trust (5), or even a thanksgiving for help already given (8).

To a first approximation, the speakers are a king (1–5) and someone praying *for* the king (6–7), after which the king briefly responds (8). But we could also imagine an ordinary person speaking throughout, including a prayer for the king because the king embodies God's protection. Once again, as in Ps 89, we see *ḥesed* and Faithfulness appointed to attend the king. If no monarch presently reigns, one may read 6–7 in future tense: "You will prolong the life of the king." Ancient Greek translators adopted this strategy, producing a messianic psalm.

The fact that Ps 61 makes equally good sense as a king's prayer or a private individual's underscores again the appropriability of royal psalms for general spirituality. Inclusion of prayer for the king (present or future) in so personal an appeal reminds us how important the ruler was as an embodiment of God's protection of the people at large—at least from the standpoint of the Psalter's writers and editors.

PSALM 72

Psalm 72 proper consists of verses 1–17. (The doxology in verses 18–19 separates Books 2 and 3 of the Psalter, and verse 20 is an ancient editorial note.) By now we recognize many elements of prayer for the king. An impossibly long royal life span (5–7, 15–17) will stave off internal and external risks of the transition between monarchs. The king enacts justice within his realm (1–4, 12–14) while dominating foreign nations and receiving rich gifts from them (8–11, 15).[41]

Psalm 72 also stresses the motif of fertility for the land. Verses 3 and 7 speak of *šālôm* (peace/health/prosperity); verse 6 likens the king to life-bringing rain.[42] The prosperity theme returns in 15–17. The Hebrew text of 16 is a little unclear but seems to speak of both vegetative and human fertility.

Verses 1–17 by themselves might, like Ps 45, apply to any ancient Near Eastern king. However, the Psalter supplies a more specific imaginative context. The psalm is headed *lišlōmōh*: "to/for/of Solomon." By itself this might be taken to mean that Solomon wrote the psalm, just as *lĕdāvid* is usually taken to indicate Davidic authorship. (Both headings consist of the preposition *lĕ* plus a proper name.) However, Book 2's concluding notice that "the prayers of David son of Jesse are ended" (72:20) implies that Ps 72 is a prayer of David. We might then understand the heading as meaning that this is a prayer by David *for* (*lĕ*) Solomon—the "king's son" of 72:1.[43]

Looking back, we recall that the royal psalm sequence began with a coronation psalm (2). The next two royal psalms contained the king's (18) and people's (20) prayers for the king in battle, followed by a thanksgiving (21). Next we encountered a royal wedding psalm (45), then one praying for the king's long reign (61). Now the royal life cycle comes full circle as the king prays for his heir (72 as a prayer by David for Solomon) or as the heir himself begins speaking (72 as a psalm *of* Solomon). The next royal psalm, 89, reports the apparent fall of the dynasty.

Returning now to 72, we find appended to it the doxology (72:18–19), which divides Books 2 and 3 of the Psalter. The doxology, unlike the psalm proper, calls Israel's God by name. Its assertion that God "alone does wondrous things" relativizes Ps 72's elaborate royal claims. In postmonarchic times it might reassure readers that the benefits which Ps 72 seeks through a now-gone king ultimately come from God (still in office). From there, however, it is only a step to literalization of the psalm's promises as a description of eschatological bliss.

PSALM 78

Psalm 78 presents us with a new kind of content—extended historical review. I have classified it as a praise psalm because it extols God's power and care. But it also criticizes the people's ungrateful response, warning its hearers that unlike their ancestors they must "not forget the works of God, / but keep his commandments" (7).

The history contains elements familiar from other biblical texts—crossing the sea behind a pillar of smoke/fire (12–14 and 53), food and water in the wilderness (15–31), Egypt's afflictions (43–51), settlement in the land (55), and loss of the ark in Eli's time (60–64)[44]—although details differ slightly from those in other accounts. (For instance, 78:12 and 43 are the only texts mentioning "Zoan" in connection with the exodus.) Periodic assessments point up Israel's error: "in spite of all this they still sinned" (32). However, the psalm closes on an upbeat note. God awakes "as from sleep," routs the adversaries, and establishes David as "shepherd of Israel" (65–66, 70–71). Verse 69's statement that *God* built the sanctuary, a replica of the cosmos ("like the high heavens, like the earth"), is the highest temple theology we have yet seen.

To whom do "Jacob" and "Israel" refer in 78:71? Looking at 67–68, we could say they refer to Judah alone, in which case "we" and the faithful "ancestors" of 3–7 would be Judean, whereas "they" with the rebellious ancestors in verse 8 would be northern. We can imagine such polemic emerging from the split of the kingdoms in Rehoboam's time, after Samaria's fall, or in Ezra/Nehemiah's returnee community.

However, Ps 78 mentions no historical event beyond David's—or possibly Solomon's—time.[45] For it, God's determinative choices lie in the era from exodus to the united monarchy—a time when, according to biblical history, the twelve tribes were one flock. Within this horizon, the northern tribes are "rejected" only insofar as the king does not come from them and the ark no longer lodges in their shrine. Now the introduction's "we" and "they" converge as different parts of a single heritage. The psalm disclaims the heritage of rebellion ("they"). It affirms ("our ancestors") a tradition of divine care which was once centered in Shiloh but is now administered by David from Zion. One can imagine this as an exhortation to disaffected northerners in David's own time, but also as an invitation from Jerusalem to the north after the split of the kingdoms, especially after Samaria's fall. It might also summon "all Israel" to David's legacy as represented by the Second Temple.

Although Ps 78 allows the first interpretive option (utter rejection of Ephraim), I find the second (inclusion of Ephraim in David's "Israel") more convincing. It respects the traditionally northern connotations of "Jacob" (71), makes sense of the introduction's overlapping good and bad ancestors, and above all honors David's reign as a symbolic time of national unity. The psalm's final verse is cleverly ambiguous: "he" could be either David (most obvious meaning) or God (harmonic resonance). That such ambiguity could be possible is a measure of the extent to which David's power is identified with God's.

We close with the following observations about David's role in the psalm:

1. Psalm 78 portrays David as worthy of being chosen: he has both an "upright heart," denoting both moral integrity and ritual purity/acceptability, and a "skillful hand" (72).

2. David appears as God's "servant" and "shepherd" (70–71). As a reference to humble beginnings, "shepherd" aligns David with the people. As a royal motif, it aligns him with God, who shepherds earlier in the psalm (52–53).

3. The preceding psalm's closing verse reads, "You led your people like a flock / by the hand of Moses and Aaron." Psalm 78 closes with David as shepherd. Its internal move from exodus/wilderness motifs to temple/monarchy language reinforces the image of David as Moses' successor.

4. Like 132, Ps 78 closely associates David and Zion. (Note especially the parallel applications of "choose" in 68 and 70.)

5. With an inclusive reading of "Israel," Ps 78 presents David as God's chosen ruler (and Zion as God's chosen place) for *all* the tribes. But we cannot exclude a reading in which Judah replaces Ephraim, showing the ease with which a theology of election (God chooses Judah) becomes one of supercession (Judah replaces Ephraim as the true "Israel").

PSALM 101

After Ps 89's lament for God's apparent abandonment of the Davidic monarchs, it comes as something of a surprise to find a royal psalm in Book 4—a royal psalm with a Davidic heading, no less.

Not surprisingly, that royal psalm, Ps 101, deals with kingly issues in a subdued tone. At first glance it does not appear royal at all—no "king," "throne," "crown," or "dominion." Modern readers may see only a psalm about keeping good company (or about self-righteous intolerance).

The speaker of 101, however, is someone with whom others "live" (101:6 NRSV)—or "sit," in which aspect this verb may connote seating in a place of power. Others "minister" (a word used to describe the activity of both priests and government officials, 6) to or on behalf of the psalmist. The speaker asserts power to destroy the wicked and cut off evildoers throughout the land (8). All this leads us to suspect that the psalmist's "house" (2, 7) is not just any house but the palace, seat of government.

The opening verse pairs *ḥesed* (NRSV "loyalty") with justice, thus balancing God's faithfulness toward the king with the king's corresponding responsibilities in government. Refusal to tolerate evildoers (3b-5, 7–8) would then suggest not personal shunning but maintenance of an honest administration. Each of the positive and negative steps outlined in the psalm leads toward a more just government.

The psalm's king of clean "heart" carefully attends to God's "way" (2). This king, who refuses to look upon "anything that is base [any matter of *bĕlîyaʿal*]" (3)—is quite different from the David who led "worthless fellows [men of *bĕlîyaʿal*]" in 1 S 30:22 and whose own eyes strayed in 2 S 11:2.

Questions of just government account so satisfactorily for Ps 101's features that even if we do not understand the psalmist to be a king, we must still posit a person of substantial authority—if we assume a single speaking voice throughout the psalm (the most obvious possibility). One might also distinguish two voices: a human one in the introduction (1–3a) and a divine one from 3b to the end of the psalm. "Minister" in 6 may then carry its usual cultic nuances; the psalm becomes one about God's standards for temple personnel. The psalm's insistence on rooting out corruption (8) remains intact, as does the principle that human administrators (now temple personnel) must reflect divine justice. The coexistence of this interpretation with the first shows the overlap between royal and priestly roles.

PSALM 110

Psalm 110 has incited speculative commentary from Roman times to the present.[46] Jesus' application of the psalm in Mk 12:36 and parallels assumes David himself as the psalm's speaker, an interpretation reinforced by the psalm's Davidic heading; but in itself the text reads more like an address *to* the king.[47] Many commentators divide the psalm into two parts, each beginning with a quoted promise from God (110:1, 4). I prefer an alternative proposal suggested by the Hebrew layout and partly reflected in NRSV's stanza divisions:

	Part 1	Part 2
The right-hand relationship of God and king	1	5a
God gives victory to the king	2–3	5b-6
The king's installation	4	7

This proposal treats 1 and 4 as brackets for Part 1 rather than the openings of separate parts. It reinforces the conclusion, already suggested by activities named in various verses, that "the Lord" and "he" in 5–6 refer to God (subduing the king's enemies), whereas the "he" who drinks in 7 is the king. (Remember to differentiate between "LORD"—the translators' respectful rendition of the divine proper name YHWH—and "Lord," a title which can be applied to either God or a human being.) The drinking may refer to some rite of installation at a spring: Gihon is mentioned repeatedly in connection with Solomon's investiture (1 K 1:33, 38, 45).

Psalm 110's forceful military language reminds us of Ps 2.[48] However, 110 also speaks of the king as "priest forever" in the tradition of Melchizedek—a tradition known to us only from this psalm and Gen 14:18–20, in which Melchizedek is both king of "Salem"[49] and "priest of God Most High." Although this psalm seems to look back toward ancient royal ritual, its royal/priestly language also resonates with the forward-looking messianic image of the priestly Branch (discussed earlier in connection with Ps 132), or at least allows one to understand priests as heirs of the kingly role.

156

PSALM 122

Psalm 122 bears a *lĕdāvid* heading, often understood as an indication of authorship. However, the psalmist speaks of visiting "the house of the LORD" (1), which did not (according to Samuel and Chronicles) exist until after David's death.[50] Some reply that David wrote for the future under prophetic inspiration, but even this hypothesis moves the interpretive context, the literary horizon of the psalm, out of David's own time.

The Ascents collection to which the psalm belongs was probably intended for pilgrimage or festival use. Psalm 122 would be appropriate for either arrival or departure. After the introductory statement about going to Jerusalem (1–2), the psalm describes the city's significance, underscoring it by both alliteration[51] and keywords: "house," "LORD," "Jerusalem," and "peace"—all in triplicate.[52] Such stress on Jerusalem qualifies Ps 122 as a Zion psalm, even though it does not use the word "Zion."

Features which account for Jerusalem's interest include its physical character ("built," "bound firmly"[53]), religious authorization ("as was decreed"), and association with David's dynasty—"for there the thrones for judgment were set up, / the thrones of the house of David" (5). References to God's "house" in the first and last verses bracket a center reference to David's "house," calling attention once again (as in Samuel and Chronicles) to the relation between God's house and David's.

"The thrones of the house of David" stand poetically parallel to "the thrones for judgment [*mišpāṭ*]" (122:5),[54] associating David's house with internal justice. (Remember that *mišpāṭ* means "justice" and "governance" as well as "judgment."[55]) Although the English term "throne" refers almost exclusively to a reigning monarch's chair (or figuratively to the monarch and the monarch's job), the corresponding Hebrew term is used for a variety of seats, often associated, as here, with justice/judgment.[56] Allen translates, "there sits the tribunal of justice, the tribunal of the Davidic court."[57]

We can easily imagine Ps 122 in a monarchic context, but what does it mean in the Second Temple context suggested by the Ascents collection? NRSV's past-tense verb ("the thrones . . . *were set up*," 122:5, emphasis added) makes the reference to David's house a historical one, a report on the city's glorious past. Implicit contrast between that past and the present then motivates prayers for the city's *šālôm*.

But because a "throne" was not necessarily occupied by an independent monarch, one could also suppose with Allen ("there sits the tribunal") that occupied thrones still dispense justice in the psalmist's time.[58] Possibly Davidic descendants held these positions. Possibly justice was, as prescribed by Dt 17:8–13, administered by priests and Levites who would also trace their authority to David.[59] In this reading, Davidic justice becomes part of Jerusalem's šālôm.

PSALM 144

We pass over Ps 132 (with which we have already spent a great deal of time) to arrive at the Psalter's last explicitly royal psalm, 144. It presents the now-familiar image of a warrior king, strengthened, protected, and given dominion by God.[60] The psalmist reminds God of human frailty (3–4, reminiscent of 89:47–48), then appeals for rescue using both the dramatic language of theophany (5–7, reminiscent of 18:7–15) and the more earthly language of "aliens" or foreigners who speak lies and deal falsely (7–8, 11). The speaker's royal identity is suggested not only by the warrior imagery but by his appeal to "the one who gives victory to kings" and explicit mention of David (10).

In verses 12–15 we encounter a collective voice—either the people or the king speaking on their behalf. In language reminiscent of Ps 72 they pray for human, plant, and animal fecundity (12–14a). A closing reference to international security (14b) links this prayer to the king's plea for divine support. The psalm's final verse declares the well-being of a people blessed by God. In it the king drops out of sight—present, if at all, only as part of the people who pray.

SUMMARY

Our survey of the psalms which specifically mention David shows less interest in his personal life than in his role as king, recipient of God's promises and God's protection. Both these psalms and the royal psalms (an overlapping group) portray the king foremost as battle leader and secondarily as bringer of justice and prosperity within the kingdom. Moving through these psalms in sequence, we saw that they present a rough history of kingship, from coronation (Ps 2) through battle, marriage, and installation of an heir (72) to the dynasty's fall (89). Later royal psalms show more emphasis on justice (especially 101) and introduce priestly themes (110, 132).

Although I have approached the royal psalms primarily as prayers which would have been used in connection with real historical kings, we have noted that they can also be interpreted "messianically," with reference to an ideal future king. Such interpretation is emphasized by James Luther Mays in a very readable article on "The David of the Psalms." "When the psalms attributed to David are read in light of what is said in the psalms about him, a messianic construal is cast over the collection. It was inevitable that the psalms would be read in the light of promises of a future Davidic messiah. . . . Prophecy has become a rubric in terms of which all the psalms may be read."[61] In my judgment, this development is more "inevitable" from the standpoint of the New Testament and Christian tradition than it is from the Psalter itself. Mays is certainly right that all the psalms *may* be read in light of messianic expectations. Whether they *must* be so read is quite a different question. Even in postmonarchic settings, these psalms can be appropriated in a variety of ways.

CHAPTER 14

THE PSALMS OF DAVID

We turn now from psalms which speak *about* David or his royal role to those psalms which have traditionally been understood as spoken *by* David—the seventy-two[1] psalms, almost half the Psalter, which bear the heading *lĕdāvid* (NRSV "of David"). A large block of them (3–41, excepting 10—which belongs with 9—and 33) occurs in Book 1 of the Psalter. Book 2 contains a large Davidic block (51–65) and a smaller one (68–70); it closes with a notice that "the prayers of David son of Jesse are ended" (72:20). Nonetheless we find occasional *lĕdāvid* psalms in the final three books: Ps 86 in Book 3; Pss 101 and 103 in Book 4; Pss 108–110, 122, 124, 131, and 138–145 in Book 5. We have already looked at eight of these psalms (18, 20, 21, 61, 101, 110, 122, and 144). In this chapter we will look carefully at two more (51 and 23) and survey characteristics of the rest.

The heading itself—the preposition *lĕ* plus "David"—could mean a variety of things including "dedicated to David" or "in Davidic style" as well as "belonging to David." It has also been proposed that "David" was not originally a proper name but a title, "beloved."[2] However, the *lĕdāvid* headings clearly came to be understood as statements of authorship by the person David.[3] Evidence for this is the fact that thirteen David psalms—and even more in the Greek and Aramaic translations—were given headings tying them to situations in David's life. These headings now reinforce the tradition of reading *lĕdāvid* psalms as David's own prayers.

THE SITUATIONAL HEADINGS

We begin with a simple survey of the situational headings. Situations are quoted verbatim from the headings, with narrative parallels suggested in parentheses:

Psalm	Situation
3	When he [David] fled from his son Absalom (2 S 15–17)
7	Which he sang to the LORD concerning Cush, a Benjaminite (perhaps 2 S 15:5–8)

18 On the day when the LORD delivered him from the hand of all his enemies and from the hand of Saul (2 S 22)

34 When he feigned madness before Abimelech, so that he drove him out, and he went away (probably 1 S 21:13)

51 When the prophet Nathan came to him, after he had gone in to Bathsheba (2 S 12)

52 When Doeg the Edomite came to Saul and said to him, "David has come to the house of Ahimelech" (1 S 22:9–10)

54 When the Ziphites went and told Saul, "David is in hiding among us" (1 S 23:19, 26:1)

56 When the Philistines seized him in Gath (1 S 21:14)

57 When he fled from Saul, in the cave (1 S 22:1, 24:3)

59 When Saul ordered his house to be watched in order to kill him (1 S 19:11)

60 When he struggled with Aram-naharaim and with Aram-zobah, and when Joab on his return killed twelve thousand Edomites in the Valley of Salt (probably 2 S 8, paralleled in 1 C 18)

63 When he was in the Wilderness of Judah (1 S 23–30)

142 When he was in the cave (1 S 22:1; 24:3; or 2 S 23:13 paralleled in 1 C 11:15)

The headings connect more closely to Samuel's version of David's story than to Chronicles' (although even Samuel is not an exact fit[4]). They portray David as a character in conflict—with Saul, other domestic opponents, foreigners, and God. But the Samuel books seldom show us David praying or illuminate his thoughts and feelings. Psalms shows David praying continuously, partly because it is a book of prayers, but also through statements such as, "I will bless the LORD at all times; / his praise shall continually be in my mouth" (34:1). The Psalter gives us less reason than Samuel to question the honesty of these prayers.

Twelve of the thirteen psalms seem suited in type to their situational headings. But Ps 60's heading refers to a successful military campaign, whereas the text cries, "Have you not rejected us, O God? / You do not go out, O God, with our armies" (60:10). The main link between the psalm and the situation of 2 S 8 seems provided by the names of Philistia, Moab, and Edom in 60:8. The preceding psalm, by contrast, has a genre (personal lament) suited to its heading, but specific details don't fit: what has Saul's watch on David's house to do with God's derision of the nations (59:8)? Such dissonant details show up in each of the situationally headed psalms.

This means that the psalms are not tightly tied to the situations in their headings. The headings invite us to consider the psalms in Davidic contexts, but their loose fit leaves the psalms open to other applications. As an example of both the dissonance and constructive interplay that can occur between heading and psalm, we turn to Ps 51.

PSALM 51

Psalm 51's title designates it "A Psalm of David, when the prophet Nathan came to him, after he had gone in to Bathsheba." At first glance the psalm seems appropriate to that occasion. The psalmist admits to having "done what is evil in your [LORD's] sight" (4). But then questions arise. How can Uriah's murderer say, "Against you [LORD], you alone, have I sinned" (4)? And what of the declaration that "I was born guilty"? To Christians schooled in the Augustinian tradition of original sin, for which this is a key proof-text, the statement may seem unremarkable: "Isn't everyone a sinner from the moment of conception?" But although Hebrew Bible writers recognize the ubiquity of sin, they tie it to particular acts. The psalmist's reference to "bones that you have crushed" (8) lacks an anchor in the Bathsheba story (and may suggest a prayer for healing). Above all, Davidic authorship is difficult to square with the final two verses, because so far as we know Jerusalem's walls needed no rebuilding in David's time. We could translate verse 18 with "build" rather than NRSV's "rebuild," but this would not account for verse 19's suggestion that sacrifice awaits such building.

The most obvious context for verses 18–19 is not David's time, but sometime after Jerusalem's fall to Babylon in 586 BCE.[5] This raises the possibility that Ps 51 asks forgiveness and purification for the nation, rather than a single individual. The disaster of 586, we recall, was blamed on infidelity to God: "Against you, you alone, have I sinned" (4).

Exploring the possibility of a collective voice, we notice that many of the psalm's images and themes resonate with words of Jeremiah and Ezekiel—prophets associated with Jerusalem's fall—and Isaiah, whose book in its final form both predicts and reflects back upon the fall.[6] Jeremiah and especially Ezekiel speak of Judah as corrupt from the outset: "Your origin and your birth were in the land of the Canaanites; your father was an Amorite, and your mother a Hittite" (Ezek 16:3). "We have sinned against the LORD our God, we and our ancestors, from our youth even to this day" (Jer 3:25). Ezekiel and Isaiah stress the metaphor of washing: "I will sprinkle clean water upon you, and you shall be clean" (Ezek 36:25); "though your sins are like scarlet, / they shall be like snow" (Isa 1:18). Ezekiel speaks of Judah's dried and scattered bones which receive a new spirit (37:1–14), and he predicts

162

God's restoration of heart and spirit: "A new heart I will give you, and a new spirit I will put within you" (Ezek 36:26; see also Jer 31:33).

If we read Ps 51 as a national confession of sin, its closing verses become a natural culmination: genuine repentance takes priority over cult (a prominent theme in Jeremiah), but hope then turns to expression of the restored relationship in rebuilt walls and renewed national worship.

If I were forced to choose a single application for the final form of Ps 51, this would be my choice, for it clicks the psalm's pieces neatly into place. But what will we do with its Davidic heading?

One point can be stated rather simply. David sinned grievously, as the kingdom he founded has since sinned. In fact, adultery—the specific aspect of David's sin to which the psalm heading alludes—is one of the major metaphors used to describe the national sin.[7] But David was not utterly cast off for his sin, and the nation hopes for similar mercy. David's story provides resonances both fitting and hopeful.

In Chapter 3 we noted Polzin's proposal that Nathan's parable (2 S 12) is also a parable of the nation's history—the same interpretive connection we have just made in the psalm. Fokkelman took Nathan's parable in a different direction: "*everyone* has the choice to live either as the poor man or as the rich man and to change his course at any moment."[8] This application also works for Ps 51, which has in fact been used predominantly as a general individual prayer.

So there are three feasible readings: Ps 51 as national prayer, as any individual's prayer, and as the prayer of David, who is both national representative and an individual in personal relationship to God.

READING DAVID PSALMS WITHOUT SITUATIONAL HEADINGS: PSALM 23

The situationally headed psalms prompt us to read other *lĕdāvid* psalms also as David's own prayers. But our experience with Ps 51 suggests that they need not be read only as David's prayers. Rather, we should ask about interplay between Davidic and other readings. Psalm 23 will serve as our example of how this works with a *lĕdāvid* psalm whose title does not point us to a particular life situation.

This brief but lovely poem offers a collection of motifs familiar from our previous study of David: shepherd language, *menûḥâ* (usually "rest"; here its plural is the "still" in "still waters"), protection and privileged treatment over against enemies, anointing, two personified virtues as attendants—one of them *ḥesed* (here translated "mercy")—and talk of God's "house." Some scholars therefore find it plausible that David himself might have written this psalm.[9]

But we also find details we would not expect in a psalm authored by—or intended with specific reference to—David. Elsewhere David has been spoken of as a literal (over sheep) or figurative (over people) shepherd, but here the speaker is a *sheep*. "Anoint" in 23:5 reflects not the special verb for royal installation (*mšḥ*) but another which seems to denote ordinary cosmetic anointing.[10] The psalm's closing line proclaims, "I shall dwell in the house of the LORD / my whole life long." But God's house was not, according to Samuel and Chronicles,[11] yet built in David's lifetime.

Modern commentators therefore tend to describe Ps 23 as a general individual prayer of confidence. Indeed one writes, "the extremely personal tone of Psalm 23 *excludes* its royal and national use."[12] Christian readers often understand verse 4's valley as death itself and hear the psalm affirm that beyond death we will feast in God's heavenly "house." But within the Psalter's horizon, the valley seems more likely to be one of mortal danger and distress, which the psalmist traverses even as he or she defiantly asserts fearlessness and confidence in God.[13] We can see in verse 5's table and cup the festal meal which the psalmist hopes to share with family and friends after deliverance, and the "house of the LORD" in the closing verse is, as usual in the Hebrew Bible, the temple.[14] NRSV's "I shall dwell," by the way, follows the ancient Greek translation. The Hebrew psalm reads, "and I shall return,"[15] meaning that we need not envision the speaker actually living at the temple.

Commentators have long noted that although the Hebrew Bible speaks of God as an *individual's* shepherd in only two places (Ps 23:1 and Gen 48:15), it frequently refers to God as the *people's* shepherd.[16] Pamela Milne points out that prophecies of restoration after exile present images especially similar to Ps 23's.[17] "I myself will gather the remnant of my flock out of all the lands . . . and I will bring them back to their fold" (Jer 23:3). "He will feed his flock like a shepherd" (Isa 40:11).[18] "I [LORD] will seek out my sheep. . . . I will feed them with good pasture . . . there they shall lie down in good grazing land" (Ezek 34:12, 14).

Psalm 23:4's striking word for darkness, *ṣlmwt*, appears with reference to exile or national defeat in Ps 44:19, Ps 107:10 and 14,[19] Isa 9:2, and Jer 13:16. In Jer 2:6 *ṣlmwt* refers to the wilderness wanderings.[20] The wilderness connection is strengthened by the fact that Ps 23's two words for "lead" also appear together in Ex 15:13: "you led the people whom you redeemed; you guided them by your strength to your holy abode." If this connection involved merely the conjunction of the two verbs, it might not be so striking, but the word which NRSV translates "abode" is closely related to the "pastures" of Ps 23:2.[21]

The feast imagery of Ps 23:5–6 also connects to traditions of God's care in the wilderness, not only through the general traditions of manna and water from the rock, but through the people's question, "Can God spread a table in the wilderness?" in Ps 78:19.[22] The overflowing cup of 23:5 contrasts with the cup of bitterness and destruction mentioned in Pss 11:6 and 75:8; Isa 51:17, 22; Jer 25:15, 17, 28 and 49:12; and Ezek 23:31–33. Meanwhile the psalm's language agrees with the promises of redemption in Jer 31.[23]

Together, these links of vocabulary and imagery suggest that the "I" of Ps 23, like that of Ps 51, could be the community—specifically, a community heartening itself in the shadow of 586 with assurance that "you are with me" (compare Isa 43:2, 5 "I am with you"). The psalm promises that they will cross the wilderness to dwell in God's land and house (23:6) once more.

A pattern emerges: again and again, psalms which could be read as David's own words may also be read as prayers of the community or prayers of an ordinary individual. We will eventually trace this phenomenon across the psalter as a whole, but first let us step back to survey some collective characteristics of the psalms with *lĕdāvid* headings.

CHARACTERIZING THE SPEAKER OF THE DAVID PSALMS

What impression do we gather of David if we take the *lĕdāvid* psalms as his words? We begin with the obvious—this David prays a lot. Table 2 shows the types of his psalms (in absolute numbers and as percentages of the *lĕdāvid* collection) compared with the occurrence of those types in the Psalter as a whole.

We note first a striking concentration of laments. Over half the David psalms (thirty-eight of seventy-two) fall into this category. To slice the information a different way, thirty-four of the Psalter's forty individual laments have David's name on them. David thus comes across as someone with problems who feels fully confident that God will take an interest in them. *All* of the Psalter's seven trust psalms[24] bear David's name, further characterizing him as a person with extraordinary confidence in God's support.

If we take the personal laments, thanksgivings, and trust songs and add personal psalms from other categories (for instance, the royal psalms 18, 61, 101, and 144), we discover that about 70 percent of "David's" psalms contain a prominent "I" voice. That voice talks primarily about present or past troubles. The picture given by David's own words (taking the *lĕdāvid* psalms imaginatively as such) in Psalms is similar to that gleaned from the situational headings: David is continually in conflict and quite keen on his own interest.

Table 2: Types of the David Psalms

	# in David	% of David	# in Psalter	% of Psalter
Laments				
Personal	34	47	40	27
Community	4	6	18	12
Thanks				
Personal	4	6	7	5
Community	2	3	5	3
Trust	7	10	7	5
Royal	7	10	12	8
Zion	1	1	5	3
Liturgy	2	3	11	7
Praise	5	7	22	15
Throne	0	—	6	4
Wisdom	5	7	12	8
Torah	1	1	3	2
Totals	72	100%	148	100%

What kind of troubles does this psalmic David find himself in?[25] We have already observed the Picasso-like quality of the Psalter's images, which makes it difficult to discern actual life situations. If pressed to identify a single concern in each psalm, however, I would say that over half the David psalms present opponents as the primary problem. (They appear as a secondary complication in additional psalms.) Some "enemy" psalms involve evildoers who seem to be close associates: "it is you, my equal, / my companion, my familiar friend" (55:13). Elsewhere the terminology suggests entire armies: "ten thousands of people / who have set themselves against me all around" (3:6). Sometimes we cannot tell whether the enemies are military troops or rivals spreading slander and discontent.

A goodly handful of enemy psalms mention false accusations or attacks on the psalmist's honor.[26] Some speculate that such psalms would have been used when seeking sanctuary at the altar (recall Joab's flight in 1 K 2:28–34), or even in ordeal situations where God was asked to provide judgment. However, the mechanisms of God's protection remain unnamed.

David's fervent pleas for punishment of the wicked suggest that he does not see himself as one of the transgressors. In a significant number of the enemy psalms (11 of 34) he explicitly affirms innocence.[27] "If you test me, you will find no wickedness in me; / . . . my feet have not slipped" (17:3, 5).

Psalms about admission to worship (15 and 24) suggest righteous confidence as well.

Christian readers, accustomed to thinking of goodness or sin as qualities of an entire life span, need to note that David claims righteousness, not sinlessness. He asserts that he is "in the right" in the psalm's specific moment, often with respect to specified relationships. Thus, Ps 5's "David" protests not that he has never done anything wrong, but that his enemies are liars (5:9)—meaning that their specific accusations against him are false. He, by contrast, cries out to, stands in awe of, takes refuge in, and loves the name of God. In Ps 69, an apparent general admission of sin ("the wrongs I have done are not hidden from you," 5) undergirds denial of present accusations ("what I did not steal must I now restore?" 4). The fact that no wrongs are hidden from God is the premise from which the psalmist argues that God can see the charges are false. Psalm 139 makes a similar appeal in more extended form.

Although most assert or quietly assume righteousness, a few David psalms do confess guilt. The collection contains five of the seven traditional "penitential psalms" (6, 32, 38, 51, and 143)[28] and four others (25 and 39–41) which admit iniquity on the speaker's part. We hear statements such as "pardon my guilt, for it is great" (25:11). But on close examination some of these psalms are not straightforward confessions of sin. Psalm 6 contains no confession; fault on the psalmist's part must be deduced from the opening request, "do not rebuke / . . . or discipline me" (6:1). Verses 7–8 seem to blame trouble on the enemies, rather than the psalmist. Psalm 143's "confession" protests that the psalmist is only human: "do not enter into judgment with your servant, for no one living is righteous before you" (143:2). Like Ps 6, it goes on to ask for help against enemies. Psalm 25, after asking "pardon my guilt, for it is great" (11), asserts that "the friendship of the LORD is for those who fear him. . . . My eyes are ever toward the LORD" (14–15) and then prays, "may integrity and uprightness preserve me" (21)! Psalm 38's confession, "I am sorry for my sin" (18), is followed by protests that the foes hate "without cause" and "wrongfully," rendering "evil for good / . . . because I follow after good" (38:19–20).

How do we make sense of these mixed signals? We have already introduced the idea that protests of righteousness are contextual rather than absolute. Thus 38:17–20 may argue, "yes, I sinned, but *this* persecution I do not deserve!" Note also the identification of righteousness with trust in God; for instance, 32:10 divides people into two categories: "the wicked" and "those who trust in the LORD." The psalm promises, with no further qualification, that ḥesed (NRSV "steadfast love) will surround the latter group. Evidently, when one seeks refuge in God, ordinary sins no longer matter. This may be why Ps 51—one of the most "sincerely" penitent psalms—focuses on sin "against you, you alone" (51:4). (For just a moment, we remember God's focus on cultic behavior in Samuel and Kings.)

We learn further (particularly in Ps 32, a thanksgiving for healing/forgiveness) that the psalmist regards forgiveness as thoroughgoingly efficacious. Once it is granted, the sin may be forgotten. This differs noticeably from Kings' notion of lingering punishment.

Finally we should note that six or seven of the "guilt" psalms, possibly all nine, speak of sickness: "I am languishing; O LORD, heal me" (6:2); "my body wasted away" (32:3); "no health in my bones" (38:3); "the fire burned" (39:3); "heal me" (41:4);[29] "bones that you have crushed" (51:8); and possibly "my spirit fails" (143:7).[30] The implications are uncomfortable for modern Western readers who shy away from interpreting physical illness as divine punishment. But the psalmist works with different assumptions.[31] "There is no soundness in my flesh / because of your indignation; / there is no health in my bones / because of my sin" (38:3). Modern readers may also reject an illness interpretation because they are confused about what to do with accompanying talk about enemies. But ancient societies generally recognized evil magic as a cause of illness. Certainly enemies could take advantage of illness even if they did not cause it.

The psalmist may then be reasoning backward from illness—understood as God's punishment—to the implied guilt. This would account well for mixed signals, such as the juxtaposition of "my pain is ever with me. / I confess my iniquity" (38:17–18) with "I follow after good" (38:20).

In all, about two-fifths of the David psalms concern God's help against enemies who are, so far as we can tell, other Israelites.[32] The enemies are so firmly characterized as wicked evildoers that it does not occur to us to ask whether this level of rebellion indicates some flaw in royal administration. Roughly another fifth of the David psalms concern divine aid for the king in battle. These are all at least implicitly royal (some explicitly so), for presumably only a king would speak of foreign armies attacking "me."[33] About 10 percent concern healing.

Prayers for such everyday blessings as good crops, healthy children, marital concord, and freedom from debt are conspicuous by their absence in the Davidic Psalter. Psalms 65 and 145 do mention food, but in contexts suggestive of national festivals.[34] Psalm 15 mentions lending at interest, but from the potential lender's viewpoint. This suggests that the David psalms were not written to cover the concerns of ordinary persons.

In Ps 89 God says of "my servant David" (20):

He shall cry to me, 'You are my Father,
my God, and the Rock of my salvation!'
(Ps 89:26)

Is this indeed how David speaks in Psalms?

Father language occurs seldom and places the psalmist in "son" position only indirectly or by innuendo: "on you I was cast from my birth" (22:10); "If my father and mother forsake me, / the LORD will take me up" (27:10); "Father of orphans and protector of widows / is God in his holy habitation" (68:5); "the child of your serving girl" (86:16); "As a father has compassion for his children, / so the LORD has compassion for those who fear him" (103:13).[35]

"My God," however, occurs thirty-eight times. "Rock of my salvation" occurs only in 89:26, but the lĕdāvid psalms contain a host of similar phrases, such as "God of my salvation," "my rock," "my fortress," and "my shield."[36] Such terms express both a personal claim on God and an expectation that God will deliver.

Modern believers usually speak of such a relationship in terms of "love," but such language is rare in psalms. Only three times do David psalms speak of humans loving God, twice in general terms (31:23 and 145:20)[37] and once (18:1) in first person. This verse employs an unusual and very warm verb (rḥm) related to the nouns for "womb" and "compassion." In 26:8 the speaker says he loves God's house.

Just as seldom do the David psalms speak of God loving humans, at least with the normal verb for love.[38] Instead they make abundant use (53 occurrences) of the term ḥesed, which denotes loyalty and kindness, usually from a superior toward an inferior.[39] This term—although not at all unique to the David psalms—suits the collection's courtly/political metaphor for relationship: David repeatedly (15 times) casts himself in the role of "servant," while referring to God as "lord" and "king." This may suggest an underlying covenantal framework, although the word "covenant" itself occurs only three times in the David psalms.[40] "You alone" (for instance, 62:5–6) presents the vassal's affirmation that he has flirted with no other overlord.

Where we might think of "loving" God, the Davidic psalms speak of taking refuge and trusting.[41] David (in the Psalter's imaginative portrayal) cries or calls out to God, in expectation that God will answer with deliverance and salvation.[42] The proper human responses to such deliverance, according to these psalms, are praising, telling, and giving thanks. We also find statements about "fear" of God, although less frequently than in non-Davidic psalms.[43] In a few places (for example, 64:8–9) this appears to mean being afraid, but more often (for example, 40:3) it seems to denote awed reverence.

169

I find myself inclined to agree with interpreters such as Eaton and Croft that the language of the David psalms was born in royal worship.[44] One clue is its association with psalms in which an "I" asks for deliverance from armies or attacking nations. Another is its neat fit with the language and concepts of the overlord/vassal covenant model. We have noted the citing of "my God" language in Ps 89:26 as a king's mode of addressing God and in Ps 18 (= 2 S 22) as a prototypical sample of royal psalmody. It often occurs in conjunction with statements or requests that the psalmist be given refuge "in the shadow/shelter of your wings," an image common in ancient Near Eastern thought (Egyptian, Mesopotamian, and Phoenician) about divine protection of the monarch.[45]

The two psalms which mention David most often present differing views on the conditionality of the divine promise to David's line (contrast 89:30–37 with 132:12). The *lĕdāvid* psalms do not resolve this issue. Statements such as "shows steadfast love to his anointed, / to David and his descendants forever" (18:50) suggest an unconditional covenant (with an unspecified amount of flexibility for discipline of the king). But many David psalms assert that God will reward the righteous and punish the wicked (see for instance 5:4–6; 7:8–13; 11:5–7; 34:15–17; 68:1–3). The psalmist does not always see such punishment and reward in action; laments protest that justice has not yet been done. But they accept, as a matter of principle, that this is how God should and eventually will act.

We must also remember that the David psalms overwhelmingly speak from a standpoint of assumed righteousness. Conditionality is not an issue so long as the conditions are not broken! The psalms do allow in principle that God punishes the wicked, but by and large that dynamic is presented as operating in the psalmist's favor. "David" appears confident that his heart is right enough for God to respond with deliverance and steadfast love.

Our survey has suggested that the Psalter's "David" speaks as king, just as he is spoken *about* in that way. The *lĕdāvid* heading then cues us to read a psalm in royal context. Psalm 8:4–5, for instance, would be a king's musings on his own status:

what is a man [that is, myself] that you are mindful of him,
a mortal that you care for him?

Yet you have made him little lower than God,
and crowned him with glory and honor.
(Ps 8:4–5, my translation.)[46]

Although the most likely background for the David psalms' intimate, confident mode of address is, in my judgment, royal tradition, this is only part of the story. Table 2 reminds us that only a minority of the David psalms (10 percent) are explicitly royal, and we saw in Chapter 13 that even many of these can be read as private individuals' prayers (61 is a good example). The allusive, nonspecific character of psalmic language allows appropriation in a variety of situations.

Take for instance Ps 22. The psalmist speaks of enemies who mock and evildoers who gloat (22:7, 16–17). Casting of lots for the psalmist's clothing (18) implies economic despoliation. But out-of-joint bones and dry mouth (14–15) sound more like wasting illness. Animal images occur in 12–13, 16, and 20–21. Suggested life contexts for this psalm have included military difficulties, legal persecution, sickness—perhaps caused by magical attack—getting lost while out hunting, or a king speaking on behalf of a besieged city. Others read it as part of an hypothesized royal "passion play."[47]

Of himself the psalmist says, "I am a worm, and not human" (22:6). No one (to my knowledge) proposes taking this line literally. But how many and which of the other statements are just as flamboyantly metaphorical? The psalm does not tell us. It makes sense against any of the suggested settings, while requiring none of them.[48]

Although Ps 22 offers an especially rich example, the language of the David psalms at large is generalizable enough to allow use by ordinary individuals in a number of different situations. Indeed, many psalms scholars would disagree with my royal reading of them, and say they were composed for such other situations. Returning to our lines from Ps 8, we see in the NRSV translation such a generalized interpretation:

> what are human beings that you are mindful of them,
>   mortals that you care for them?
>
> Yet you have made them a little lower than God,
>   and crowned them with glory and honor.
>
>   (Ps 8:4–5)

Now we hear not a king reflecting with amazement upon his high status, but an equally amazed reflection upon God's grant of near-divine status to every human being. The flexible poetic language of the Davidic psalms opens to ordinary individuals the special "my God" relationship between God and king.

171

Nor have we yet exhausted the interpretive possibilities. Many David psalms can—like 51, 23, and psalms studied in Chapter 13—be read not only as individual prayers (whether from David or someone else) but as prayers of the people collectively. This possibility is enhanced by the presence in the David psalms themselves of collective language: not only "*my* shield" and "*my* God" but "*our* shield," the "God of *our* salvation," and of course "*our* God" (emphasis added, for examples see 59:11; 65:5; 18:31, respectively). In this way, David's voice becomes the collective voice of Israel.

CHAPTER 15

DAVID AND THE BOOK OF PSALMS

Tradition has seen David not only as author of the *lĕdāvid* psalms but as patron of the Psalter at large. Such a reading is encouraged by the example of the David psalms, which are many in number and distributed throughout the collection. Although we have identified characteristic emphases and tendencies in them, they have more than enough in common with the other psalms to establish continuity through the collection. What happens to our vision of the Psalter's David when we include all of the psalms?

My handling of this question will draw heavily on recent work, especially by Gerald Wilson, on the structure of the Psalter as a whole.[1] I also bring to the task three observations from our work on the Psalter's David. First, we have noted the psalmic David's strongly royal character. Second, we have discerned a characteristic speaking style in the David psalms—an "I" calling upon "my God" for deliverance. Third, we have seen that the psalmic David's "I" can be generalized by two different strategies: by identifying the "I" as the community or by allowing the speaker to be an ordinary individual.

These qualities of Psalms' "David" will function in interactive ways as we develop two overall readings of the book of Psalms: Psalms as a community's story, and Psalms as the unfolding of a personal spirituality. A third potential reading develops the vision of an eschatological messiah. As groundwork for these readings, we turn now to the book's opening pair of psalms.

PSALMS 1 AND 2 AS CLUES TO THE PSALTER

A number of features set Pss 1 and 2 apart from the rest of the Psalter's Book 1. (For a fuller exploration of this, see Patrick Miller's essay, "The Beginning of the Psalter.") Whereas almost all the other psalms of Book 1 have *lĕdāvid* headings,[2] 1 and 2 have no headings. Each links up with psalms elsewhere in the Psalter: 1 with 19 and 119, 2 with royal psalms (especially 89) and with 148–149 (especially 148:11 and 149:7–8). They also link with one another, framed by 1:1's "happy are those" (in Hebrew, "happy is the one" or "happy is he") and 2:12's "happy are all." Psalm 1 upholds the positive example of those who "meditate" (Hebrew *hgh*, 1:2) on God's Torah (NRSV

173

"law") day and night. Psalm 2 scoffs at the negative example of those who "plot" (Hebrew *hgh*, 2:1) against God and the anointed. Psalm 1 promises that "the way of the wicked will perish" (1:6), Psalm 2 warns the nations' kings lest they "perish in the way" (2:11).

Psalm 1 prompts us to think in terms of individual piety defined by study of scripture. Its promise is summarized by the closing verse: "LORD watches over the way of the righteous." Psalm 2 moves in the world of Davidic covenant, where plotting foreign nations will soon be subdued under God's anointed. We may summarize it with the affirmation of verse 6: "I have set my king on Zion."

These two psalms suggest two ways to read the book of Psalms as a whole. We will begin with the choice offered by Ps 2, reading the Psalter as God's history with Israel among the nations—a history intricately linked to the Davidic covenant. We will then read it again as an exploration of individual piety—connected with David through the "I" of the *lĕdāvid* psalms and the prompts of the situational headings. I will not attempt to trace every possible connection, but will simply indicate the main contours of each reading. With these national and personal interpretations of the Psalter in hand, we will reflect on David's character as finally synthesized from his many modes of presence in the book of Psalms.

"I HAVE SET MY KING ON ZION" (2:6): THE PSALTER AS ISRAEL'S HISTORY

We noted in Chapter 13 that royal psalms—2, 72, and 89—sit at key junctures in the Psalter's layout, framing something like an imaginative history of the monarchy. Royal and David psalms do occur after 89, but with some changes in tone—a chastened sense of responsibility (101) and introduction of a priestly note into the royal promise (110 and 132). As a map for the journey refer to the overview of the Psalter's psalm types and headings in Table 1 (see Chapter 12, page 132). I will present my royal reading in terms of the five books into which our present Psalter is divided.

Book 1. Psalms—like Chronicles—begins Israel's story with the institution of monarchy. Only brief allusions to Torah (NRSV "law," 1:2) hint at any history prior to that. Beyond the introductory pair, Book 1 is composed almost entirely of David psalms. The very first of these (3) has a situational heading encouraging us to read it, and subsequent *lĕdāvid* psalms, as the prayers of the king, David.

Although only three of these David psalms are explicitly royal (18, 20, and 21), we saw in Chapter 14 that many more are implicitly so because of their language, the presupposed relationship to God, and the situations involved. Thirty of these thirty-nine psalms use significant "I" language, with a preponderance of individually oriented psalm types such as personal lament. This means that Book 1 presents the issues of kingship primarily from the king's own point of view. He is sensitive to the remarkable character of his position (Ps 8, royal reading), knows that responsible behavior is required of those who would approach God (Ps 15), and treasures the Torah (19). God's support of him in battle (18, 21) reinforces his own assessment that he meets the standard of righteousness.

A few features darken the fundamentally confident tone of this book. The king is, as foreshadowed by Ps 2, in almost continual conflict. Illness causes him to question his moral standing, and one of these illness psalms (41) closes Book 1. It counters Ps 2's statement, "Happy are all who take refuge in him [LORD]," with reflection on the king's social responsibilities: "Happy is the man who considers the poor" (41:1, my translation[3]). The king complains of betrayal by his own bosom friend (41:9), a haunting echo of the Absalom reference in Ps 3's heading.

Book 2 opens with a string of Korah psalms (Korah may be the name of a singer's guild). In Pss 42–43 an individual who sounds much like "David" ("my God," etc.) calls to a God who has cast him off (43:2). The rest of the Korah psalms are more communal in genre: a communal lament, a courtier's celebration of a royal wedding, two Zion psalms and one about God's kingship, and a meditation on the nature of wealth. Psalm 50, foreshadowing the Asaph series of Book 3, indicts the people as covenant-breakers (over against their protest of innocence in 44:17–18) and warns that God will not accept sacrificed bulls without accompanying true loyalty. These Korah and Asaph psalms give a voice to the rest of the worshiping community.

David psalms resume with 51, which answers 50's order to call upon God. As we have seen, this psalm superimposes communal and personal confession. In Book 2's arrangement, the confession receives no immediate answer: lament and rumination upon injustice continue through Ps 60. Only after the royal prayer in 61 does the tone lighten, with songs of trust and eventually a jubilant sequence of thanks and praise in 65–68.[4]

In 71:9 the psalmist pleads, "Do not cast me off in the time of old age; / do not forsake me when my strength is spent" (71:9).[5] Book 2 then closes with Ps 72, David's prayer (imaginatively speaking) for Solomon. This prayer reminds us, much more strongly than Ps 2 (whose "happy" motif reappears in

72:17), that the king is God's agent for justice within the country as well as its military protection.

Despite Ps 72's bright picture, Book 2 leaves us uneasy about the Davidic covenant. The king *can* sin. The people *can* suffer defeat. How will the nation fare as David's throne passes to his descendants?

Book 3 contains only one *lĕdāvid* psalm—86, a personal lament featuring such probably-royal terms as "your servant" and "child of your serving girl" (2, 4, 16). However, the book's Asaph and Korah psalms appropriate some "Davidic" language, such as "God my King," "I cry aloud," "my God," paired *ḥesed* and Faithfulness, and "God of my salvation," (74:12; 77:1; 83:13; 85:10; 88:1). This has the effect of merging the Davidic voice with the community's. Psalm 88 in particular reads like the lament of the anointed one whose fall is reported in 89.[6]

The dominant psalm type is community lament. Book 3 contains more of these than any other book of the Psalter, both in absolute number (six, or seven if we include 89) and relative concentration (over a third of the book's psalms). Several psalms seem to concern the fall of the northern kingdom (78, 80, 81), whereas others mourn the sacking of Jerusalem (74, 79).[7] The inter-mixing of community laments with joyful affirmations of God's saving love, especially in the Zion psalms, anticipates the stark contrast of these themes in the two parts of the final psalm, 89.

Book 3 also introduces a new type of psalm, the extended historical review (78–81 and 83). We got just a slight foretaste of this in Book 2 with Pss 44 and 68 (which mentions Sinai twice, 8 and 17). In Book 3 we find multiple references to deliverance from Egypt (77, 78, 80, 81) and the Psalter's first mention of Moses (77:20). On the one hand, these themes invoke the highly conditional Sinai covenant model and thus suggest why God might allow Israel to fall (81 develops this with particular clarity). On the other, the exodus/wilderness imagery prepares us for later use of the exodus as a "type" or model for deliverance from exile.

Book 3 closes with two of the Psalter's darkest psalms: 88 and 89. Psalm 88 repeats many of the motifs in 69 (mire, deep waters), and like 69 it lays blame for the difficulties squarely with God. However, 88 offers no closing promise of thanksgiving or anticipation of salvation. It closes in despair: "Your wrath has swept over me; your dread assaults destroy me" (88:16). Its final word is "darkness" (88:18). In 89 we see the consequences of aban-donment for the entire people. The promises of Ps 2 seem, at this point, bankrupt.

Book 4 introduces a new editorial style into the Psalter. Hitherto nearly every psalm has carried a Davidic or choral guild ascription. In Books 4–5 only a few psalms carry such headings. However, we find new markers such as "praise the LORD!" Table 3 (based on the type identifications of Table 1) shows us that we also encounter a new mix of psalm types. Books 1–3 have high lament content—45–50 percent if we combine individual and community laments. (Notice how the balance in these three books shifts from individual to community laments.) In Books 4–5 lament frequency drops below 30 percent, while praise psalms (of which enthronement psalms are a special category) more than double in concentration. The effect of these changes is to accent the break between Books 1–3 and 4–5.

Book 4 opens with the Psalter's one and only Moses psalm (90). The book also mentions Moses six times in psalm texts (99:6; 103:7; 105:26; 106:16, 23, 32). David's name occurs only twice (in the headings of 101 and 103), confirming the shift from Davidic to Mosaic covenant emphasis. Psalm 89:50 asked remembrance for God's servant the anointed. Psalm 90:13 and 16 ask compassion on God's *servants* the people. Psalm 102 also refers to the people as servants, whereas 105 uses servant terminology for Abraham, the people, and Moses. Book 4 never applies the term "servant" to David or a king. Psalm 89:47–48 cited the brevity of human life as a reason for God to show mercy, implicitly assuming that God's wrath was not intended unto death. Psalm

Table 3: Distribution of Psalms by Type

	Book 1		Book 2		Book 3		Book 4		Book 5	
Laments										
Personal	18	45%	11	36%	2	12%	1	6%	8	18%
Community	1	3%	3	10%	6	35%	3	18%	5	11%
Thanks										
Personal	3	8%	1	3%	0	—	1	6%	2	5%
Community	0	—	2	7%	0	—	0	—	3	7%
Trust	4	10%	2	7%	0	—	0	—	1	2%
Royal	4	10%	3	10%	1	6%	1	6%	3	7%
Zion	0	—	2	7%	2	12%	0	—	1	2%
Liturgy	2	5%	1	3%	3	18%	2	12%	3	7%
Praise	3	8%	1	3%	2	12%	4	24%	12	27%
Throne	0	—	1	3%	0	—	5	29%	0	—
Wisdom	3	8%	3	10%	1	6%	0	—	5	11%
Torah	2	5%	0	—	0	—	0	—	1	2%
Totals	40	100%	30	100%	17	100%	17	100%	44	100%

90:12 counsels that we of brief days should wise up, apparently assuming that God's wrath will not end until we quit offending. Why did the dynasty fall? Not because God is false, but because Israel[8] was (90:8). Psalm 90:14 requests—as Ps 89 did—God's *ḥesed*, but for the people directly rather than their king.

Psalm 91 returns to prayer for an individual (its "you" is singular) using language that reminds us of "David" and the royal cult: "my refuge and my fortress," "my God," "under his wings," "a shield and a buckler." However, the psalm has no Davidic heading. God's special protection can now be claimed by anyone. Psalms 92, 94, 102 continue this democratization process with anonymous versions of Davidic-type prayers.

Book 4's high number of enthronement psalms—five of the Psalter's six, comprising almost 30 percent of the book—provides another piece of its answer to the problem of the dynasty's fall. These psalms (93 and 96–99) speak not of a human king but of God as king, who will "judge the world with righteousness / and the peoples with equity" (98:9).[9]

Despite these shifts of emphasis, we do find two *lĕdāvid* psalms in Book 4. Psalm 101 addresses God's requirements for good government, perhaps tacitly admitting the Davidic dynasty's failures in this regard ("when shall I attain it?" 101:2). The voice recalls Book 1's "good David" (compare Pss 15 and 24), but he now speaks as chastened representative of his post-586 people, responding to the real king who is God.

This national-conscience David speaks again in Ps 103, affirming God's graciousness as revealed to Moses (!)(6–9; compare Ex 33:17–23; 34:6–8). The psalm speaks of God's *ḥesed*, forgiveness, compassion, and fatherly love for "us" (11–13), while stressing that the covenant and commandments must be observed (18). It points not to the "king on Zion" (2:6) but to the one in heaven (103:19). One can easily imagine the "I" of this psalm as the people.

The book ends with a review of God's mighty acts, from creation (104) through exodus (105) to alternating forbearance and punishment in the face of repeated iniquities (106). The final verses of 106 affirm God's compassion (45) and plead, "gather us from among the nations" (47). Will God respond to this as to Moses' past intercession (23)?

Book 5's opening exhortation to "those he redeemed from trouble / and gathered in" (107:2–3) suggests that Book 4's plea has been fulfilled. Backward references to exile in other psalms ("When the Lord restored the fortunes of Zion," 126:1; "By the rivers of Babylon— / there[10] we sat down and there we wept," 137:1) reinforce the sense of being back home. But we also find allusions to life in Diaspora: "I am an alien in Meshech" (120:5); "wherever I make my home" (119:54).[11]

Returning to the survey of psalm types in Table 3, we see that Book 5 contains the Psalter's highest concentrations of wisdom and praise psalms.[12] In most other respects, its percentages are intermediate between those of Book 4 (which, however, it generally resembles, especially in the preponderance of praise over lament) and Books 1–2. We encounter several psalm types which we have not seen since the opening books: community thanksgivings, a trust psalm, and a Torah psalm. This is also the first book since Book 2 to contain a situational heading (Ps 142). These features create the impression of a restored community which has been permanently stamped by the exilic experience (general stylistic similarities between Books 4 and 5) but is nonetheless reappropriating some of its early traditions. The shift from personal lament to praise as the dominant psalm type suggests that this restored community's life is more unified and joyful than that in the time of kings.

Our "map" in Table 1 brings out some additional features. The heading column (middle) shows three "thanks!" psalms (107, 118, and 136)—each beginning "O give thanks to the LORD, for he is good; / for his steadfast love endures forever." Wilson has shown that these psalms divide Book 5 into three parts (107–117, 118–135, and 136–150).[13] The opening and closing parts contain strings of David psalms (108–110 and 138–145). The middle part contains fifteen Ascents psalms (120–134), several of which also bear David headings and/or mention David (122, 124, 131, and 132). Thus David makes a comeback in Book 5, where almost a third of the psalms bear David headings.

Book 4 complicated our picture of David by putting David headings on two psalms (101 and 103) of rather different tone from most earlier David psalms, while *not* putting such headings on psalms which did sound typically "Davidic" (91 and 102). What happens to David's voice in Book 5?

We first hear it in Ps 108, which answers ("I will give thanks," 3) 107:1–3's exhortation to give thanks. This sets up David as speaker for the Second Temple congregation, but what he does is repeat pieces of David psalms (57 and 60) from Book 2. What an authorization for claiming David's psalms as the community's! If we continue that line of interpretation, 109 (written in the favorite David-genre of individual lament) becomes also a prayer for God's aid against oppressing peoples (compare its curses with those of Ps 137). Psalm 110 then assures us that God "will execute judgment among the nations" (6). We earlier noted the priestly aspect it adds to royal theology (4).

The following praise psalms (111–117[14]), although directed to the congregation, contain several "Davidic" notes. Psalm 113 echoes Hannah's song as it praises God for raising "the poor from the dust, / . . . the needy from the ash heap" (compare 7–9 with 1 S 2:5–8).[15] Psalm 115 claims "help" and "shield" language for Israel, Aaron's house, and God-fearers (9–11). Psalm

179

116 reads as a thanksgiving for the rescue requested in the Davidic Ps 86, especially in its talk of "your servant," "child of your serving girl" (116:16).

Psalm 118, opening the second part of Book 5, also looks very much like a royal thanksgiving ("nations surrounded me; / in the name of the LORD I cut them off!" [118:10]) We can easily imagine it as a festival liturgy, with its multiple voices, demand that the gates be opened (19), and climax at the horns of the altar (27). But it does not use the words "king" or even "servant," speaking instead of "the one who comes in the name of the LORD" (118:26).[16]

Psalm 118:20 declares that "the righteous shall enter" the gate of the LORD. How does one gain righteousness? Psalm 119, which shows a surprising number of verbal links to 118,[17] answers in terms of Torah and commandments. Some of its references would well suit a diaspora setting: "I live as an alien in the land" (119:19), "I will speak of your decrees before kings" (119:46), "wherever I make my home" (119:54). However, its counsel serves equally well as guidance for a nation making its way under the Mosaic covenant which Book 4 upheld as the answer to exile.

In the middle of Book 5 we also find the fifteen-psalm Ascents collection. "Ascents" comes from the Hebrew verb for "going up." Rabbinic tradition held that there was one Ascents psalm for each stairstep of the temple. "Go up" is also the standard term for travel to Jerusalem, so "goings-up" might refer to pilgrimage. Either explanation connects the Ascents psalms to temple worship. Nine of the psalms explicitly mention Zion, Jerusalem, or "the house."[18] Two which we have already studied (122 and 132) name David in association with the city, and 132 again implicitly transfers the Davidic promise from royal dynasty to Zion's priests and people. In 124 "David" leads the people ("let Israel now say," 1) in proclaiming "*our* help is in the name of the LORD" (8, my emphasis).[19] In 131—a song of trust—the psalmist declares personal humbleness, then closes by exhorting Israel to hope in God. David's presence in this section then reinforces the general shift to a communal, Jerusalem-centered piety. As elsewhere in Books 4 and 5, David psalms and anonymous psalms of the community blend in style and tone.

The opening psalm of the third and final part of Book 5 (Ps 136) stresses God's *ḥesed* to the community ("us," 136: 23–24). The specific historical references are pre-Davidic, but we feel little doubt that the psalm celebrates God's remembrance and rescue of the Second Temple community. This impression is strengthened by the psalm's juxtaposition with 137, a much darker recollection of Jerusalem's fall and the people's exile in Babylon.[20]

As 108's "I give thanks" (Davidic) responded to 107's "give thanks!" so 138's "I sing" (Davidic) answers 137's "how could we sing?"[21]—perhaps making David song leader for the diaspora as well as the Judean community. Like 108–110, 138–145 use language similar to that of Book 1. We hear pleas for exoneration from false charges (139) and for rescue from enemies and evil-doers (140–143). Overall, however, these psalms seem brighter in tone than the Book 1 collection; the balance of lament and thanksgiving has tipped toward the latter. Psalm 144 echoes 18's heavenly warrior images and 65's vision of domestic prosperity. In 145—the Psalter's final *lĕdāvid* psalm—David himself falls nearly out of sight beneath a paean of exuberant praise for God's power, goodness, and providence.

In 107–108 and 137–138 David's voice responded to a summons or question of the community at large. Now the process reverses. At the close of 145 "David" pledges, "My mouth will speak the praise of the LORD, / and all flesh will bless his holy name." The subsequent "praise!" psalms offer just such praise (146–150). Denying trust in human princes (146:3), the congregation assigns to God the royal duties of protection and justice. It is no longer the king whom God sets on Zion (2:6), but the "outcasts of Israel" (147:2). The children of Zion rejoice in God self as their king (149:2). With God's help they will fetter the rebellious kings of the nations (149:6–8; contrast 2:2–3, 8–9) and receive glory (*hdr*, 149:9; contrast the king's *hdr*—translated as "majesty"—in 21:5, 45:3; 45:4).[22] In a triumphant crescendo, Ps 150 bids "everything that breathes" (150:6, compare 145:21) to join the praise which resounds through God's sanctuary.

The community reading which we have just traced moves from a rather naive royal theology in Book 1 to a complex picture in which people and priests take the king's place as recipient of God's promises. Instead of God shielding the king who shields the people, God shields the people directly. In Books 4 and 5 of the Psalter, a somewhat chastened "David" speaks less as an individual than as spokesperson for the nation. This enhances the already present possibility of reading even the earlier psalms as prayers of a communal "I."

"I WILL CAUSE A HORN TO SPROUT UP FOR DAVID" (132:17): AN ALTERNATIVE COMMUNITY READING

We noted in Chapter 13 that many royal psalms and psalms mentioning David—including the key psalms 2, 72, 110, and 132—may be read "messianically" with reference to a future, more glorious ruler.[23] This opens a second option for community reading, one in which the expansive rhetoric of royal theology acquires literal force. The failings and fall of the dynasty do not now discredit the theology's bold claims but merely show that its true fulfillment has not yet occurred. The joy of Book 5 now anticipates the messianic age rather than springing from life beyond monarchy. Centuries of

Christian commentary and some threads of Jewish interpretation bear witness to this secondary interpretive possibility.

"LORD WATCHES OVER THE WAY OF THE RIGHTEOUS" (1:6): THE PSALTER AND PERSONAL PIETY

We now reread the assembled Psalter, still cognizant of the structural patterns pointed out by Wilson but this time emphasizing the reading clues provided by Psalm 1. By their kinship with Ps 1, wisdom psalms will acquire greater prominence (see Mays, "The Place of the Torah-Psalms"). If our previous reading generalized David as voice of the community, this one will claim his intensely personal relationship to God (as portrayed in the David psalms) as a model for ordinary individuals.

Psalm 1 contrasts two "ways"[24]—that of the righteous who meditate on Torah (NRSV "law") and prosper like deep-rooted trees, and that of the wicked who keep bad company, follow poor advice, and perish like wind-blown chaff. The psalm tells us both *how* to be righteous—study Torah and avoid the way of the wicked—and *why*: the righteous are "happy,"[25] prosperous, and "watched over" by God. The reference to Torah (1:2, NRSV "law") is double-edged. To a first approximation Torah denotes the five so-called books of Moses (Genesis through Deuteronomy). But it also refers to God's "teaching" (the etymological meaning of *tôrâ*; see for instance Ps 78:1) in a broader sense which might also encompass the five books of the Psalter itself. The psalm's advice to meditate on Torah then inclines us to approach the Psalter less as a community hymnal than as devotional reading.[26] As before, we will proceed book by book. Links between Pss 1 and 2 (discussed at the beginning of this chapter) now prompt us to equate the contrasts presented by the two psalms, taking the Davidic king as model of a righteous person and his enemies as examples of wickedness.[27]

Book 1's David psalms generally accept and reinforce the equation of David with the righteous and his enemies with the wicked, starting already in 3:7. If David is a model of righteousness, then the righteous can aspire to be like David; after all, every human is royal in God's eyes (8:4–8)! So we generalize both the rights and privileges of the relationship described in the David psalms. God will answer anyone who calls (4:3 and many other places). The book's closing angle on who is happy—"happy the one who considers the poor" (41:1, my translation[28])—describes an obligation of the righteous rather than a specifically royal responsibility.

Psalm 19, near the center of Book 1, picks up the opening psalm's motifs of Torah (NRSV "law," 7), meditation (14), and assurance of benefit (11).[29] Here as elsewhere the righteous person of whatever station becomes "your servant" (11 and 13), claiming God as "my rock and my redeemer" (14).

Promises of safety and great reward stand in some tension with the individual lament type which dominates Book 1. Will the righteous really prosper and the wicked perish? Psalm 37 asks the question with particular directness. "Yet a little while," it then answers, "and the wicked will be no more" (37:10).

Book 2 brings a strengthened communal emphasis. The Korah psalms speak of Zion, temple, and altar, and so does "David": "Happy are those whom you choose and bring near to live in your courts" (65:4). At the same time, God's promises of salvation come under question. "You have rejected us and abased us / . . . yet we have not forgotten you, / or been false to your covenant" (44:9, 17). Psalm 49's meditation (a noun related to the verb in Ps 1) on "times of trouble, / when the iniquity of my persecutors surrounds me" (5) offers the only partially consoling answer: "when they die they will carry nothing away" (17).

Book 2 also deals, more seriously than Book 1, with possible error on the petitioner's own part. Once again David shows the way: "I know my transgressions / . . . create in me a clean heart, O God / . . . then I will teach transgressors your ways" (51:3, 10, 13). A "broken spirit" (51:17) will be accepted, enabling resumption of communal worship at Zion (18–19). In the next psalm David is once again, like the righteous person of Ps 1, planted firm as a tree (52:8).

Book 3 turns in its very first psalm (73) to the nagging issue of life's fairness: "I saw the prosperity of the wicked. / for they have no pain" (3). "Always at ease, they increase in riches. / All in vain I have kept my heart clean / and washed my hands in innocence" (12–13, with an echo of 26:6). The premise of the two ways may seem vindicated by realization that "those who are far from you will perish" (27, compare 1:6 and 2:12). But assurance of prosperity for the righteous is conspicuous by its absence. Instead we hear, "My flesh and my heart may fail, / but God is the strength of my heart and my portion forever" (26). God provides comfort, strength, and inner peace even when outer deliverance or healing are not forthcoming.[30]

The Hebrew text of 73 begins, "Truly God is good to Israel" (*lyśr'l*). NRSV offers a corrected reading, "truly God is good to the upright" (*lyšr'l*), which makes sense insofar as 73 concerns the fates of the upright and the wicked. The Hebrew text foreshadows Book 3's concern with national disas-

183

ter. It offers a clue for coping: when God's goodness to Israel fails, even then "it is good to be near God; / . . . to tell of all your works" (73:28). The same answer appears in other Book 3 psalms. "Has God forgotten to be gracious?" asks 77:9. Verse 12 answers, "I will meditate [*hgh*] on all your work, / and muse on your mighty deeds." The historical review psalm type which this book introduces shows how to accomplish such musing.

Psalm 84 insists, "Happy are those whose strength is in you, / . . . happy is everyone who trusts in you" (5, 12). But the question of 89:46 remains: "How long will your wrath burn like fire?" In an individual reading of the Psalter as in a communal one, Book 3 portrays a crisis.

Book 4 explains divine wrath as a response to Israel's iniquities and "secret sins" (90:8), implying a failure in the central duty of studying Torah (compare 19:11–13). Some of its psalms reassert the premise of reward, insisting that the righteous flourish like trees (92:12–15; compare 1:3). Yet the apparent ascendance of the wicked cannot be completely denied. Psalm 94 responds to this vexing problem with a new benediction: "Happy are those whom you discipline, O LORD" (12).[31] It commends Torah as a "respite from days of trouble" (13), until that time when "justice will return to the righteous" (15).

David models the appropriate attitude in 101's ethical pledges and 103's deeply thankful blessing. Psalm 103:17–18 detaches *hesed* from the Davidic promise (contrast 89's usage of the term) and offers it "to those who keep his covenant / and remember to do his commandments." Psalm 105:45 identifies such obedience as God's whole purpose in giving Israel land: "that they might keep his statutes and observe his laws." Earlier in the Psalter, we might have thought that simply taking refuge in God brought happiness. Book 4's final psalm sets the record straight: "Happy are those who observe justice, who do righteousness" (106:3).

Book 5 in an individual reading, as in a communal, continues the new direction of Book 4 while offering a rapprochement to the world of Books 1 and 2. It can speak of God's unqualified support for David "forever" (110:4), but it knows also that God's precepts are "established forever and ever, / to be performed with faithfulness and uprightness" (111:7–8). "Happy are those who fear the LORD, / who greatly delight in his commandments. / . . . who deal generously and lend, / who conduct their affairs with justice / . . . Their righteousness endures forever" (112:1, 5, 9).

Hitherto we have emphasized the Ascents collection at the heart of Book 5, but an individual reading emphasizes the book's other heart—the massive Ps 119, which has more verses (176) than all the Ascents psalms combined (101). Psalm 119 picks up the Torah theme with a vengeance, containing twenty-five of the Psalter's thirty-five occurrences of the word *tôrâ*. It does not mention Israel, Jacob, David, Zion, Jerusalem, or the temple at all. Nor does the psalmist ever use the words "we," "us," or "our." The psalm's first person is singular and its piety individual. If we had any doubt about the ability of an ordinary person to be "your servant" (thus far the phrase has appeared eleven times in David psalms, three times elsewhere with clear reference to David or Davidic kings—89:39, 50, and 132:10—and twice in 116:16, which is closely tied to 86), the twelve occurrences of this phrase in 119 would resolve them.

We noted in our community reading that "wherever I make my home" (119:54) hints at life in the Diaspora. Certainly the psalm offers a mode of piety which would not be tied to life in Jerusalem or Judah. But 120—the first of the Ascents psalms—also seems to speak of life in a foreign land: ("an alien in Meshech / . . . among the tents of Kedar," 5) as if to say that Diaspora Jews need not confine themselves to Torah but are invited to make pilgrimage to the temple. The general structure of Book 5 sends the same message. Although 119 and other individually oriented psalms certainly offer an individual piety, they are embraced by praise and liturgical psalms which affirm the goodness and joy of life in a worshiping congregation. Perhaps this suggests that in the very act of meditating on Torah an individual is drawn into the life of the community.

In our individually oriented reading of the Psalter, the king's vassal/sovereign relationship to God becomes a model for general individual piety. However, the simple equation of the wicked with the psalmist's opponents and the assumption that righteousness will bring prosperity are progressively challenged. Books 4 and 5 emphasize anew the justice and righteousness required of the individual. In one sense, the individual reading climaxes in Ps 119, which affirms Torah study as a pathway not just to prosperity but to the intimate relationship with God ("your servant") spoken of in the earlier David psalms. In another sense, Book 5's structure places even the Torah-studying individual within the larger matrix of the worshiping community.

DAVID IN THE PSALTER: A SUMMARY

Psalm texts speak *about* David as king and recipient of covenant promises. Situational headings and the preponderance of individual psalm types in the *lĕdāvid* collection (psalms *of* David) hint at a character somewhat like the one we saw in Samuel—passionate and enmeshed in conflict. He seems to grapple more fiercely with Israelite opponents than with foreign enemies, although subduing foreign nations is a primary component of his job description. As we move through the books of the Psalter, this "David"—now symbolic of the royal dynasty—moves from naive confidence in his own righteousness and God's support through experiences of defeat and finally the dynasty's fall, emerging somewhat chastened (Book 4) and aware that the promises of the royal covenant are subordinate to the demands of the Mosaic one. His voice becomes progressively less distinct from the people's as he leads them in worship in the restored community. As symbolic voice of a congregation united in joyful worship, this final "David" of the Psalter resembles the worship-organizing king we met in Chronicles.

Figure 1 provides a simplified graphic summary of the Psalter's dynamics. Movement from top to bottom takes us sequentially through the book of Psalms, from the introductory Pss 1 and 2 to the closing David and Hallelujah sequences. A horizontal line halfway down the page marks the break between crisis in Book 3 and the responses in Book 4. Themes in Books 1–3 (top half of the diamond) are very sketchily summarized as a move from psalms proclaiming trust and asking help to those which consider community consequences and theodicy issues. Developing themes in Books 4–5 are summarized by allusion to Book 5's centerpieces, Ps 119 ("Study Torah") and the Ascents collection ("Go to Zion").

Figure 1's horizontal dimensions represent different interpretive strategies. The left side summarizes a community reading (cued especially by the royal psalms), which begins by accepting Ps 2's presentation of the king as divinely appointed protector, wrestles with the crisis of the dynasty's fall in Ps 89, turns to Moses for an answer, and eventually reassimilates the royal traditions as expressions of the community's relationship to God. On this side, movement from Ps 1 to 150 is also an imaginative historical movement from the monarchy's founding to restored worship in the Second Temple.[32]

The right side of the diamond tracks an individually oriented reading, which claims the royal prayers as models for personal trust in God. This reading too arrives at a crisis in which it becomes evident that life is not just (Ps 73) and simply crying out to God does not assure well-being (88 and 89). Torah study seems to provide the answer, but in the end this will not suffice: one also needs to engage in community worship. On this side, movement from Ps 1 to 150 traces a process of individual spiritual growth from naive claims on God through a struggle with theodicy issues to mature Torah study and involvement in community.

Down the center of the diamond, we track a messianic (eschatological) reading which interprets the whole sequence, from Ps 2's promises to 138–145's royal reprise, as prediction of a fulfillment yet to come.

Thus the highly symbolic, Picasso-like images of David's story in Psalms support several interpretive strategies. The Psalter imaginatively sketches Is-

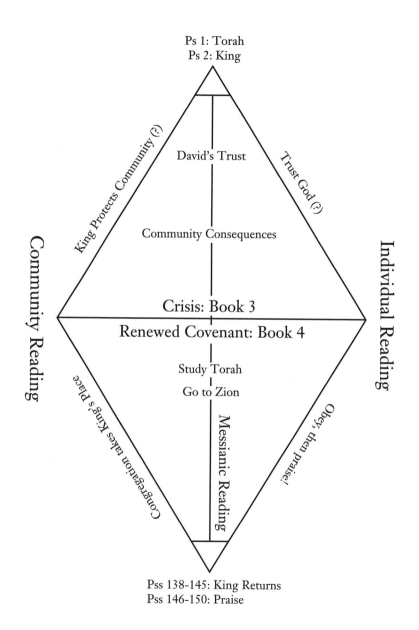

Ps 1: Torah
Ps 2: King

David's Trust

King Protects Community (?)

Trust God (?)

Community Consequences

Community Reading

Crisis: Book 3

Renewed Covenant: Book 4

Individual Reading

Study Torah

Go to Zion

Congregation takes King's Place

Messianic Reading

Obey, then praise!

Pss 138-145: King Returns
Pss 146-150: Praise

Figure 1. Dynamics of the Psalter

rael's history, moving from naive petition for special favors to a complex theology in which God both punishes and forgives. Although the dynasty's fall signals primarily a shift to direct relationship between God and community, rather than relationship mediated through the king, it secondarily hints that the Davidic ideal and associated promises have not yet found their true fulfillment (the messianic reading of Psalms). The book of Psalms is also a journey in personal spirituality. Its "David" leads us from rather simplistic expectations (I am righteous and I expect God to help me succeed) through crisis to a more humble but joyful spirituality, centered in Torah but cognizant of the wider congregation's life. In the completed Psalter, as in so many individual psalms, David's voice is simultaneously any individual's and the community's.

PART 5

REFLECTIONS

CHAPTER 16

DAVID: A SYNTHESIS

"[The Psalter] might well be called a little Bible. In it is comprehended most beautifully and briefly everything that is in the entire Bible. . . . Anyone who could not read the whole Bible would here have anyway almost an entire summary of it, comprised in one little book."

(Martin Luther, 1528)[1]

We began our inquiry into the Hebrew Bible's portraits of David with a quotation from the book of Psalms. We will return to Psalms because its collage incorporates pieces of all the Hebrew Bible's David portraits. Before we attempt to integrate them, however, let us briefly survey the Hebrew Bible's scattered references to David outside the three main portraits.

THE FOURTH DAVID: SKETCHES AND GLIMPSES

David's name appears in the Hebrew Bible forty-two times outside of the books we have already studied (Samuel and Kings, Chronicles and Ezra-Nehemiah, and Psalms). Twenty-eight times it appears in prophecies of deliverance. Seven pertain to current affairs during the Judean monarchy; twenty-one look forward to restoration of that monarchy, usually over a united Israel.[2] Eleven times David's name occurs in connection with the historical Judean monarchs, primarily in prophetic words of judgment.[3] Twice it occurs in literary figures, once in a geographical reference and once transferring the Davidic promise to the people.[4]

Proverbs and Ecclesiastes both claim in their opening verses to be written by sons of David; this tells us more about Solomon's reputation for wisdom than about David. The Song of Solomon associates David with military glory (4:4). We hear twice of David's descent from Ruth's son Obed (Ruth 4:17,

22), reinforcing David's role as symbol of inclusiveness (Ruth was from Moab). The northern prophet Amos remembers David as musician (6:5, a rather uncomplimentary association), but in their present forms the books of both Amos (9:11) and Hosea (3:5) look forward to Israel's restoration under Davidic kings.

The books which mention David most frequently (outside of the major portraits) are Isaiah, Jeremiah, Ezekiel, and Zechariah. Isaiah mentions David mostly in connection with the reigning dynasty.[5] For instance, the prophet addresses King Ahaz as "house of David" (7:13) and tells Hezekiah that God will defend Jerusalem for God's sake and the sake of David (37:35). The name "David" has very positive associations here despite the prophet's criticism of current rulers.

Only three of Isaiah's ten references involve future restoration. One of these, 9:6–7's announcement that "a child has been born for us," was probably originally composed for a royal birth or, more likely, coronation (compare Ps 2). But it is now prefaced by reference to "the latter time," inviting us to understand the Prince of Peace as an eschatological ruler. Isaiah 16:5's prediction of "a ruler who seeks justice" (notice "steadfast love" and "faithfulness" earlier in the verse) also seems to point forward. Isaiah's final reference to David comes in the section which celebrates Cyrus's advent: "I will make with you [plural] an everlasting covenant, my steadfast, sure love for David" (55:3). We saw in Chapter 13 how this passage transfers the Davidic promise to the people at large.

Jeremiah's allusions to David are more mixed in tone. The eight which refer to current rulers entail warning, condemnation, and curse. The other seven occur in Jeremiah's "comfort" chapters (30–33) and predict restoration:[6] "In those days . . . I will cause a righteous Branch to spring up for David; and he shall execute justice and righteousness in the land" (33:15).

Ezekiel does not name David at all in connection with the pre-586 rulers he so bitterly condemns. But four references at the end of the book look forward to a new day: "I will set up over them one shepherd, my servant David, and he shall feed them: he shall feed them and be their shepherd" (34:23; see also 34:24 and 37:24–25).

In Chapter 13 we noted that Zechariah appears to think in terms of two anointed leaders: Zerubbabel and the priest Joshua. But history did not fulfill the prophet's hopes for these leaders. As it has so many other times, disappointment led to new and more radical hope. Zechariah 12 envisions direct action by the divine warrior who will restore Judah with the house of David, "like God, like the angel of the LORD, at their head" (12:8). But this house of David will not set itself up over the people. Judah will be restored *before* Jerusalem, lest the Jerusalemites be exalted over them (12:7). David's house will weep for "the one whom they have pierced" (12:10–12), but God will open a fountain to cleanse David's house and Jerusalem from impurity (13:1).

For Isaiah, David's charisma outlasts his dynasty and devolves on the people themselves. For Jeremiah, the Davidic kings are as corrupt as the rest of the people's leaders—but after punishment, God will remake the dynasty, as well as the people, in a more faithful form. Zechariah also foresees eschatological glory, but in terms which bespeak bitter memories of oppression by David's house. Ezekiel uses David's name only in association with the glorious image of restoration.

Finally, we recall that although Genesis never mentions David's name, its ancestor stories echo many themes from Samuel's tales about David's family.

SUMMARIZING OUR FINDS

We have now looked at three major presentations of David—the primary history's realistic mural, Chronicles' stained-glass window, and the Psalter's collage—as well as scattered reflections elsewhere in the Hebrew Bible. Each major portrait exhibits a unique character. The books of Samuel show a flamboyant, successful leader whose greatest difficulties arise in his personal life. We are never quite sure of his motives, but we cannot deny that "LORD is with him." Chronicles plays down the personal aspects, good and bad, of David's life to emphasize his unity with "all Israel" and especially its leaders—a unity undergirding temple arrangements right down to the readers' present. In Psalms David starts out confident that God will answer his cries. He emerges from the crisis of defeat in Book 3 with a new consciousness of covenant, community, and the joy of life before God.

Every portrait situates David at the point where God, in that portrayal, most affects human existence. Samuel and Kings stress the king's role in national well-being and the terrible ways in which his personal misdeeds can impact the nation. Chronicles also sets David at the heart of community life, but Chronicles' heart is the temple. The Psalter's David promises both refuge for individuals who place their trust in God and joyous celebration for the congregation whose king is God. Elsewhere, God's help comes in David's name (Isaiah of Jerusalem) and God's punishment upon David's house (Jeremiah's warnings and condemnations; here, the junction of human life and divine intervention is not a pleasant location). When hope turns to God's future intervention, "David" becomes the promised messianic king (Jeremiah, Ezekiel, Zechariah) or paradigm for a redeemed people (Isa 55).

Each portrait has its own tensions. In 1 and 2 Samuel, uncertainty over David's own character swells outward into questions about God's justice and benevolence without erasing the assertion of divine favor for David. The prophets wrestle with the balance between God's loyalty to David's house and discipline for a nation gone astray. Chronicles, at first glance, seems free of tension. God's rules are clear, and David conducts himself in accord with them. But intertextual ties to Kings and Ezra-Nehemiah raise questions. How do we square David the temple-planner with the charming rogue of Samuel and the dynastic founder of Kings? Shall Israel's boundaries be defined by Moses and his disciples Ezra and Nehemiah, who command the exclusion of "foreigners," or by David—himself an alien and transient[7] before God?

Psalms asks again about the relationship of Mosaic and Davidic covenants. It ponders the relationship of individual trust (royal or otherwise) to communal celebration, and asks—more straightforwardly than the other books under discussion here—what we should think when the wicked prosper at the expense of the righteous. David flickers in and out of focus—now himself, now Israel, now any worshiper.

In a sense, the book of Psalms embraces and integrates the Hebrew canon's other David portraits. Figure 1 sketched the Psalter's dynamics on a diamond grid. Figure 2 takes the same grid (with some labeling removed to reduce clutter) and locates the other David portraits on it with respect to their interpretations and interests.

I locate the books of Samuel near the top of the diamond for three reasons. First, the Samuel portrait stresses David's historical context (whether or not it gives us an accurate picture of that context). If Samuel were performed on stage, it would call for exotic, antique-looking sets and costumes. (Sets and costumes for Chronicles would need a minimalist touch, using stylized designs with contemporary overtones.) To the extent that the Psalter is also an imaginative history of Israel, Samuel's David belongs near the beginning of it. The *lĕdāvid* and situational headings in Books 1 and 2 of the Psalter—and repetition of 2 S 22 in Ps 18—also pull Samuel to this position. Finally, Book 1's type profile (heavy concentration of individual laments) suits David's self-interestedness in Samuel.

The books of Samuel balance interest in David's personal affairs with a firm insistence on his royal status and its consequences for the nation. For this reason I center Samuel horizontally between the individual and community readings.

The books of Kings do something a little different with David, relocating him in a line that stretches from God's contract with Israel at Sinai (the Torah emphasis of Ps 1) to a point just past the dynasty's fall (halfway down the diamond). The strong national orientation of this treatment puts it on

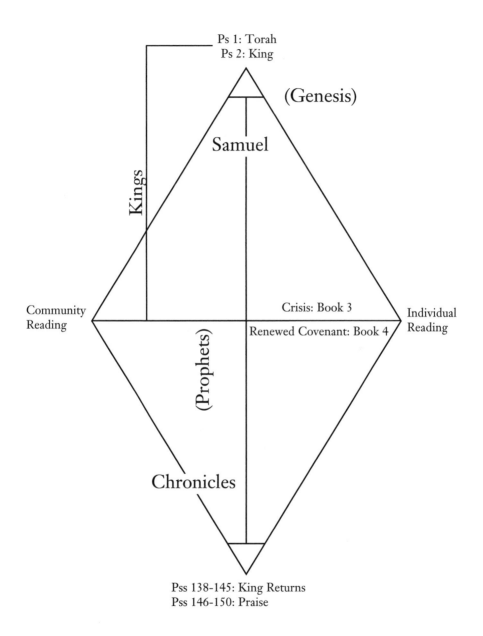

Figure 2. Relative Locations of David Portraits

the left (community) side of the grid. This line does not enter the study-and-worship dynamics of the Second Temple portion of the diamond.

Chronicles also belongs on the community side of the diagram, but it has little concern with the monarchic questions of the top half, nor even much interest in the Torah dynamics which stretch from Ps 90 to Ps 119. It has great affinity indeed for the Jerusalem-oriented Ascents collection, David's trust in God in 138–145, and the closing Hallelujah psalms.

Prophetic references to David scatter beyond the area indicated in Figure 2, but frequent eschatological references put the prophetic allusions, as a group, close to the messianic interpretive line. The second most common type of David reference—warning and condemnation—pulls the group leftward (in the direction of community concern) a little. I put prophetic references below the centerline because they share Book 4's sense of deserved judgment, rather than interpreting disaster as a breach of contract on God's part or simply appealing for rescue (as psalms prior to 89 more commonly do).

I have placed Genesis above Samuel because it occurs in a time frame prior to the monarchy, and somewhat to the right because its stories, with all their Davidic innuendoes, emphasize personal relationship to God. One could argue, however, that its promises of national blessing and concern about boundaries (may the patriarch marry a foreigner?) should put it nearer to Chronicles.

Now, what do we do with all this? As I reflect on my years of work with David, I note how difficult it has been to break free of the "good David" reading of 1 and 2 Samuel. Having been taught that the Samuel books defend David—and God—I had difficulty crediting the many troubling details in the primary history's mural. In my struggle to understand the Hebrew Bible's cumulative picture of David, I now find it easier to begin with the royal psalms and their fairly standard ancient Near Eastern picture of the deity and king as mutually supportive "father" and "son." Chronicles, seeing the positive aspects of this relationship, depicts it in stained glass as a model for community life. Messianic prophetic passages, seeing more discrepancy between the ideal and life, refract the picture forward to a utopian future.

Samuel (with resonant echoes in Genesis) and Kings contextualize the royal rhetoric in a "realistic" mural, forcing us to confront the practical implications of claims for special divine favor. The imaginative horizon of this presentation is, as we have seen, exile, but that may simply be a way of reinforcing its shadows and denying the legitimacy of the Davidic tradition's later claimants. The Samuel-Kings presentation of royal tradition problematizes our understanding not only of the Davidic kings but of the God who supports (and eventually rejects) them.[8]

Were this shadowed picture the only one we had of David, I think he would be less popular than he is. But a purely idealized picture would, I think, have perished even faster. We can see already, in the situational psalm headings, how the primary history's complex picture of David captured imaginations. It surely enhanced the movement by which private individuals found themselves emboldened to pray the king's prayers.

The Hebrew Bible's David stands perpetually at the point where divine power enters our world. We are fascinated by both his charisma (in all senses) and his flaws. We embrace him as a concrete and very human individual (1 and 2 Samuel), yet we are also invited, individually and communally, to enter into his relationship with God (Chronicles and Psalms). We can see in him, if we like, confirmation of our most cynical suspicions about the ways of power. But most people, along with the Hebrew Bible's prophets, see something else. It can seem that God—if there is one—is mostly a God of anger. "Weeping may linger for the night," David responds (Ps 30:5), "but joy comes with the morning."

NOTES

CHAPTER 1—AN INVITATION

1. The Hebrew Bible mentions David about 1,080 times, compared with 772 for Moses, 359 for Jacob, and 236 for Abraham/Abram. The New Testament also mentions David frequently (58 times), although less frequently than Moses (80 times) or Abraham (75 times).
2. Christians especially seem to look for a single, unified biblical system. Jewish commentary is typically more willing to see diversity in both the Bible and the interpretation thereof.
3. Not all critical scholars rule out miracles or inspired prediction, although in the present generation a heavy majority are dubious about "miracles." This scepticism is partly learned from previous generations of critical scholars who did believe in miracles, sought to prove that they had really happened, and discovered—to their dismay—that they could not produce such proof. The search for evidence of Joshua's conquest at Jericho is a famous example of such failure (Holland, "Jericho," 736).
4. I follow the *Journal of Biblical Literature*'s system which gives each Hebrew consonant a one-letter English equivalent. Pronounce š as "sh," ṣ as "ts," and ḥ as a cross between "h" and "k" (like the "ch" in the Scottish word "loch"). ʾ and ʿ are silent.

CHAPTER 2—LOOKING FOR DAVID

1. Dempster, "Elhanan." The Chronicles parallel (1 C 20:5) makes the father's name Jair and the victim "Lahmi, the brother of Goliath the Gittite, the shaft of whose spear. . . ." "Lahmi" is the second half of the word "Bethlehemite" which appears in Samuel but not in Chronicles.
2. Levenson, "1 Samuel 25," 27; Levenson and Halpern, "Political Import."
3. Edelman, "Ahinoam," 118.
4. The Hebrew reads "your master's women" (there is no separate word for "wife"), but I think NRSV has correctly interpreted the implications.
5. Besides Ahinoam, one may certainly point to Michal, Abigail, and Maacah. Levenson and Halpern, "Political Import."
6. Mettinger speaks of trying to "reconstruct a reality that can explain the historical evidence" (the "historical evidence" being scripture). *King and Messiah*, 16.
7. McCarter, "The Historical David," quotes from 121 and 128. Several other articles on David appear in the same issue of *Interpretation*.

8. The inscription was first announced in the popular article "'David' Found at Dan" (listed in the bibliography under that title). A more technical analysis by Biran and Naveh appeared later ("An Aramaic Stele Fragment from Tel Dan"). The find ignited a bitter controversy. For arguments against the "House of David" translation, see the articles by Lemche and Thompson ("Did Biran Kill David?"), Davies ("*Bytdwd* and *Swkt Dwyd*") and Ben Zvi ("On the Reading '*bytdwd*'"). These articles give further bibliography, including reference to a claim that another long-known ancient inscription actually contains David's name. Baruch Halpern ("Erasing History") reviews arguments in favor of the David translation. "City of David" excavations in Jerusalem purport to show us a piece of the Davidic city wall, but we have no way of knowing whether the wall in question was associated with anyone named David.

9. Flanagan, *David's Social Drama*. The book—which unfortunately is rather difficult for lay readers to penetrate—explores relationships between archaeological impressions of Israelite society, patterns observed in contemporary communities of similar social structure, and David's role in the various biblical texts. The main discussion of Ibn Saud comes in Appendix 2.

10. Dever, "Archaeology and the 'Conquest,'" 549. Shanks et al., *The Rise of Ancient Israel*, offers the lay reader a more extended glimpse of debate on the subject.

11. Thompson, *Early History of the Israelite People*, 409–11.

12. This scheme is especially associated with the name of Leonhard Rost. His seminal work has been published in English as *The Succession to the Throne of David*.

13. Anderson, *Understanding the Old Testament*, 228.

14. Delekat, "Tendenz und Theologie," quotes from 28 and 34–35, my translation, author's emphasis.

15. Whybray proposes the education hypothesis in *The Succession Narrative*; Gunn proposes entertainment in *King David*, 61–62.

16. Noth, *Deuteronomistic History*, 89–92; von Rad, "The Deuteronomic Theology of History in I and II Kings," 219–20; Japhet, "The Supposed Common Authorship" and *I & II Chronicles*, 3–7; Williamson, *Israel in the Books of Chronicles*. With regard to Chronicles, Williamson's pages on ideology (60–70) would be the most interesting reading for nonspecialists.

17. Gunn, *King David*, 32–33 and 46–62 (these arguments are more technical than his interpretive discussion in Chapter 5); Flanagan, "Court History or Succession Document?"; Van Seters, *In Search of History*, 277–91.

18. McKenzie, *The Chronicler's Use of the Deuteronomistic History*. Different versions of the Samuel book may have existed in different geographical regions.

19. The Hebrew word in Ps 51:18 could be translated simply "build." However, this does not remove the problem, for David reportedly captured the city with its walls intact (1 S 5:6–8). If these verses have been added (an explanation proposed by many commentators), then the psalm as it stands is not written by David.

20. Childs summarizes these expansions, with references, in "Psalm Titles and Midrashic Exegesis," 142–43.

21. Wilson, "The Use of the Royal Psalms." For more information on the overall structure of Psalms, see *The Editing of the Hebrew Psalter*, also by Wilson, and *The Shape and Shaping of the Psalter*, edited by J. Clinton McCann, Jr.

22. The window/picture figure comes from Trible (*Rhetorical Criticism*, 97), who attributes it to Macky, "The Coming Revolution." On 98–99, Trible discusses an additional metaphor, the text as mirror.

23. Sternberg, *Poetics of Biblical Narrative*, 193–96.

24. My translation. The NRSV translators, knowing something has been left out, insert ellipses here.

25. Sternberg, *Poetics of Biblical Narrative* (mentioned earlier in conjunction with 2 S 11:1). In "Reading Right," Gunn criticizes Sternberg's position. He and Fewell have a nice discussion of God as character in *Narrative in the Hebrew Bible*, especially 81–89.

26. Wesley Kort in *Story, Text and Scripture* offers an interesting discussion of types of literary approaches to the Bible.

27. A comparison stressed, for instance, by Harold Bloom in the concluding chapter to *The Book of J*.

28. In general terms, Sternberg, Fokkelman, Polzin, and Brueggemann could all be described as "critical" interpreters, but in various ways their work still seems deeply shaped by traditional assumptions, especially about God's character. Brueggemann, to his credit, openly acknowledges such commitments.

29. Polzin, *David and the Deuteronomist*, 96–98.

30. The American Standard Version (1901) uses a very "literal" translation style and can be another helpful tool for following literary arguments. Except for this specialized purpose, I prefer a translation such as NRSV, which uses more recent textual scholarship and renders meaning in more fluent English.

31. For a brief and clearly written exploration of this ambiguity, see Perdue, "Is There Anyone Left?"

32. Bakhtin, *Dialogic Imagination*, 420–21.

33. Polzin, *David and the Deuteronomist*, discussion of the parable from 122–30, quote from 122. This is one volume of a series which also includes *Moses and the Deuteronomist* and *Samuel and the Deuteronomist*. (A volume or volumes on the kings and the Deuteronomist will presumably follow.)

34. Polzin, *David and the Deuteronomist*, 128–30.

35. Fokkelman, *King David*, discussion of the parable 71–87, quote from 79–80. This book is one of a four-volume series entitled *Narrative Art and Poetry in the Books of Samuel*.

36. For discussions of this phenomenon with respect to the succession narrative, see Gunn, *Story of King David*, 81–84; and Ackroyd, "The Succession Narrative (So-Called)."

CHAPTER 3—SAMUEL'S DAVID: PRELUDE

1. Many Bible passages refer to God as "the LORD," with "LORD" in large and small capital letters. The Hebrew text of these verses contains a proper name,

YHWH, which was probably pronounced "Yahweh." ("Jehovah" is an incorrect medieval reconstruction of this same name.) For various reasons, most Jews and Christians during the last two thousand years have not used the proper name. Instead they say "the Lord." NRSV, like many other English translations, follows this custom, but it uses large and small capital letters to show that LORD represents God's name and not just the ordinary Hebrew title "Lord" (which also appears occasionally). Since Lord actually represents a name, I will use it without a preceding "The" (for instance, "LORD says" rather than "The LORD says"), except when I am quoting someone else's work.

2. Polzin, *Samuel and the Deuteronomist*, 22–30.
3. Quite a lot of ink has been spilled on the subject of whether Samuel himself is priest or prophet. Many of the most famous prophets (including Isaiah, Ezekiel, and Jeremiah) apparently *were* priests. Our own tendency to see the roles as opposed may derive from Protestant biblical scholars who have seen the Roman Catholic hierarchy as "priests" and themselves as "prophets." Although I think the priest/prophet disjunction has been overemphasized, in this passage both similarity (*neʾeman*) and difference (priest/prophet) seem significant. Samuel both is and is not the promised leader.
4. Most Hebrew words are built by adding vowels and modifiers to a three-consonant core. For instance, the core consonants *špṭ* underlie the verb "he judged/ governed" (*šāpaṭ*), the noun "judge/governor" (*šōpēṭ*), and the noun "justice/ judgment" (*mišpāṭ*). Here I use the core consonants for a collective reference to various conjugated forms of the verb. If I said "words of the *špṭ* family," I would be referring not only to the verb, but also nouns and adjectives built on that three-consonant core.
5. Fokkelman, *Vow and Desire*, 326.
6. Eslinger, *Kingship of God in Crisis*, 252–82.
7. Miscall, *1 Samuel*, 47.
8. Gunn, *Fate of King Saul*, 59.
9. NRSV follows the Greek text here (as the translation's textual footnote tells us) in rendering "just as they have done *to me*." Whether or not this was part of the original Hebrew text, it is certainly implied.
10. Miscall, *1 Samuel*, 48.
11. Polzin, *Samuel and the Deuteronomist*, 87–88.
12. Fokkelman, *Vow and Desire*, 323 and 340.
13. Gunn, *Fate of King Saul*, 61; Polzin, *Samuel and the Deuteronomist* 87; Eslinger, *Kingship of God in Crisis*, 251–82, quote from 269.
14. Augustine, "On Christian Doctrine," Chapter III, 154.
15. Miscall, *1 Samuel*, 49; Bakhtin, *Dialogic Imagination*, 420–21.
16. Polzin, *Samuel and the Deuteronomist*, 87.
17. Mettinger, *King and Messiah*, 151–84.
18. It is grammatically possible (barely) to understand the Hebrew sentence so that the "he" of the verb refers to Samuel and the "he" of "his words" refers to God, thus: "Samuel let none of LORD's words fall to the ground." However, inter-

preters of widely varying ideologies overwhelmingly opt, with good reasons, for a reading such as NRSV's.

CHAPTER 4—SAMUEL'S DAVID AS INNOCENT AND ATTRACTIVE HERO

1. Levenson rejects "fool" (see the NRSV textual note on 1 S 25:25 NRSV) on the grounds that *nābāl* means "not a harmless simpleton, but rather a vicious, materialistic, and egocentric misfit" ("1 Samuel 25," 13).
2. NRSV follows Chronicles in naming the son Ishbaal. Samuel's Hebrew text gives the name as Ishbosheth, with *bōšet* ("shame") taking the place of *baʿāl* ("Lord," title of a Canaanite god and possibly also for Israel's God in Saul's time).
3. "Father" here is used in the sense of "forefather" or "ancestor."
4. Elsewhere Kings says of Josiah, "Before him there was no king like him, who turned to the LORD with all his heart, with all his soul, and with all his might, according to all the law of Moses; nor did any like him arise after him" (2 K 23:25; compare Dt 6:5).

CHAPTER 5—TROUBLING DETAILS: READING DAVID'S HEART

1. Sternberg, *Poetics of Biblical Narrative*, 326 and 348.
2. I follow and extend the contrasts of Fokkelman's chart, *Vow and Desire*, 548.
3. For a wonderfully detailed discussion of the nuances of such literary technique, see Lanser, *The Narrative Act*. Berlin's *Poetics and the Interpretation of Biblical Narrative* is a good introduction to point-of-view theory as it applies specifically to the Hebrew Bible.
4. NRSV glosses over the impact: "When David and his men came to the city, they found it burned down." Compare KJV: "So David and his men came to the city, and, behold, it was burned with fire." The term which KJV translates "behold" often marks entry into a character's point of view (Berlin, *Poetics*, Chapter 3).
5. 1 Samuel 17:23; 20:39; 23:26; 26:3–5; 30:3, 16; 2 S 1:2; 13:36, and all the instances in 2 S 15 and 16.
6. Paley was a student of Polzin, who quotes her in *David and the Deuteronomist*, 91 and 222 n.
7. Fokkelman, *Crossing Fates*, 261 n. 23. On the good, "giving" (passive) David and the bad, "grasping" David, see Gunn, *King David*, 85–111.
8. Klein, *1 Samuel*, 234.
9. Fokkelman, *Crossing Fates*, 453.
10. Fokkelman, *Crossing Fates*, 455. The Hebrew text does not contain the word "cloak." NRSV and most other English translations, like the ancient Greek, fill it in.
11. Fokkelman, *Crossing Fates*, 453–59. *Māšîaḥ* (anointed one) occurs twelve times in 1 Samuel, seven of which are in 1 S 24 and 26.
12. Polzin, *Samuel and the Deuteronomist*, 210.
13. Perdue, "Is There Anyone Left?" 80.

14. Polzin, *Samuel*, 71. The pronoun in the last part of 1 S 6:20 is ambiguous: I refer it to the ark ("it"), whereas NRSV refers it to God ("he").

15. David's linen ephod creates another parallel with Samuel.

16. 2 S 5:20—*pāraṣ* "burst forth," *pereṣ* an "outburst" of water, and *pĕrāṣîm* (twice) in "Baal-*Perazim*"; 2 S 6:8—*pāraṣ* "burst forth," *pereṣ* "outburst" and *pereṣ* in "*Perez-Uzzah*." Fokkelman, *Throne and City*, 195.

17. Brueggemann comments, "the death has its salutory effect; David becomes freshly afraid of Yahweh" (*First and Second Samuel*, 249).

18. NRSV interpretively expands: "to me" becomes "into my care."

19. Obed-Edom is identified as a Gittite, that is, a citizen of Gath, which is one of the five Philistine cities. Polzin offers the intriguing observation that only here, in the entire deuteronomic history, is God said to bless a house/household (*David and the Deuteronomist*, 65).

20. Fokkelman, *Throne and City*, 180 and 190.

21. Fokkelman, *Throne and City*, 210–11.

22. Bailey, *David in Love and War*, 85.

23. Sternberg, *Poetics of Biblical Narrative*, Chapter 6.

24. Fokkelman, *King David*, 76.

25. Polzin, *David*, 124.

26. Polzin, *David*, 125–26.

27. Linafelt ("Taking Women in Samuel") and Fewell and Gunn ("In the Shadow of the King," Chapter 7 of *Gender, Power, and Promise*) explore the meaning of this for women in David's story. Both discussions accuse the narrator of not caring about the women's fates. Why else, however, do we see Paltiel weeping in 2 S 3:16 or hear about the concubines' "widowhood" in 2 S 20:3?

28. Other possible instances are 1 S 16:21 (Saul), 18:3, and 20:17 (Jonathan). Each of these statements takes the form "he loved him." In each, it is not absolutely clear who loved whom, but interpreters overwhelmingly (and I think correctly) understand David as the beloved rather than the lover in all three cases.

29. If there is an insinuation of pretense in 2 S 14:2, it lies not in the basic meaning of the verb, but in the particular form of it (hithpaʿel) which is used.

30. The verb *tkl* calls for a feminine subject, which we have if we take the "spirit of" the king as subject, per some of ancient Greek manuscripts and (apparently) 4QSam^a at Qumran (which shows part of the word "spirit," although not the whole word). McCarter, *II Samuel*, 338.

31. This third possibility is endorsed by Fokkelman (*King David*, 126), who credits it to his colleague K. Jongeling.

32. NRSV translates "mind."

33. McCarter, *II Samuel*, 338; Anderson, *2 Samuel*, 187.

34. Fokkelman, *King David*, 126, referring to an article by K. Jongeling. McCarter and Anderson follow a minority manuscript tradition which changes "all the days" to "many days." (It is not clear which reading NRSV follows with "day after day.") Polzin says the matter "remains opaque" (*David and the Deuteronomist*, 133).

35. At a few points during the intervening narration we may share David's perception (2 S 15:24, 32; 16:1, 5, 14), but these brief glances outward tell us nothing about his inner life.

36. Fokkelman, *King David*, 263.

37. Brueggemann, "2 Samuel 21–24: An Appendix of Deconstruction?"; Gunn, "In Security." Gunn's arguments appear in briefer form in "2 Samuel," 302–4; and in Gunn and Fewell, *Narrative and the Hebrew Bible*.

38. Cazelles, "David's Monarchy and the Gibeonite Claim"; Kapelrud, "King and Fertility" and "King David and the Sons of Saul."

39. Brueggemann, "Appendix of Deconstruction?" 390–92 and 386; Gunn, "In Security," 134–36.

CHAPTER 6—TROUBLING DETAILS: DAVID'S WORDS AND DEEDS

1. Steussy, "The Problematic God of Samuel."

2. Alter, *The Art of Biblical Narrative*, 118. Clines points out in the introductory essay of *Telling Queen Michal's Story* (33) that the same point was made by N. J. D. White in a 1902 *Encyclopaedia Biblica* entry on Michal.

3. Porter, "The Interpretation of 2 Samuel 6 and Psalm 132," esp. 164–67.

4. Brueggemann, *First and Second Samuel*, 251.

5. Clines, "The Story of Michal," 139.

6. Clines, "The Story of Michal," 139; Exum, "Murder They Wrote," 185.

7. J. J. Glück argues for the originality of the "Michal" reading ("Merab or Michal?"). He says a scribe would have been unlikely to err on the mother's name, because the maternal connection to Saul is the reason for execution. This requires us to understand 2 S 6:23 as saying that she had *no more* children until she died. Most commentators disagree; for a clear statement of the reasons, see McCarter, *II Samuel*, 439.

8. The Hebrew of 1 S 18:3 has "Jonathan and David" making covenant, but the verb is singular and appears next to Jonathan's name (hence NRSV "Jonathan made a covenant with David"). 1 Samuel 20:16–17 portrays Jonathan as initiator. Only in 23:18 is the act apparently mutual: "they made, the two of them, a covenant" (my translation).

9. Levenson and Halpern, "Political Import," 511. In Hebrew as in NRSV, there is a slight difference in the spelling of the names, but this is not uncommon. For instance, Michal's husband is referred to as Palti in 1 S 25:44 and Paltiel in 2 S 3:15. 1 Chronicles 2:16 spells "Abigail" as 1 S 25 does.

10. The narrator calls Abigail "Nabal's wife" in 1 S 27:3 and 30:5 as well as 2 S 2:2 and 3:3. NRSV smooths things over by changing "wife" to "widow." Compare the references to Bathsheba as Uriah's wife in 2 S 11:26, 12:9–10, 15. Levenson speaks of the Nabal episode as "the very first revelation of evil in David's character" ("1 Samuel 25," 23).

11. The word translated "blameless" is *ṭôb*, which we earlier discussed in connection with the meanings "good" and "handsome."

12. Susanna's story appears as Daniel 13 in Roman Catholic Bibles and as an "Addition to Daniel" in the Protestant Apocrypha.
13. Fokkelman, *King David*, 147.
14. Gunn, "In Security," 135.
15. NRSV's textual note indicates a slight difficulty with this verse, but it does not affect the points made here.
16. Delekat, "Tendenz und Theologie," 29.
17. Levenson and Halpen, "Political Import," discussed earlier in this chapter in connection with 1 S 25:42.
18. Fokkelman, *King David*, 292, commenting on 2 S 19:11–12.
19. Gunn, "2 Samuel," 303.
20. Gunn, "2 Samuel," 303–4; Brueggemann, "2 Samuel 21–24: An Appendix of Deconstruction?" 392–93.
21. Delekat, "Tendenz und Theologie," 33–34.

CHAPTER 7—SAUL, DAVID, AND GOD

1. The passages listed here all use the same Hebrew verb, *ḥml*, meaning to have pity on someone or something, or to spare them. In his response to Nathan's parable, David condemns the man who has no pity, using the same verb *ḥml* (2 S 12:6).
2. Gunn, *Fate of King Saul*, 33–40.
3. Ibid., 41–56.
4. Perhaps Samuel believes that God will not repent because Samuel already asked for such a change of mind in 15:11 when he "cried out to the LORD all night." This is, however, sheer speculation; we do not know exactly what Samuel was upset about or what if anything he requested. At best, such an explanation would yield a Samuel convinced that if he himself got no results, there should be no further trying.
5. An intertextual note: Saul's family finally finds vindication (over a descendant of Agag, no less) in the story of his descendants Esther and Mordecai.
6. Von Rad, "The Beginnings of Historical Writing in Ancient Israel," 204.
7. Bailey, "They're Nothing but Incestuous Bastards."

CHAPTER 8—DAVID'S LEGACY

1. We have already looked at the narrator's handling of Samuel and Nathan. Elisha's cursing (2 K 2:23–24) is a good example of unsympathetic portrayal in Kings. The narrator specifies that the scoffers are *small* boys, and that Elisha sees them—and thus knows they are small boys—before he curses them. Why tell us this if we are to feel unreserved approval of Elisha's curses? An even more complex instance—moving from prophets to the God they serve—involves the lying spirit who enacts God's decree of disaster in 1 K 22:22–23.
2. Eslinger says they accede to God and Samuel's program in 1 S 12 because they realize that "no human power could ever deliver them from this potential enemy [God]" (*Kingship of God in Crisis*, 414).

3. Gunn asks relative to these narratorial evaluations, "what if it is the *narrator* . . . who is the object of the irony?" ("New Directions," 72, author's emphasis). I suggest that the irony twists instead against the prophets (and God) whose voice the narrator mimics. Lyle Eslinger studies "deuteronomistic" evaluative language at length in *Into the Hands of the Living God*. His final chapter has, in addition to a technical analysis of the locations of such language, some interesting comments on narratorial irony in Kings.

CHAPTER 9—CHRONICLES: AN OVERVIEW

1. Jewish tradition divides the Hebrew canon into three parts: the Torah (Genesis through Deuteronomy); the Prophets (subdivided into the Former Prophets— Joshua through Kings, excepting Ruth—and the Latter Prophets, which are Isaiah, Jeremiah, Ezekiel, and Hosea through Malachi); and the Writings (all the rest of the books including Psalms, Daniel, Chronicles, and Ezra-Nehemiah).
2. Japhet, "The Supposed Common Authorship" and *I & II Chronicles*, 3–7; Williamson, *Israel in the Books of Chronicles*. Williamson's pages on ideology (60–70) would be the most interesting reading for nonspecialists. Klein conveniently summarizes the issues in "Chronicles," 993.
3. For a concise survey of the historical problem and proposed solutions, see Klein, "Ezra-Nehemiah," 735–37.
4. Cyrus conquered Babylon about half a century after Babylon captured Judah. The middle portion of Isaiah, which most scholars think was written in Cyrus's time, refers to Cyrus as God's "anointed one" (*māšîaḥ*, see Isa 45:1).
5. NRSV follows the Greek text in which Ezra gives this lecture (Neh 9:6). According to the Hebrew text (see NRSV's textual note), Levites deliver the speech.
6. Van Seters, *In Search of History*, 277–91, argues that the succession narrative was added in a late (postexilic) revision of Samuel rather than being one of its earliest sources. Auld, *Kings Without Privilege*, argues for a common Samuel/Chronicles source which would not have included this material or anything else not held in common.
7. Duke, *Persuasive Appeal*, 36–37.
8. For more on mixed marriages in Chronicles, see Williamson, *Israel*, 60–61.
9. On the form and function of genealogies, see Wilson, "Genealogy, Genealogies." De Vries' commentary in the Forms of the Old Testament Literature series also attends carefully to genres of lists and genealogies.
10. Osborne, *The Genealogies of I Chronicles 1–9*, referenced repeatedly by Duke, *Persuasive Appeal*.

CHAPTER 10—DAVID'S DEEDS IN CHRONICLES

1. This account telescopes the entire period up to and including the investiture in Hebron. The Hebrew terms used for these warriors suggest something like knights—not merely good military athletes, but men with the wealth to equip themselves well.

2. This may be the same person referred to in 2 S 23:8 as Josheb-basshebeth ("the one who sits in the seat"). For speculation on the original form of the name, see Duke, "Jashobeam." What interests me is not what the man might actually have been called but the form his name takes in Chronicles.

3. For information on various groups of singers, see the *Anchor Bible Dictionary* under the Levitical names (Asaph, Korah, etc.).

4. If David remained at Jerusalem, how did he take the crown from Milcom's head? His remaining makes sense in Samuel's story, which also explains David's later arrival at Rabbah (2 S 12:26–29). It makes less sense in Chronicles. On the other hand, the previous chapter (in both books) also reports that David "sent Joab" (2 S 10:7, 1 C 19:8) against the Ammonites, apparently not accompanying the army himself.

5. NRSV and other translations going all the way back to the ancient Greek have read "Satan" as a proper name, but it could equally well be an indefinite common noun. Chronicles generally does *not* depict the universe dualistically; it ascribes both good and ill fortune to God. If the writer does allude to a supernatural adversary, it is probably—like the *śāṭān* of Job 1–2—a prosecuting attorney in God's own court rather than a demonic rival (Japhet, *I and II Chronicles*, 374–75).

6. 1 Chronicles 4:10; 5:20; 21:28; 2 C 12:7, 12; 14:11–12, 15:2–7, 15; 20:9, 15; 30:18–20; 32:20–21, 24–26; 33:12–13; 34:26–27. In Samuel, David's statement echoes those in 2 S 12:22 and 16:12.

7. The *biographical* location of the census/plague story is unclear, especially in 2 Samuel: we do not know exactly when it is supposed to have occurred vis-à-vis other events in David's life. *Narratively*, however, both Samuel and Chronicles put the story just before their discussions of Solomon's succession.

8. Negative for Joab and Shimei, positive for Barzillai's sons.

9. 2 Chronicles 1:4; 2:7, 12, 14; 3:1; 5:1; 6:7–8; 7:6; 8:14; 23:18; 29:25–27, 30; 33:7; 35:4, 15.

10. 2 Chronicles 1:8–9; 6:4, 6, 10, 15–17, 42; 7:18; 13:5, 8; 21:7; 23:3.

11. 2 Chronicles 7:17; 11:17; 24:2; 28:1; 29:2.

12. 2 Kings 14 and 15 refer to this king sometimes as Uzziah, sometimes as Azariah. Perhaps these are his throne and personal names, respectively.

13. 1 Kings 14:25–28 records only Shishak's attack and Rehoboam's substitution of bronze shields for gold; the entire interchange involving Shemaiah is lacking.

14. 2 Chronicles 10:13–17, 15:9–12, 28:8–15, 30:11, 18–20.

CHAPTER 11—DAVID'S MESSAGE TO YEHUD

1. The "rest" verb under discussion also appears in conjunction with sabbath legislation (Ex 20:11, 23:12, Dt 5:14). I mention it here because sabbath and temple are closely connected. The temple is a sacred location in *space*, sabbath a sacred location in *time*.

2. Japhet, *I and II Chronicles*, 333. The alliteration of *b* and *n* sounds is missing in Samuel, where God will "make" (*yaʿăśeh*, 2 S 7:11) a house and raise one "out of thy bowels" (7:12 KJV, *mimmaʿêkā*) to build the house.

3. Church Bible study materials often use the same technique. Writers restate and paraphrase Bible material in a form similar enough to the source story that most users accept the retellings as accurate renditions. In fact, however, the retellings drop, add, and alter details in ways which may substantially change perception of the story. For instance, many mainline Protestant Sunday School books interpret the flood story as an example of God's love for all creatures, glossing over the destruction of all creatures not on the ark.

4. Joshua hears this from Moses in Dt 31:7–8, 23. He also hears it from God (Josh 1:6–7, 9) and the people (Josh 1:18). Exact wording varies slightly from occurrence to occurrence. Braun, "Solomon, the Chosen Temple Builder," 587.

5. Braun, "Solomon, the Chosen Temple Builder," 589.

6. 1 Chronicles 12:38 uses a different word for "single" than the other three verses discussed here.

7. 1 Chronicles 29:5, 6, 9 (twice), 14, and 17 (twice). 2 Chronicles uses words from this family in association with the David-like kings Hezekiah (29:31 and 31:14) and Josiah (35:8).

8. This charge from David forms the basis of William How's hymn "We Give Thee but Thine Own."

9. Carroll comments, "a squalid deportation of disruptive elements has been thereby [by the ideology of exile and return] transformed into a significant exile of leadership elements awaiting the work of Yahweh in restoration" ("Israel, History of," 574–75). The first part of his sentence describes the situation as both Babylonians and the other Judeans may have understood it; the second part expresses the viewpoint of the exiles themselves, or their descendants, as handed down in the Bible.

10. Stern, *Material Culture*, 229.

11. For more on the ideology of this argument, see Carroll, "The Myth of the Empty Land."

12. Hanson, *The People Called*, 264.

13. For an excellent summary of Chronicles' position relative to Ezra-Nehemiah's on the genealogical boundaries of Israel, see Williamson, *Israel in the Books of Chronicles*, 60–61 and 87–140.

14. 1 Chronicles 15:1, 3, 12; 22:3, 5 twice, 14 twice; 28:2, 29:2, 3, 19; 2 C 1:4, 2:6, 3:1.

15. De Vries gives a nice discussion of this position in *1 and 2 Chronicles*, 114–15. From the discussion on 230 I gather that de Vries may see somewhat more hope in Chronicles than I do for restoration of the monarchy, but by and large I find myself in agreement with his comments.

16. I speak here in terms of my artistic metaphor, which compares Chronicles to a stained-glass window. I do not mean to imply that the Second Temple's congregation gathered inside their building (the public worshiped in outdoor courts), much less that the temple actually had stained-glass windows. The "building" in this metaphor is the community and its religious life, not the temple itself.

CHAPTER 12—THE PSALTER: AN OVERVIEW

1. For the convenience of non-Hebrew readers, I have replaced the *w* in the ancient pronunciation of David's name with its modern equivalent, *v*.
2. Interpreting Ps 139 as a psalm of innocence provides a logical bridge between the psalmist's appeal to God's knowledge in 1–18 and the outcry against the wicked in 19–24. Allen provides a nice discussion of the psalm from this angle (*Psalms 101–150*, 260–63).
3. Almost any book about Psalms will supply a list of classifications. Stuhlmueller's introduction to Psalms in *Harper's Bible Commentary* also offers a detailed table (435) which lists composite and contested psalms under multiple headings. Gerstenberger's volume on Psalms in the Forms of the Old Testament Literature series discusses genre in rigorous detail. Readers familiar with the field will notice that I have not distinguished between hymns and songs of praise; so far as I could discern, this distinction had no relevance for my characterization of David.
4. "Cult" because holding a recognized part in officially organized worship (cult); "prophet" because acting as a spokesperson for God. Unfortunately the term suggests a contrast between "cult" and "real" prophets, and also between prophets and priests.
5. The form-critical distinction between songs of praise and hymns bears little relevance for our study of David. For praise hymns from other parts of the ancient Near East, see Pritchard, *Ancient Near Eastern Texts*, Chapter 5.
6. I thank my colleague D. Newell Williams, an American church historian, for this observation. William Bellinger, in his excellent little handbook on Psalms, recommends alertness to this generalizing tendency as a standard part of psalms study (*Psalms*, 29 and 31–32).
7. A late date for the Psalter's final form is suggested by variant forms of the book at Qumran as well as differences between the current Hebrew text and ancient translations (Sanders, *The Dead Sea Psalms Scroll*).
8. In the Psalter as in Chronicles, "Israel" refers to the people as an ideal unity, not (as in most of Samuel) to the northern tribes.

CHAPTER 13—PSALMS SPEAKING ABOUT DAVID

1. "Steadfast love" appears in verses 1, 2, 14, 24, 28, 33, and 49, and "faithfulness" in 1, 2, 5, 8, 24, 33, and 49. The most common Hebrew word for "forever" (*'ôlām*) occurs in 1, 2, 4, 28, 36, and 37, whereas a different one (*neṣaḥ*) appears in 46. Perhaps the *'ôlām* pattern is filled out by a related word *'ălûmāyw* ("his youth") in 45.
2. For a book-length study of this word, see Sakenfeld's *Faithfulness in Action*.
3. Weinfeld, "The Covenant of Grant." For more on Israel's two covenant traditions I highly recommend Levenson's *Sinai and Zion*.
4. For more about this dragon, see Day, "Dragon and Sea." Levenson probes the image's theological significance in *Creation and the Persistence of Evil*.

5. A Babylonian version of this story appears in Pritchard's *Ancient Near Eastern Texts*, 60–72 and 501–3. Thorkild Jacobsen provides an illuminating discussion in *Treasures of Darkness*, Chapter 6. A version from the Syrian city of Ugarit, featuring Baal as the dragon-slaying conqueror, appears in Pritchard (129–42) and Coogan's more readable translation, *Stories from Ancient Canaan*, 86–115.

6. Kraus says that *ḥāsîd* "certainly refers to Nathan" (I disagree) but admits that the relationship between 2 S 7 and Ps 89 is not straightforward (*Psalms 60–150*, 200 and 208). In Chronicles, we recall, David reports being spoken to directly by God. Some Hebrew manuscripts and the Greek refer to "faithful *ones*," so in them the transaction involves three parties: God, David, and the "faithful ones" who have a stake in David's rule.

7. Remember that vowels were added to written Hebrew in the Middle Ages. We know of the old-fashioned word for "lad" through texts from Ugarit, an ancient city which used a language closely related to Hebrew. Dahood explores this (*Psalms*, 2:316) and thousands of other possible connections between Ugaritic and Hebrew poetry in his Anchor Bible commentary on Psalms.

8. We discussed this word in connection with 1 S 9:2, which describes Saul as *bāḥûr*. Joel 2:28 is a good example of *bāḥûr* used with reference to age. (There NRSV translates its plural as "young men.")

9. Fensham, "Father and Son as Terminology for Treaty and Covenant"; Moran, "The Ancient Near Eastern Background of the Love of God in Deuteronomy"; Weinfeld, "The Covenant of Grant."

10. Verses 14 and 24 use different but related words for faithfulness.

11. For instance, Eaton, *Kingship and the Psalms*, 109–11, 121–22. Goulder develops a similar theory but locates the ritual at Dan in the northern kingdom (*Psalms of the Sons of Korah*); he considers that these particular verses in Ps 89 derive not from the ritual but in fact from the fall of the Davidic dynasty (234-38).

12. Sheol seems to have been imagined as a sort of storage pit for the spirits of the dead. It differs from hell in that it is not particularly associated with judgment or punishment, and from heaven in that existence there cannot properly be described as "life." "Who can escape the power of Sheol?" asks exactly the same thing as its parallel, "who can live and never see death?"

13. Even lament psalms usually end with thanks, although not always (see 88).

14. Key comments on the connection between this passage and Ps 89 come from Otto Eissfeldt, "The Promises of Grace to David," and Westermann, *Isaiah 40–66*, 283–84.

15. See Davies, "The Ark in the Psalms." Here, the terms "Mighty One of Jacob" (2 and 5) and "footstool" (7) may also refer to the ark.

16. Chronicles rearranges events so that David receives his palace after the first phase of the ark's relocation (1 C 14:1–6).

17. "Place" in English has no particular religious associations, but Hebrew *māqôm* not infrequently appears in connection with or as a synonym for God's dwelling in Jerusalem. This is the path by which rabbinic interpreters came to regard Morde-

211

cai's statement that "deliverance will rise . . . from another quarter (*māqôm*)" (Esth 4:14) as the book of Esther's one reference to God.

18. We have already seen the importance of *měnûḥâ* ("rest") in Chronicles and associated texts. Numbers 10:33 also speaks of transporting the ark to a place of *měnûḥâ*.

19. Sakenfeld argues that "faithful [ones]" (132:9, 16) may also be a priestly term (*The Meaning of Hesed*, 244).

20. In Hebrew, an oath not to do something is phrased "if (*ʾim*) I do this thing"—presumably short for "if I do this thing may I be cursed." NRSV translates "I will not."

21. In Table 1, I list Ps 132 as a royal psalm because of its concern with dynastic promise. However, the petition/response form qualifies it as a liturgy (recall our earlier discussion of "prophetic liturgies" containing first person address by God). One might also consider it a Zion psalm.

22. Those who suppose an annual ritual of humiliation for the king find reference to it here (Johnson, *Sacral Kingship*, 18). 1 Samuel 6:20–23 also connects humility and the ark transfer, although it uses different vocabulary and a quite different tone.

23. Both Dahood (*Psalms*, 3:238–39) and Crow (*Songs of Ascents*, 97–98) identify the language of Ps 131 as royal.

24. This rule applies even more strongly for those who must work with the text in English translation. Test ideas about meaning by whether they fit with the passage as a whole, rather than building theories upon a single word, which was, after all, chosen by a translator!

25. I do not consider this decisive for interpretation, because a king might well speak of himself in the third person, but it does factor in.

26. The ark's ultimate fate cannot be ascertained from the Hebrew Bible, but it appears to have been lost or destroyed by 586 at the latest, perhaps much earlier. The Bible says nothing about an ark in the Second Temple, despite the attention given it by texts from that period.

27. In "literal" usage *ṣmḥ* describes the growth of hair or vegetation. Metaphorical usages not clearly associated with kingship occur in Isa 42:9 (new things), 43:1 (new thing = return under Cyrus), 44:4 (the people after return), 45:8 (righteousness), 55:8 (your healing), 61:11 (righteousness and praise), and 85:11 (faithfulness), plus a couple of negative instances in Job. Isa 4:2 uses the noun metaphorically for Israel replanted in Zion. The famous "branch" passage in Isa 11:1 uses a similar image but different vocabulary.

28. The first part of Zechariah contains dates from 520 to 518 BCE. The final chapters (9–12) contain no dates and probably come from a later writer.

29. We do hear of a throne (132:11–12) and crown (18), but the high priest in Zechariah has these too.

30. A high-priestly "Branch" might still have military enemies. In Roman times there were certainly groups who expected a priestly messiah to provide military leadership against the forces of evil.

31. The consonants of *tr'm*, "you shall break," could also be read as "you shall shepherd/rule." Ancient Greek and Syriac translators followed the latter option, but the parallel with "dash them in pieces" suggests the former.

32. Possibly they are asked to acknowledge the anointed as well; it depends upon how we translate the very garbled text at the junction of verses 11 and 12. The Hebrew as it stands appears to say "serve LORD fearfully, rejoice tremblingly, kiss son lest he anger . . ." (11–12, my translation). The word translated "son" is not the one used in verse 7 nor one we would expect in this psalm.

33. Compare the strong conflict themes in the *Enuma Elish*, a Mesopotamian story told in support of the monarch (Pritchard, *Ancient Near Eastern Texts*, 60–72 and 501–3).

34. Craigie lists and discusses parallels (*Psalms 1–50*, 173–74). Dahood pursues the possibilities much more aggressively (*Psalms*, 1:101–19).

35. Here we touch upon Zion's status as "navel of the earth"—not merely earth's center, but its junction with the divine realm. For more, see Levenson, *Sinai and Zion*, 115–26.

36. Commentators sometimes identify the king as Ahab, who marries a Phoenician princess (1 K 16:31) and lives in an ivory house (1 K 22:39). Most suppose an Israelite rather than Judean king because Ps 45 belongs to the "Elohistic Psalter" (Pss 42–83), which may be a northern collection. These clues are suggestive rather than definitive, and they are not determinative for our literary reading.

37. Christians read Isa 9:6–7 messianically, but "a son given to us" suggests the birth/adoption language of coronation (compare Ps 2:7).

38. Craigie, *Psalms 1–50*, 338. Royal language in the Song of Solomon has been similarly interpreted.

39. The word which NRSV translates "earth" may also be rendered "land." Recall that Zion is spoken of as the center of the earth.

40. Dahood argues vigorously for this, translating "from the brink of the nether world" (*Psalms*, 1:84–85). I prefer to leave the options open.

41. Verse 8 exhibits mythological dimensions comparable to the sea/rivers language of 89:25. Some assign mundane meanings to each phrase and argue that at its greatest extent the Israelite empire reached these borders, but the realm described by Ps 72 *has* no borders: it includes all the inhabited world.

42. Farmers may be troubled at the image of rain on mown grass. Biblical scholars, some of whom grew up on farms, puzzle over it as well. Some assign other, less common meanings to the word which NRSV translates "mown grass." Alternatively, the image may involve promoting growth prior to or after mowing.

43. Wilson, "The Use of the Royal Psalms."

44. "Power" in 78:61—the same word translated as "might" in 132:8—probably refers to the ark.

45. Whether David or Solomon depends on whether we think the sanctuary of 78:69 is the earthly temple. We simply don't know what event verses 9–10 refer to; scholars have proposed at least half a dozen candidates scattered across seven or eight centuries of "Israel's" history (Tate, *Psalms 51–100*, 284–85 and 288–89).

46. Allen points out that 110:1 is quoted or alluded to more times by the New Testament than any other verse in the Hebrew Bible (*Psalms 101–150*, 87). The psalm is full of text and translation problems. Among them: Do we understand verse 3's *yldtyk* as "your youth" with the Hebrew text, or as "I have begotten you" with the Greek? Is *mlky-ṣdq* in 4 a proper name (Melchizedek, as in NRSV) or a description ("a rightful king," the option given in NRSV's textual note)? I find NRSV's handling of the problems satisfactory.

47. Jesus plays on precisely this tension in Mt 22:44, Mk 12:36, and Lk 20:42, although he applies "my Lord" to an eschatological messiah rather than a past Davidic king. He appears to be arguing that the messiah need not be of Davidic descent—a peculiar agenda if he claimed to be the messiah and was a descendant of David.

48. The connections become even closer if we follow the ancient Greek translation and read "I have begotten you" rather than "your youth" in the second part of verse 3.

49. A shortened name for Jerusalem, found also in Psalm 76:2.

50. In 2 S 12:20 David goes to "the house of the LORD," but elsewhere, as we know, Samuel and Kings identify Solomon as house-builder.

51. "Jerusalem" (*yĕrûšālayim*), "to it" (*šĕššām*), "name" (*šēm*), "there" (*šāmmāh*), "peace of" (*šĕlôm*), "prosper" (*yišlāyû*), "security" (*šalwâ*).

52. "LORD" occurs four times in NRSV because the translation does not distinguish between the four-letter name YHWH used in 1, 4b, and 9, and a shortened form (YH) used in 4a.

53. The verb "bound" is usually used for human bonds rather than architectural ones. But the parallelism of the line suggests physical rather than social binding. The city's physical qualities reappear as a motif in 7's "walls" and "towers."

54. This parallel is more evident in Hebrew, which uses the same preposition in both parts: "thrones *lĕ*-judgment, thrones *lĕ*-the-house of-David."

55. We discussed this family of words in connection with 1 S 7:15–8:6, where an aging Samuel appoints his sons as *šōpṭîm*, but they corrupt *mišpāṭ*, and Israel's elders respond by asking for a king to *špṭ* the people.

56. The word translated as "throne" in Ps 122 is also used of the priest Eli's seat (1 S 1:9; 4:13, 18), the queen mother's seat (1 K 2:19), a chair in Elisha's lodgings (2 K 4:10), and the sitting-place of the proverbial "foolish woman" (Pr 9:13). In Persian-era context, we hear of thrones for the emperor's adviser Haman (Esth 3:1) and a provincial governor (Neh 3:7, NRSV translates "jurisdiction"). For examples of "thrones" associated with justice/judgment, see Isa 9:7 and 16:5 (David's throne); Pr 16:12, 20:8, and 29:14 (kingly thrones in general); and Ps 9:4, 7; 11:4; 89:14; 97:2 (God's throne). Daniel 7:9, written in Aramaic, offers a related image. Anderson (*Psalms 73–150*, 107) mentions this connection between thrones and justice.

57. Allen, *Psalms 101–150*, 155. He assumes that the occupants, rather than seats, are subject of the verb "sit."

58. Hebrew verbs are less definite about time frame than English ones, so Allen's "sits" (quoted above) does not require a change in the text.
59. A connection with Deuteronomy seems feasible given the reference to decree in 122:4. The Deuteronomy passage designating the central sanctuary as a center of justice appears immediately before the "law of the king" (Dt 17:14–20).
60. Over whom is the king given dominion? The standard Hebrew text of 144:2 reads "who subdues *my people* under me" (NRSV textual note, emphasis added). However, some Hebrew manuscripts and several ancient translations read "peoples" (NRSV main text) rather than "my people." Because the verb in question is normally used for international dominion rather than the king's governing of his own people, "peoples" is probably the correct choice.
61. Mays, "The David of the Psalms," 153–54. The article appears in an issue of *Interpretation* devoted to different portraits of David.

CHAPTER 14—THE PSALMS OF DAVID

1. Be reminded that I do not include Ps 133 in the *lĕdāvid* collection (my reasons appear in Chapter 12).
2. "Beloved" might further have been either a royal title or a divine one. Lemche and Thompson ("Did Biran Kill David?," 11–15), Davies (*"Bytdwd* and *Swkt Dwyd"*), and Ben Zvi ("On the Reading '*bytdwd*,'" 27–28) all address the divine-title possibility in connection with the inscription mentioned in Chapter 2.
3. Brevard Childs suggests that the relationship between Ps 18 and 2 S 22 played a pivotal role in development of the situational titles ("Psalm Titles and Midrashic Exegesis," 138–43).
4. Discrepancies do exist between the titles and the Samuel narrative. The books of Samuel do not mention "Cush the Benjaminite" (Ps 7), unless this is another name for Shimei. In Samuel, David feigns madness before Achish, not Abimelech (Ps 34). Samuel and Chronicles put the number of Edomite dead in the Valley of Salt (Ps 60) at *eighteen* thousand and attribute the killings to David (2 S 8:13) or Abishai (1 C 18:12), not Joab—although 1 K 11:15 does speak of Joab killing an unspecified number of Edomites.
5. Commentators who assign the bulk of the psalm to David, plus many who read it as an anonymous penitential psalm, usually regard 51:18–19 as later additions. My own final-form approach requires that we interpret the psalm as it stands.
6. Isaiah of Jerusalem, for whom the book is named, prophesied about a century and a half before Jerusalem's fall. Isaiah 40–66, plus scattered other sections, seem to have been added (probably in more than one installment) after Cyrus's appearance on the international scene in the mid-500s BCE (see Isa 44:28 and 45:1). The idea of a community "I" has been around a while, but it was Stuhlmueller's discussion of it in "Psalms," 457–58, that made me appreciate its relevance for Ps 51.
7. Hosea gives the best-known presentation of the adultery metaphor, but the metaphor also appears in Jeremiah (for instance, 2:2, 20, 33; 3:1) and Ezekiel (for instance, Ezek 23).
8. Fokkelman, *King David*, 80, emphasis added.

9. For instance, Holladay, *Psalms Through Three Thousand Years*, 9–10, 23. Though Holladay finds Davidic authorship believable, he also terms it unprovable.

10. The verb *dšn* is employed for anointing (royal or otherwise) only here in Ps 23. Other allusions to nonroyal anointing, using slightly different vocabulary, occur in Eccl 9:8 and Isa 61:3.

11. Only 2 S 12:20 seems to point the other way.

12. Gerstenberger, *Psalms: Part I*, 115, emphasis added.

13. I base this assertion on (1) other usages of the term *ṣlmwt* (NRSV "darkest," KJV "of the shadow of death"), (2) the close connection between trust psalms and laments, and (3) the general absence of hope for an afterlife in the Psalter. For a dissenting opinion on afterlife in Psalms (in general and 23 in particular), see Dahood, *Psalms*, 1:148–49.

14. A few scholars, such as Koehler ("Psalm 23") argue that the shepherd metaphor continues throughout the psalm. Gerstenberger places the psalm in a family/small group worship context and argues that "the role of the sanctuary need not be overemphasized. The psalm mentions neither Zion nor Jerusalem" (*Psalms, Part 1*, 116). But in the present form of the Psalter, if not in the original setting of the psalm, "house of the LORD" does point to Jerusalem. Smith ("Setting and Rhetoric in Psalm 23") reads Ps 23 as a pilgrimage psalm.

15. We have mentioned that the Hebrew text was standardized and provided with vowels by Jewish scholars in the early middle ages. "Dwell" can be derived from the present Hebrew consonants in two ways: by restoring a supposedly lost *y* to the consonantal text or by assigning different vowels to the consonants as they stand.

16. Given the associations we have noted (Chapter 7) between David and the ancestral stories in Genesis, it is interesting that one of the "individual" shepherd references is a *lĕdāvid* psalm, the other a statement by Jacob.

17. Milne, "Psalm 23: Echoes of the Exodus." Most although not all of the examples in these two paragraphs come from Milne's article.

18. Remember that chapters 40–55 of Isaiah concern return from exile.

19. Shepherd imagery appears later in this psalm, 107:41.

20. We find the word elsewhere only in Amos (5:8, a reference to midnight darkness) and nine times in Job (generally dated to sometime after 586).

21. A Qumran manuscript uses this same expression—"holy abode"—in Ps 93:5 (*nwh*, in place of *n'wh* "befits your holiness"), yielding "your house is a holy abode, O LORD" (my translation) and connecting the "pasture" language with God's house (Tate, *Psalms 51–100*, 474; citing Howard, *The Structure of Psalms 93–100*). The closing Hebrew words of 93:5 (NRSV "forevermore") are identical to those of 23:6 (NRSV "my whole life long").

22. Psalm 78 also makes repeated use (78:14, 53, 72) of 23:3's word for "lead." Remember that it uses shepherd imagery for both God and David (78:52, 71–72).

23. See especially 31:14, which echoes Ps 23's verb for "overflowing." The term "fatness" comes from the same *dšn* family as Ps 23's "anoint."

24. Different interpreters find slightly different numbers of trust or confidence psalms. I was encouraged to find that my list coincides with that of Limburg, "Psalms," 532.

25. My discussion of David's situation will parallel, in many ways, the observations offered by Steven Croft (*Identity of the Individual*), although my analysis is confined to David psalms, whereas Croft looks at all "I" psalms regardless of heading. Both my sample and Croft's have a high proportion of individual laments and therefore strongly reflect the features of that genre. It is, after all, the favorite prayer form of the Psalter's David!

26. David psalms which mention false legal charges or attacks on honor include 4, 5, 17, 26, 35, 69, 70, and 139.

27. David laments which affirm the speaker's innocence include 4, 5, 7, 17, 26, 35, 55, 59, 109, 140, and 69 (which we will discuss shortly).

28. Psalms 102 and 130 (both non-Davidic) fill out the traditional list of seven.

29. Note references to sickbed, illness, and infirmities in the preceding verse. This psalm can be read either as petition or as thanksgiving for a healing which has already occurred. Such uncertainty (petition or thanksgiving?) is not unusual in individual laments.

30. These are not the only phrases in these psalms which reflect sickness, nor is it impossible that the two remaining psalms (25 and 40) address such a situation, given the similarities of their language to other psalms which more clearly address sickness.

31. We also saw sickness attributed to God in 2 S 12:15 and 24:15.

32. Psalms which seem to portray foes within the nation include those mentioned in the previous note and 7, 9–10, 11, 25, 27 (?), 28, 36, 54, 55, 57, 59, 62, 63, 64, 109, 138 (?), 140, 141, and 142 (?).

33. Psalms that seem to envision national enemies include 3, 7, 9–10, 18, 20, 21, 27 (?), 56, 60, 68, 86, 108, 110, 124, 143, and 144.

34. Psalm 65 speaks of those who "live in your courts" (4); both psalms mention "awesome deeds" (65:5; 145:6); 65 alludes to a battle with the sea and stilling of "the peoples" (7); 145 wants God's dominion proclaimed to "all people" (12).

35. Outside the David collection, we have royal uses of father/son language in 89:26 and 2:7 plus possibly 80:17 ("and upon the son you made strong for yourself," my translation of the phrase in NRSV's textual note). A general application appears in 73:15 ("the circle of your children"). Psalm 116:16 ("I am your servant, the child of your serving girl") may or may not be royal.

36. "My God" occurs an additional twenty times outside the David psalms. "God of my salvation" (which should arguably be translated "my saving God") is used four times in the David psalms, once elsewhere. Psalm 18:2 uses the related phrase "horn of my salvation." "My rock" appears nine times in the David collection and three times outside, translating two different Hebrew terms. It also appears in NRSV's translation of 144:2, but there the Hebrew reads "my ḥesed." "My fortress" appears nine times in *lĕdāvid* psalms and three times elsewhere, translating two different Hebrew expressions. "My shield" occurs four times in *lĕdāvid*

psalms and once outside. Croft (*Identity of the Individual*, 78) provides a chart listing twenty-three such expressions, although his findings are not organized into Davidic vs. non-Davidic psalms. For several epithets his counts differ from mine, probably because he includes only "I" psalms. For illustrations showing how such concepts were visualized in the ancient Near East, see Keel, *Symbolism of the Biblical World*.

37. These verses use the ordinary Hebrew equivalent of our term love (*'hb*). The only non-David psalm to use *'hb* with God as object is 116:1. Psalm 119 uses "love" (*'hb*) repeatedly for objects such as Torah, commandments, and promise.

38. Five psalms (three of them Davidic) speak of God loving (*'hb*) righteousness and justice and those who enact such. Three psalms, all non-Davidic, mention God's love for Jacob, Judah, and the gates of Zion.

39. Sakenfeld (*Faithfulness in Action*) speaks of loyalty "to a person in need by a person who has the ability to help" (131). In practice this usually means a social superior.

40. Psalms 25:10, 14, and 103:18. Covenant is mentioned sixteen times in non-Davidic psalms. I exclude two references to covenants between human parties.

41. Refuge in God is mentioned thirty-five times in the *lĕdāvid* psalms and thirteen times in other psalms. Trust in God is mentioned seventeen times in the *lĕdāvid* psalms and ten times in other psalms.

42. The David psalms mention crying or calling out (*qr'*) to God thirty times; such language appears nineteen times elsewhere in Psalms. David psalms speak twenty-five times of God answering, with ten instances elsewhere in Psalms. In NRSV, talk of "deliverance" and "salvation" most commonly reflects words in the *yš'* family, occurring seventy-six times in David psalms and fifty-nine times in other psalms.

43. The David psalms speak twenty-five times of fearing God; other psalms use this terminology an additional thirty-one times.

44. Eaton, *Kingship and the Psalms*, especially 70–72, "the king's designations for God as his personal saviour." Croft (*Identity of the Individual*, 77–80) notes that although such terms do occur in nonroyal psalms, they are considerably more frequent in those psalms which he has—on other grounds—judged royal. Although their conclusions reinforce mine, neither studies the David collection as such.

45. In Psalms we find such phrases in 17:8, 57:2, 61:4, 63:7 and (as a possibility for all humankind) 36:7, also in the non-Davidic (but probably royal) Ps 91:4. A connection has been drawn to the cherubim wings which arched over the ark in the Holy of Holies (1 K 6:27 and 8:6–7). For similar images, see Pritchard, *Ancient Near East in Pictures*, figures 377, 379, 416, 458, and 544. Some of these show wings wrapped directly over the king's head; others show them incorporated into the architecture of thrones. Such visual portrayals (in drawings, not photographs) may also be found in Keel's *Symbolism*, figures 19, 21–22, and 260–62, with discussion on 190–92. One could argue on the basis of passages such as Dt 32 (which uses rock, father, apple of eye, and eagle wing language for the people as a whole) that this is not royal language, but I am presently more inclined to think that Deuteronomy deliberately reapplies royal language.

46. NRSV's plurals in these lines attempt to provide inclusiveness, in line with an interpretation we will consider later. The Hebrew singular may be read as either generic (RSV, "what is man") or indefinite ("what is a man"). Patrick Miller relates this psalm to the king's pledge in 7:17 to "sing praise to the name of the LORD, the Most High" ("Beginning of the Psalter," 89–90).

47. For more about this hypothesized royal humiliation, see Klein, "Akitu." The theory of an Israelite New Year Festival is especially associated with Mowinckel (*Psalms in Israel's Worship*, Volume 1, Chapter 5). More recent advocates include Johnson (*Sacral Kingship in Ancient Israel*) and Eaton (*Kingship and the Psalms*). You can read the text of the Babylonian festival in Pritchard, *Ancient Near Eastern Texts*, 331–34.

48. The passion stories of the Christian Gospels provide the best fit, probably because their writers deliberately draw upon the psalm.

CHAPTER 15—DAVID AND THE BOOK OF PSALMS

1. Wilson presents much of this work in summary form in "Shaping the Psalter." It appears in the company of several other very helpful essays in *Shape and Shaping of the Psalter*, edited by McCann.

2. The other Book 1 psalms which lack headings are 10 and 33. Ps 10 lacks one because it continues a psalm begun in 9. There is some evidence that 32 and 33 should also be considered a single psalm (Wilson, *Editing of the Hebrew Psalter*, 173–76).

3. NRSV's plural ("happy are those") respects the inclusive possibilities of Hebrew's masculine singular, but obscures the line's potential royal dimensions. Wilson hesitates to call this a royal psalm but agrees that in a Davidic reading this "would be taken to refer to the *King's* responsibility to protect the poor, widows orphans, etc." (*Editing of the Hebrew Psalter*, 208 n. 15, Wilson's emphasis).

4. Psalms 65 and 68 are Davidic; 66 and 67 anonymous.

5. Walton ("Psalms: A Cantata About the Davidic Covenant") argues that a biographical framework exists in the first two books of the Psalter. Although I do see a life-sequence framework in very broad terms, I find the detailed aspects of Walton's proposal unconvincing. If such a sequence were intended in the arrangement of the Psalter, it was not perceived by the contributors of the situational headings (which do not appear in chronological sequence).

6. Several terms and motifs link the two psalms, as do heading references to Ethan the Ezrahite.

7. Features which suggest northern provenance include references to Joseph and Ephraim. Psalms 74 and 79 may originally have concerned the north before adaptation to the south by Zion and Jerusalem references.

8. "Israel" now, as throughout almost all of this chapter, in its inclusive, "spiritual" sense as the people of God, an identity claimed at this point in history by the remnant of Judah.

9. DeClaissé-Walford concurs in identifying God's kingship as the central theme of the Psalter and especially Book 4 ("Anzu Revisited," 363–64).

10. "There" suggests that the psalm recollects Babylon, rather than speaking directly from it.
11. In the previous note I took "there" in 137:1 and 3 as an indication that in its primary sense Ps 137 looks *back* upon Babylon. The interpretive tradition bears abundant witness, however, that this psalm too may be read as a diaspora prayer.
12. If, however, we include the enthronement psalms in the praise category, Book 4 has the highest concentration.
13. Each of these "thanks!" psalms follows one or more "praise!" psalms which begin and/or end, "Praise the Lord!" (in Hebrew, *halĕlû-yāh*). Wilson, *Editing of the Hebrew Psalter*, 125–29; "Shaping the Psalter," 79–80.
14. Psalm 114 lacks "Praise the LORD!" but may originally have been joined with 113 (Wilson, *Editing of the Hebrew Psalter*, 179–80).
15. Christian readers will note the recurrence of this theme in the Magnificat (Lk 1:46–55).
16. This verse nonetheless appears to have been understood as a royal acclamation by the New Testament's Gospel writers, all four of whom quote it in their Palm Sunday stories (Mt 21:9; Mk 11:9; Lk 19:38; Jn 12:13).
17. Verbal links include "righteous" and "righteousness" (three times in 118, fourteen in 119), *ḥesed* (five times in 118, seven in 119) and "salvation" (three times in 118, five in 119).
18. Psalm 27:1's "house" is double-edged. A Solomonic superscript and parallel mention of "the city" prompt us to interpret the house as temple, but later verses about sons (3–5) open an interpretation of "house" as family line.
19. In 129:1 an anonymous voice makes the same exhortation, "let Israel now say." This is a good example of the way in which the language of Davidic and non-Davidic psalms converges in Book 5.
20. Croft posits an exiled temple singer—recruited by the Babylonians for service in their own temples—as Ps 137's speaker (*Identity of the Individual*, 175). Although in general I resist such specific attempts to locate the psalmists—I have already commented on the kinds of results this can produce with a psalm such as 22—for 137 his proposal works well.
21. Wilson, *Editing of the Hebrew Psalter*, 221–22. Wilson takes references to singing "before the gods" and bowing *toward* the temple in 138:1–2 as descriptive of a diaspora situation. However, 5:7 uses the same "toward" phraseology in parallel with "entering" the house.
22. Psalm 110:3 may also contain a reference to royal *hdr* (NRSV changes the word to *hrr*, "mountains"). The Psalter uses *hdr* seven times with reference to God's glory and majesty, but only here and possibly in 8:5 (which can be read either generally or royally) is it applied to humans other than the king.
23. Psalms 2 and 72 are crucial because of their structural functions in the Psalter. Psalms 110 and 132 are important because they speak of David so intensively and because they give Book 5's royal psalmody a priestly accent. I have put quotation marks around the term "messianic" as a reminder that the word "messiah" originally referred to ancient Judean kings, not a future ruler. Mays's article on "The

David of the Psalms," which moves in generally the same directions as I do, gives much more emphasis to the messianic reading: "When the psalms attributed to David are read in light of what is said in the psalms about him, a messianic construal is cast over the collection" (153).

24. Hebrew *drk*, translated by NRSV as "path" in 1:1 and "way" (twice) in 1:6.

25. Earlier English translations said "blessed," but this is slightly misleading because for many people it suggests spiritual well-being, whereas the Hebrew term connotes worldly well-being (although not to the exclusion of spiritual well-being).

26. Kraus, *Psalms*, 1:116; Brueggemann, "Bounded by Obedience and Praise," 63–66; Miller, "Beginning of the Psalter," 84–86.

27. Miller, "Beginning of the Psalter," 87–88.

28. As in 1:1, the Hebrew text uses a masculine singular, which NRSV shifts to plural in order to honor its presumed gender inclusivity.

29. Allen, "David as Exemplar of Spirituality."

30. Psalm 73's struggle with the question of God's justice has interested many writers. Among those who have enriched my own reflections on this psalm—and my sense of its importance in the Psalter's structure—are Buber, "The Heart Determines," in *Right and Wrong*; Crenshaw, "Standing Near the Flame," in *A Whirlpool of Torment*; Ross, "Psalm 73"; McCann, "Psalm 73"; and Brueggemann, "Bounded by Obedience and Praise," 80–86.

31. The logic here is very similar to the Beatitudes of the New Testament (Mt 5:3–11, Lk 6:20–22), which declare various apparently oppressed categories of people "blessed" (a Greek term equivalent to the "happy" in Ps 94) because of the rewards they will enjoy in God's near-at-hand realm.

32. Roughly speaking, this may also be a movement through the history of the book of Psalms, but the imaginative dynamic I describe is not dependent upon this historical-critical judgment.

CHAPTER 16—DAVID: A SYNTHESIS

1. "Preface to the Psalms," quoted by Kraus, *Theology of the Psalms*, 12.

2. Short-term: Isa 7:2, 13; 22:22; 29:1; 37:35; 38:35; Jer 17:25. Long-term: Isa 9:7; 16:5; Jer 23:5; 30:9; 33:15, 17, 21–22, 26; Ezek 34:23–24; 37:24–25; Hos 3:5; Amos 9:11; Zech 12:7, 8 (twice), 10, 12; 13:1. Isa 9:7 may originally have referred to a contemporary, but I judge it "messianic" in its present application.

3. Ruth 4:17, 22; Prov 1:1; Eccl 1:1; Jer 13:13; 21:12; 22:2, 4, 30; 29:16; 36:30.

4. Literary: Cant 4:4; Amos 6:5. Geographical: Isa 22:9. Transfer: Isa 55:3.

5. Isa 7:2, 13; 22:9, 22; 29:1; 37:35; 38:5. The Ariel prophecy (29:1–8) is a mixed bag but seems to end on a positive note. "David" in NRSV 29:3 is conjectural.

6. Warning/condemning: Jer 13:13; 17:25; 21:12; 22:2, 4, 30; 29:16; 36:30. (Jeremiah 17:25 is an "if," not a promise.) Restoration: Jer 23:5; 30:9; 33:15, 17, 21–22, 26.

7. 1 Chronicles 29:15.

8. For more on how this works in Samuel, see my essay on "The Problematic God of Samuel."

BIBLIOGRAPHY

Achtemeier, Paul J., ed. *HarperCollins Bible Dictionary*. Rev, ed. San Francisco: HarperCollins, 1996.

Ackerman, James. "Knowing Good and Evil: A Literary Analysis of the Court History in 2 Samuel 9–20 and 1 Kings 1–2." *Journal of Biblical Literature* 109 (1990): 41–64.

———. "Who Can Stand Before YHWH, This Holy God? A Reading of 1 Samuel 1–15." *Prooftexts* 11 (1991): 1–24.

Ackroyd, Peter R. "The Succession Narrative (So-Called)." *Interpretation* 35 (1981): 383–96.

———. "The Theology of the Chronicler." *Lexington Theological Quarterly* 8 (1973): 101–16.

Allen, Leslie C. "David as Exemplar of Spirituality: The Redactional Function of Psalm 19." *Biblica* 67 (1986): 544–46.

———. *Psalms 101–150*. Word Biblical Commentary. Waco, Texas: Word, 1983.

Alonso Schökel, L. "David y la Mujer de Tecua: 2 Sm 14 Como Modelo Hermenéutico." *Biblica* 57 (1976): 192–205.

Alter, Robert. *The Art of Biblical Narrative*. New York: Basic Books, 1981.

Anderson, A. A. *Psalms*. 2 vols. New Century Bible Commentary. Grand Rapids: Eerdmans, 1972.

———. *2 Samuel*. Word Biblical Commentary. Waco, Texas: Word, 1989.

Anderson, Bernhard W. *Understanding the Old Testament*. 4th ed. Englewood Cliffs, N.J.: Prentice-Hall, 1986.

Augustine, Bishop of Hippo. "On Christian Doctrine." In *Documents in Early Christian Thought*, edited by Maurice Wiles and Mark Santer, 154–58. London: Cambridge University, 1975.

Auld, A. Graeme. *Kings Without Privilege: David and Moses in the Story of the Bible's Kings*. Edinburgh: T & T Clark, 1994.

Bailey, Randall C. J. *David in Love and War: The Pursuit of Power in 2 Samuel 10–12*. Sheffield: JSOT Press, 1990.

———. "They're Nothing but Incestuous Bastards: The Polemical Use of Sex and Sexuality in Hebrew Canon Narratives." Paper Presented at the Annual Meeting of the Society for Biblical Literature. Kansas City, 1991.

Bakhtin, Mikhail M. *The Dialogic Imagination: Four Essays*. Austin: University of Texas, 1981.

Bal, Mieke. *Lethal Love: Feminist Literary Readings of Biblical Love Stories*. Bloomington: Indiana University, 1987.

Bar-Efrat, Shimon. *Narrative Art in the Bible*. Sheffield: Almond, 1989.

Bassler, Jouette M. "A Man for All Seasons: David in Rabbinic and New Testament Literature." *Interpretation* 40 (1986): 156–69.

Bellinger, William H., Jr. *Psalms: Reading and Studying the Book of Praises*. Peabody, Massachusetts: Hendrickson, 1990.

Bellis, Alice Ogden. *Helpmates, Harlots, and Heroines: Women's Stories in the Hebrew Bible*. Louisville: Westminster John Knox, 1994.

Ben Zvi, Ehud. "On the Reading *'bytdwd'* in the Aramaic Stele from Tel Dan." *Journal for the Study of the Old Testament* 64 (1994): 25–32.

Berlin, Adele. *Poetics and Interpretation of Biblical Narrative*. Sheffield: Almond, 1983.

Berquist, Jon L. *Judaism in Persia's Shadow: A Social and Historical Approach*. Minneapolis: Fortress, 1995.

Biran, Avraham, and Joseph Naveh. "An Aramaic Stele Fragment from Tel Dan." *Israel Exploration Journal* 43 (1993): 81–98.

Bloom, Harold. *The Book of J*. New York: Grove Weidenfeld, 1990.

Braun, Roddy L. *1 Chronicles*. Word Biblical Commentary. Waco, Texas: Word, 1986.

———. "Solomon: The Chosen Temple Builder: The Significance of 1 Chronicles 22, 28, and 29 for the Theology of Chronicles." *Journal of Biblical Literature* 95 (1976): 581–90.

Brueggemann, Walter. "Bounded by Obedience and Praise: The Psalms as Canon." *Journal for the Study of the Old Testament* 50 (1991): 63–92.

———. "David and His Theologian." *Catholic Biblical Quarterly* 30 (1968): 156–81.

———. *David's Truth in Israel's Imagination and Memory*. Philadelphia: Fortress, 1985.

———. *First and Second Samuel*. Interpretation. Atlanta: John Knox, 1990.

———. "Kingship and Chaos: A Study in Tenth Century Theology." *Catholic Biblical Quarterly* 33 (1971): 317–32.

———. "Life and Death in Tenth Century Israel." *Journal of the American Academy of Religion* 40 (1972): 96–109.

———. "On Coping with Curse: A Study of 2 Sam 16:5–14." *Catholic Biblical Quarterly* 36 (1973): 175–92.

———. "On Trust and Freedom: A Study of Faith in the Succession Narrative." *Interpretation* 26 (1972): 3–19.

———. "Samuel, Book of 1–2: Narrative and Theology." *Anchor Bible Dictionary*, 5:965–73. New York: Doubleday, 1992.

———. "2 Samuel 21–24: An Appendix of Deconstruction?" *Catholic Biblical Quarterly* 50 (1988): 383–97.

———. "The Triumphalist Tendency in Exegetical History." *Journal of the American Academy of Religion* 38 (1970): 367–80.

———. "The Trusted Creature." *Catholic Biblical Quarterly* 31 (1969): 484–98.

Buber, Martin. "The Heart Determines." In *Right and Wrong: An Interpretation of Some Psalms*, 34–52. London: SCM, 1952.

Camp, Claudia V. "The Wise Women of 2 Samuel: A Role Model for Women in Early Israel." *Catholic Biblical Quarterly* 43 (1981): 14–29.

Campbell, A. F. *The Ark Narrative (1 Sam 4–6; 2 Sam 6): A Form-Critical and Traditio-Historical Study.* Missoula: Scholars Press, 1975.

———. "Psalm 78: A Contribution to the Theology of Tenth Century Israel." *Catholic Biblical Quarterly* 41 (1979): 51–79.

Cargill, Jack. "David in History: A Secular Approach." *Judaism* 35 (1986): 211–22.

Carlson, R. A. *David the Chosen King: A Traditio-Historical Approach to the Second Book of Samuel.* Uppsala: Almquist and Wiksells, 1964.

Carroll, Robert P. "Israel, History of (Post-Monarchic Period)." In *Anchor Bible Dictionary*, 3:567–76. New York: Doubleday, 1992.

———. "The Myth of the Empty Land." *Semeia* 59 (1992): 79–93.

Cartun, Ari. "Topography as a Template for David's Fortunes During His Flight Before Avshalom." *Journal of Reform Judaism*, Spring 1991, 17–34.

Caspari, Wilhelm. "The Literary Type and Historical Value of 2 Samuel 15–20." Originally published in 1909 as "Literarische Art und Historischer Wert von 2 Sam. 15–20." In *Narrative and Novella in Samuel: Studies by Hugo Gressmann and Other Scholars 1906–1923*, edited by David M. Gunn, 59–88. Sheffield: Almond, 1991.

Cazelles, H. "David's Monarchy and the Gibeonite Claim (II Sam XXI, 1–14)." *Palestine Exploration Quarterly* 87 (1955): 165–75.

Childs, Brevard S. "Psalm 8 in the Context of the Christian Canon." *Interpretation* 23 (1969): 20–31.

———. "Psalm Titles and Midrashic Exegesis." *Journal of Semitic Studies* 16 (1971): 137–50.

Clifford, Richard J. "In Zion and David a New Beginning: An Interpretation of Psalm 78." In *Traditions in Transformation*, edited by B. Halpern and J. D. Levenson. Winona Lake, Ind.: Eisenbrauns, 1981.

———. "Psalm 89: A Lament Over the Davidic Ruler's Continued Failure." *Harvard Theological Review* 73 (1980): 38–47.

Clines, David J. A. "Michal Observed: An Introduction to Reading Her Story." In *Telling Queen Michal's Story: An Experiment in Comparative Interpretation*, edited by David J. A. Clines and Tamara C. Eskenazi, 24–63. Sheffield: Sheffield Academic Press, 1991.

———. "The Story of Michal, Wife of David, in Its Sequential Unfolding." In *Telling Queen Michal's Story: An Experiment in Comparative Interpretation*, edited by David J. A. Clines and Tamara C. Eskenazi, 129–40. Sheffield: Sheffield Academic Press, 1991.

Clines, David J. A., and Tamara C. Eskenazi, eds. *Telling Queen Michal's Story: An Experiment in Comparative Interpretation.* Sheffield: Sheffield Academic Press, 1991.

Coats, George W. "Parable, Fable, and Anecdote: Storytelling in the Succession Narrative." *Interpretation* 35 (1981): 368–82.

Cohen, Martin A. "The Rebellions During the Reign of David: An Inquiry into Social Dynamics in Ancient Israel." In *Studies in Jewish Bibliography, History, and Literature in Honor of Edward Kiev*, edited by Charles Berlin, 91–112. New York: Ktav, 1971.

Cohn, Robert L. "1 Samuel." In *Harper's Bible Commentary*, edited by James L. Mays, 268–86. San Francisco: Harper & Row, 1988.

Collins, T. "Decoding the Psalms: A Structural Approach to the Psalter." *Journal for the Study of the Old Testament* 37 (1987): 41–60.

Conroy, C. *Absalom Absalom! Narrative and Language in 2 Sam 13–20*. Rome: Biblical Institute, 1978.

Coogan, Michael David. *Stories from Ancient Canaan*. Philadelphia: Westminster, 1978.

Coote, Robert B. *Early Israel: A New Horizon*. Minneapolis: Fortress, 1990.

Craigie, Peter C. *Psalms 1–50*. Word Biblical Commentary. Waco, Texas: Word, 1983.

Crenshaw, James L. *A Whirlpool of Torment: Israelite Traditions of God as an Oppressive Presence*. Philadelphia: Fortress, 1984.

Croft, Steven J. L. *The Identity of the Individual in the Psalms*. Sheffield: JSOT Press, 1987.

Crow, Loren D. *The Songs of Ascents (Psalms 120–134): Their Place in Israelite History and Religion*. Atlanta: Scholars Press, 1996.

Cryer, F. H. "David's Rise to Power and the Death of Abner: An Analysis of 1 Samuel 26:14–16 and Its Redaction-Critical Implications." *Vetus Testamentum* 35 (1985): 385–94.

Culley, Robert C. *Studies in the Structure of Hebrew Narrative*. Missoula: Scholars Press, 1976.

Dahood, Mitchell. *Psalms: A New Translation with Introduction and Commentary*. 3 vols. Anchor Bible. New York: Doubleday, 1965/1968/1970.

"'David' Found at Dan." *BAR* 20 (March/April 1994): 26–39.

Davies, G. Henton. "The Ark in the Psalms." In *Promise and Fulfillment*, edited by F. F. Bruce, 51–61. Edinburgh: T & T Clark, 1963.

Davies, Philip R. "*Bytdwd* and *Swkt Dwyd*: A Comparison." *Journal for the Study of the Old Testament* 64 (1994): 23–24.

———. *In Search of Ancient Israel*. Sheffield: JSOT Press, 1992.

Day, John. "Dragon and Sea, God's Conflict With." In *Anchor Bible Dictionary*, 2:228–31. New York: Doubleday, 1992.

DeClaissé-Walford, Nancy. "Anzu Revisited: The Scribal Shaping of the Hebrew Psalter." *Word and World* 15 (1995): 358–66.

Delekat, Lienhard. "Tendenz und Theologie der David-Salomo-Erzählung." In *Das ferne und nahe Wort*, edited by F. Maass, 26–36. Berlin: Töpelmann, 1967.

Dempster, Stephen G. "Elhanan." In *Anchor Bible Dictionary*, 2:455–56. New York: Doubleday, 1992.

Dever, William G. "Archaeology and the 'Conquest'" In *Anchor Bible Dictionary*, 1:545–58. New York: Doubleday, 1992.

226

De Vries, Simon J. *1 and 2 Chronicles*. Forms of the Old Testament Literature. Grand Rapids: Eerdmans, 1989.

———. "Moses and David as Cult-Founders in Chronicles." *Journal of Biblical Literature* 107 (1988): 619–39.

Duke, Rodney K. "Jashobeam." In *Anchor Bible Dictionary*, 3:647–48. New York: Doubleday, 1992.

———. *The Persuasive Appeal of the Chronicler*. Sheffield: Almond, 1990.

Eaton, John H. *Kingship and the Psalms*. 2d ed. Sheffield: JSOT Press, 1986.

———. "The Psalms and Israelite Worship." In *Tradition and Interpretation*, edited by G. W. Anderson, 238–72. New York: Oxford University, 1979.

Edelman, Diana V. "Ahinoam." In *Anchor Bible Dictionary*, 1:117–18. New York: Doubleday, 1992.

Eissfeldt, Otto. "The Promises of Grace to David in Isaiah 55:1–5." In *Israel's Prophetic Heritage (Fs. J. Muilenburg)*, edited by Bernhard W. Anderson and Walter Harrelson, 196–207. New York, Harper & Brothers: 1962.

Eslinger, Lyle M. "'A Change of Heart': 1 Samuel 16." In *Ascribe to the Lord: Biblical and Other Studies in Memory of Peter C. Craigie*, edited by Lyle M. Eslinger and Glen Taylor, 341–61. Sheffield: JSOT Press, 1988.

———. *House of God or House of David: The Rhetoric of 2 Samuel* 7. Sheffield: JSOT Press, 1994.

———. *Into the Hands of the Living God*. Sheffield: Almond, 1989.

———. *Kingship of God in Crisis*. Sheffield: Almond, 1985.

———. "Viewpoints and Points of View in 1 Samuel 8–12." *Journal for the Study of the Old Testament* 26 (1983): 61–76.

Exum, J. Cheryl. *Fragmented Women: Feminist (Sub)versions of Biblical Narratives*. Sheffield: JSOT Press, 1993.

———. "Murder They Wrote: Ideology and the Manipulation of Female Presence in Biblical Narrative." In *Telling Queen Michal's Story: An Experiment in Comparative Interpretation*, edited by David J. A. Clines and Tamara C. Eskenazi, 176–98. Sheffield Academic Press, 1991.

———. *Tragedy and Biblical Narrative*. Cambridge: Cambridge University, 1992.

Fensham, F. C. "Father and Son as Terminology for Treaty and Covenant." In *Near Eastern Studies in Honor of W. F. Albright*, edited by H. Goedicke, 121–35. Baltimore, Johns Hopkins: 1971.

Fewell, Danna Nolan, and David M. Gunn. *Gender, Power, and Promise: The Subject of the Bible's* First Story. Nashville: Abingdon, 1993.

Fishbane, Michael. "I Samuel 3: Historical Narrative and Narrative Poetics." In *Literary Interpretations of Biblical Narrative II*, edited by Kenneth R. R. Gros Louis and James Ackerman, 191–203. Nashville: Abingdon, 1982.

———. *Text and Texture: Close Readings of Selected Biblical Texts*. New York: Schocken, 1979.

Flanagan, James W. "Court History or Succession Document? A Study of II Samuel 9–20 and I Kings 1–2." *Journal of Biblical Literature* 91 (1972): 172–81.

———. *David's Social Drama: A Hologram of Israel's Early Iron Age*. Sheffield: Almond, 1988.

———. "Samuel, Book of 1–2: Text, Composition, and Content." In *Anchor Bible Dictionary*, 5:957–65. New York: Doubleday, 1992.

Fokkelman, J. P. *The Crossing Fates*. Vol. 2 of *Narrative Art and Poetry in the Books of Samuel*. Assen: Van Gorcum, 1986.

———. *King David (II Samuel 9–20 and I Kings 1–2)* Vol. 1 of *Narrative Art and Poetry in the Books of Samuel*. Assen: Van Gorcum, 1981.

———. *Throne and City*. Vol. 3 of *Narrative Art and Poetry in the Books of Samuel*. Assen: Van Gorcum, 1990.

———. *Vow and Desire*. Vol. 4 of *Narrative Art and Poetry in the Books of Samuel*. Assen: Van Gorcum, 1993.

Freedman, David Noel. "The Chronicler's Purpose." *Catholic Biblical Quarterly* 23 (1961): 436–42.

Freedman, David Noel, and David Frank Graf, eds. *Palestine in Transition: The Emergence of Ancient Israel*. Sheffield: Almond, 1983.

Fretheim, Terence E. "Psalm 132: A Form-Critical Study." *Journal of Biblical Literature* 86 (1967): 289–300.

Garsiel, Moshe. *The First Book of Samuel: A Literary Study of Comparative Structures, Analogies, and Parallels*. Jerusalem: Rubin Mass, 1985.

Gerstenberger, Erhard S. *Psalms: Part I, with an Introduction to Cultic Poetry*. Forms of the Old Testament Literature. Grand Rapids: Eerdmans, 1987.

Glück, J. J. "Merab or Michal?" *Zeitschrift für die alttestamentliche Wissenschaft* 77 (1965): 72-81.

Good, Edwin M. *Irony in the Old Testament*. 2d ed. Sheffield: Almond, 1981.

Gordon, R. P. "David's Rise and Saul's Demise: Narrative Analogy in I Samuel 24–26." *Tyndale Bulletin* 31 (1980): 37–64.

Goulder, M. D. "The Fourth Book of the Psalter." *Journal of Theological Studies* 26 (1975): 269–89.

———. *The Psalms of the Sons of Korah*. Sheffield: JSOT Press, 1982.

Gressmann, Hugo. "The Oldest History Writing in Israel." Selections from *Die älteste Geschichtsschreibung und Prophetie Israels*, 1921. In *Narrative and Novella in Samuel: Studies by Hugo Gressmann and Other Scholars 1906–1923*, edited by David M. Gunn, 9–58. Sheffield: Almond, 1991.

Gros Louis, K. R. R. "The Difficulty of Ruling Well: King David of Israel." *Semeia* 8 (1977): 15–33.

———. "King David of Israel." In *Literary Interpretations of Biblical Narrative II*, 204–19. Nashville: Abingdon, 1982.

Gunn, David M. "David and the Gift of the Kingdom (2 Sam 2–4, 9–20, 1 Kgs 1–2)." *Semeia* 3 (1975): 14–45.

———. *The Fate of King Saul: An Interpretation of a Biblical Story*. Sheffield: University of Sheffield, 1980.

———. "In Security: The David of Biblical Narrative." In *Signs and Wonders: Biblical Texts in Literary Focus*, edited by J. Cheryl Exum, 133–51. Atlanta: Scholars Press, 1989.

———. "Narrative Patterns and Oral Tradition in Judges and Samuel." *Vetus Testamentum* 24 (1974): 286–317.

———. "New Directions in the Study of Biblical Hebrew Narrative." *Journal for the Study of the Old Testament* 39 (1987): 65–75.

———. "Reading Right: Reliable and Omniscient Narrator, Omniscient God, and Foolproof Composition in the Hebrew Bible." In *The Bible in Three Dimensions*, edited by David J. A. Clines, 53–64. Sheffield: Sheffield Academic Press, 1990.

———. "2 Samuel." In *Harper's Bible Commentary*, edited by James L. Mays, 287–304. San Francisco: Harper & Row, 1988.

———. *The Story of King David: Genre and Interpretation*. Sheffield: University of Sheffield, 1978.

Gunn, David M., and Danna Nolan Fewell. *Narrative in the Hebrew Bible*. New York: Oxford University, 1993.

Hagan, H. "Deception as Motif and Theme in 2 Sm 9–20; 1 Kgs 1–2." *Biblica* 60 (1979): 301–26.

Halpern, Baruch. "Erasing History: The Minimalist Assault on Ancient Israel." *Bible Review*, December 1995, 26–47.

Hanson, Paul D. *The People Called: The Growth of Community in the Bible*. San Francisco: Harper & Row, 1986.

Hoftijzer, J. "David and the Tekoite Woman." *Vetus Testamentum* 20 (1970): 419–44.

Holladay, William L. *The Psalms Through Three Thousand Years: Prayerbook of a Cloud of Witnesses*. Minneapolis: Augsburg Fortress, 1993.

Holland, Thomas A. "Jericho." In *Anchor Bible Dictionary*, 3:723–37. New York: Doubleday, 1992.

Howard, David M., Jr. "A Contextual Reading of Psalms 90–94." In *Shape and Shaping of the Psalter*, edited by J. Clinton McCann, Jr. Sheffield: JSOT Press, 1993.

———. "Editorial Activity in the Psalter: A State-of-the-Field Survey." *Word and World* 9 (1989): 274–85.

———. *The Structure of Psalms 93–100*. Dissertation, University of Michigan. Ann Arbor: University Microfilms International, 1986.

Humphreys, W. Lee. "The Tragedy of King Saul: A Study of the Structure of I Samuel 9–31." *Journal for the Study of the Old Testament* 6 (1978): 18–27.

———. *The Tragic Vision and the Hebrew Tradition*. Overtures to Biblical Theology. Philadelphia: Fortress, 1985.

Im, Tae-Soo. *Das Davidbild in den Chronikbüchern*. Frankfurt am Main: Peter Lang, 1985.

Jackson, Jared J. "David's Throne: Patterns in the Succession Story." *Canadian Journal of Theology* 11 (1965): 183–195.

229

Jacobsen, Thorkild. *The Treasures of Darkness: A History of Mesopotamian Religion.* New Haven: Yale, 1976.

Japhet, Sara. *I & II Chronicles: A Commentary.* OTL. Louisville: Westminster John Knox, 1993.

———. "The Supposed Common Authorship of Chronicles and Ezra-Nehemiah Investigated Anew." *Vetus Testamentum* 18 (1968): 330–71.

Jobling, David. "Deuteronomic Political Theory in Judges and 1 Samuel 1–12." In *The Sense of Biblical Narrative: Structural Analyses in the Hebrew Bible II*, 44–87. Sheffield: Almond, 1986.

———. "Jonathan: A Structural Study in I Samuel." In *The Sense of Biblical Narrative: Structural Analyses in the Hebrew Bible, I*, 12–30. Sheffield: JSOT Press, 1978.

Johnson, Aubrey R. *Sacral Kingship in Ancient Israel.* 2d ed. Cardiff: University of Wales, 1967.

Kapelrud, A. S. "King and Fertility: A Discussion of II Sam 21:1–14." *Norsk Teologisk Tidsskrift* 56 (= *Interpretationes ad Vetus Testamentum pertinentes Sigmundo Mowinckel septuagenario missae*, Oslo: land og kirche) (1955): 113–22.

———. "King David and the Sons of Saul." In *La Regalità Sacra: Contributi al di delle VIII Congresso Internazionale Di Storia Delle Religioni (Rome, April 1955)*, 294–301. Leiden: Brill, 1959.

Keel, Othmar. *Symbolism of the Biblical World: Ancient Near Eastern Iconography and the Book of Psalms.* New York: Seabury, 1978.

Kelly, Brian E. *Retribution and Eschatology in Chronicles.* Sheffield: Sheffield Academic Press, 1996.

Klein, Jacob. "Akitu." In *Anchor Bible Dictionary*, 1:138–40. New York: Doubleday, 1992.

Klein, Ralph W. "Chronicles, Book of 1–2." In *Anchor Bible Dictionary*, 1:992–1002. New York: Doubleday, 1992.

———. "Ezra-Nehemiah, Books of." In *Anchor Bible Dictionary*, 2:731–42. New York: Doubleday, 1992.

———. *Samuel.* Word Biblical Commentary. Waco, Texas: Word, 1983.

Koehler, Ludwig. "Psalm 23." *Zeitschrift für die Alttestamentliche Wissenschaft* 68 (1956): 227–234.

Koopmans, W. T. "The Testament of David in 1 Kings 2:1–10." *Vetus Testamentum* 41 (1991): 429–49.

Kort, Wesley. *Story, Text and Scripture: Literary Interests in Biblical Narrative.* University Park: Pennsylvania State, 1988.

Kraus, Hans-Joachim. *Psalms.* 2 vols. Continental Commentaries. Minneapolis: Augsburg, 1988/1989.

———. *Theology of the Psalms.* Continental Commentaries. Minneapolis: Augsburg, 1986.

Kuntz, J. K. "King Triumphant: A Rhetorical Study of Psalms 20 and 21." *Harvard Annual Review* 10 (1986): 157–76.

Lanser, Susan S. *The Narrative Act: Point of View in Prose Fiction.* Princeton: University Press, 1981.

Lemche, Niels Peter. "David's Rise." *Journal for the Study of the Old Testament* 10 (1978): 2–25.

Lemche, Niels Peter, and Thomas L. Thompson. "Did Biran Kill David? The Bible in Light of Archaeology." *Journal for the Study of the Old Testament* 64 (1994): 3–22.

Levenson, Jon D. *Creation and the Persistence of Evil.* San Francisco: Harper & Row, 1988.

———. "The Davidic Covenant and Its Modern Interpreters." *Catholic Biblical Quarterly* 41 (1979): 214–15.

———. "1 Samuel 25 as Literature and as History." *Catholic Biblical Quarterly* 40 (1978): 21–22.

———. *Sinai and Zion: An Entry into the Jewish Bible.* Minneapolis: Winston, 1985.

Levenson, Jon D., and Baruch Halpern. "The Political Import of David's Marriages." *Journal of Biblical Literature* 99 (1980): 507–28.

Limburg, James. "Psalms, Book of." In *Anchor Bible Dictionary*, 5:522–36. New York: Doubleday, 1992.

Linafelt, Tod. "Taking Women in Samuel: Readers/Responses/Responsibility." In *Reading Between Texts: Intertextuality and the Hebrew Bible*, edited by Danna Nolan Fewell, 99–113. Louisville: Westminster John Knox, 1992.

Long, Burke O. "Framing Repetitions in Biblical Historiography." *Journal of Biblical Literature* 106 (1987): 385–99.

———. "The 'New' Biblical Poetics of Alter and Sternberg." *Journal for the Study of the Old Testament* 51 (1991): 71–84.

———. "Wounded Beginnings: David and Two Sons." In *Images of God and Man: Old Testament Short Stories in Literary Focus*, 26–34. Sheffield: Almond, 1981.

McCann, J. Clinton, Jr. "Books I–III and the Editorial Purpose of the Hebrew Psalter." In *The Shape and Shaping of the Psalter*, edited by J. Clinton McCann, Jr., 93–107. Sheffield: Sheffield Academic Press, 1993.

———. "Psalm 73: A Microcosm of Old Testament Theology." In *The Listening Heart*, edited by K. Hoglund, 247–57. Sheffield: JSOT Press, 1987.

———. "The Psalms as Instruction." *Interpretation* 46 (1992): 117–19.

———, ed. *The Shape and Shaping of the Psalter.* Sheffield: Sheffield Academic Press, 1993.

McCarter, P. Kyle, Jr. "The Apology of David." *Journal of Biblical Literature* 99 (1980): 489–504.

———. "The Historical David." *Interpretation* 40 (1986): 117–29.

———. "Plots, True or False: The Succession Narrative as Court Apologetic." *Interpretation* 35 (1981): 355–67.

———. *Samuel: A New Translation with Introduction, Notes and Commentary.* 2 vols. Anchor Bible. Garden City: Doubleday, 1980/1984.

McKenzie, Steven L. *The Chronicler's Use of the Deuteronomistic History.* Atlanta: Scholars Press, 1985.

Macky, Peter W. "The Coming Revolution: The New Literary Approach to the New Testament." In *A Guide to Contemporary Hermeneutics*, edited by Donald K. McKim, 263–79. Grand Rapids: Eerdmans, 1986.

Marcus, David. "David the Deceiver and David the Dupe." *Prooftexts* 6 (1986): 163–71.

Mays, James Luther. "The David of the Psalms." *Interpretation* 40 (1986): 143–55.

———. "The Place of the Torah-Psalms in the Psalter." *Journal of Biblical Literature* 106 (1987): 3–12.

———. *Psalms*. Interpretation. Louisville: Westminster John Knox, 1994.

Mettinger, Trygve N. D. *King and Messiah: The Civil and Sacral Legitimation of the Israelite Kings*. Lund: CWK Gleerup, 1976.

Miles, Jack. *God: A Biography*. New York: Random House, 1995.

Miller, Patrick D. "The Beginning of the Psalter." In *The Shape and Shaping of the Psalter*, edited by J. Clinton McCann, Jr., 83–92. Sheffield: Sheffield Academic Press, 1993.

———. *Interpreting the Psalms*. Philadelphia: Fortress, 1986.

———. "Power, Justice, and Peace: An Exegesis of Psalm 72." *Faith and Mission* 4 (1986): 65–70.

Miller, Patrick D., and J. J. M. Roberts. *The Hand of the Lord: A Reassessment of the "Ark Narrative" of 1 Samuel*. Baltimore: Johns Hopkins, 1977.

Milne, Pamela. "Psalm 23: Echoes of the Exodus." *Studies in Religion/Sciences Religieuses* 4 (1974/5): 237–47.

Miscall, Peter D. "For David's Sake: A Response to David M. Gunn." In *Signs and Wonders: Biblical Texts in Literary Focus*, edited by J. Cheryl Exum, 154–163. Atlanta: Scholars Press, 1989.

———. *1 Samuel: A Literary Reading*. Bloomington: Indiana University, 1987.

———. *The Workings of Old Testament Narrative*. Philadelphia: Fortress, 1983.

Moran, W. L. "The Ancient Near Eastern Background of the Love of God in Deuteronomy." *Catholic Biblical Quarterly* 25 (1967): 77–87.

Morgenstern, Julian. "David and Jonathan." *Journal of Biblical Literature* 78 (1959): 322–25.

Mowinckel, Sigmund. *The Psalms in Israel's Worship*. 2 vols. Nashville: Abingdon, 1962.

North, R. "Theology of the Chronicler." *Journal of Biblical Literature* 82 (1963): 369–81.

Noth, Martin. *The Deuteronomistic History*. Sheffield: JSOT Press, 1981.

Osborne, W. L. *The Genealogies of I Chronicles 1–9*. Ph.D. Dissertation. The Dropsie University. 1979.

Perdue, Leo G. "'Is There Anyone Left of the House of Saul . . .?' Ambiguity and the Characterization of David in the Succession Narrative." *Journal for the Study of the Old Testament* 30 (1984): 67–84.

Petersen, David L. "Portraits of David: Canonical and Otherwise." *Interpretation* 40 (1986): 130–42.

Polzin, Robert. *David and the Deuteronomist: A Literary Study of the Deuteronomic History—Part Three: 2 Samuel.* Bloomington: Indiana University, 1993.

————. *Moses and the Deuteronomist.* In *A Literary Study of the Deuteronomic History.* Bloomington: Indiana University, 1993.

————. *Samuel and the Deuteronomist: A Literary Study of the Deuteronomic History.* San Francisco: Harper & Row, 1989.

Porter, J. R. "The Interpretation of 2 Samuel 6 and Psalm 132." *JTS* 5 (1954): 161–73.

Pritchard, James B., ed. *Ancient Near Eastern Texts Relating to the Old Testament.* 3d ed. Princeton: University Press, 1969.

————, ed. *The Ancient Near East in Pictures Relating to the Old Testament.* 2d ed. Princeton: University Press, 1969.

Riley, William. *King and Cultus in Chronicles.* Sheffield: JSOT Press, 1993.

Rosenberg, Joel. *King and Kin: Political Allegory in the Hebrew Bible.* Bloomington: Indiana University, 1986.

Ross, J. F. "Psalm 73." In *Israelite Wisdom*, edited by J. G. Gammie, 161–75. Missoula: Scholars Press, 1978.

Rost, Leonhard. *The Succession to the Throne of David.* Sheffield: Almond, 1982.

Roth, Wolfgang M. W. "You Are the Man! Structural Interaction in 2 Samuel 10–12." *Semeia* 8 (1977): 1–13.

Sakenfeld, Katharine Doob. *Faithfulness in Action: Loyalty in Biblical Perspective.* Philadelphia: Fortress, 1985.

————. *The Meaning of Hesed in the Hebrew Bible: A New Inquiry.* Missoula: Scholars Press, 1978.

Sanders, J. A. *The Dead Sea Psalms Scroll.* Ithaca: Cornell University, 1967.

Schniedewind, William H. *The Word of God in Transition: From Prophet to Exegete in the Second Temple Period.* Sheffield: Sheffield Academic Press, 1995.

Schulz, Alfons. "Narrative Art in the Books of Samuel." (Originally published in 1923 as *Erzählungskunst in den Samuel-Büchern.*) *Narrative and Novella in Samuel: Studies by Hugo Gressmann and Other Scholars 1906–1923*, edited by David M. Gunn, 119–70. Sheffield: Almond, 1991.

Schwartz, Regina M. "Adultery in the House of David: The Metanarrative of Biblical Scholarship and the Narratives of the Bible." *Semeia* 54 (= *Poststructuralism as Exegesis*, edited by David Jobling and Stephen D. Moore) (1992): 35–55.

Seow, C. L. "Ark of the Covenant." In *Anchor Bible Dictionary*, 1:386–93. New York: Doubleday, 1992.

Shanks, Herschel, William G. Dever, Baruch Halpern, and P. Kyle McCarter, Jr. *The Rise of Ancient Israel.* Washington, D.C.: Biblical Archaeology Society, 1993.

Sheppard, Gerald T. "'Blessed Are Those Who Take Refuge in Him': Biblical Criticism and Deconstruction." *Religion and Intellectual Life* 5 (1988): 57–66.

Smith, Mark S. "Setting and Rhetoric in Psalm 23." *Journal for the Study of the Old Testament* 41 (1988): 61–66.

Stern, Ephraim. *Material Culture of the Land of the Bible in the Persian Period, 538–332 B.C.* Warminster: Aris & Phillips, and Jerusalem: Israel Exploration Society, 1982.

Sternberg, Meir. *The Poetics of Biblical Narrative: Ideological Literature and the Drama of Reading.* Bloomington: Indiana University, 1985.

Steussy, Marti J. "People, Power, and Providence: Preaching the Lections from Second Samuel." *Quarterly Review* 14 (1994): 107–24.

———. "The Problematic God of Samuel." In a festschrift for James L. Crenshaw, edited by David Penchansky, forthcoming.

Steussy, Marti J., and Richard Davies. "The Storyteller and the Biblical Scholar: Exegesis in the Form of Dialogue (2 Samuel 11:27b-12:25)." *Journal of Biblical Storytelling* 6, no. 1 (1996): 21–30.

Stuhlmueller, Carroll. "Psalms." In *Harper's Bible Commentary*, edited by James L. Mays, 433–94. San Francisco: Harper & Row, 1988.

Talmon, S. R. "1 and 2 Chronicles." In *The Literary Guide to the Bible*, edited by Robert Alter and Frank Kermode. Cambridge, Massachusetts: Belknap, 1987.

Tate, Marvin E. *Psalms 51–100.* Word Biblical Commentary. Waco, Texas: Word, 1990.

Thompson, J. A. "The Significance of the Verb *love* in the David-Jonathan Narratives in 1 Samuel." *Vetus Testamentum* 24 (1974): 334–38.

Thompson, Thomas L. *Early History of the Israelite People.* Leiden: Brill, 1992.

Throntveit, M. A. *When Kings Speak: Royal Speech and Royal Prayer in Chronicles.* Atlanta: Scholars Press, 1987.

Trible, Phyllis. *Rhetorical Criticism: Context, Method, and the Book of Jonah.* Minneapolis: Fortress, 1994.

———. *Texts of Terror.* Philadelphia: Fortress, 1984.

Tsevat, M. "The House of David in Nathan's Prophecy." *Biblica* 46 (1965): 353–356.

Vanderkam, James C. "Davidic Complicity in the Deaths of Abner and Eshbaal: A Historical and Redactional Study." *Journal of Biblical Literature* 99 (1980): 521–39.

Van Seters, John. *In Search of History: Historiography in the Ancient World and the Origins of Biblical History.* New Haven and London: Yale, 1983.

———. "Problems in the Literary Analysis of the Court History of David." *Journal for the Study of the Old Testament* 1 (1976): 22–29.

von Rad, Gerhard. "The Beginnings of Historical Writing in Ancient Israel." In *The Problem of the Hexateuch and Other Essays*, 166–204. Edinburgh: Oliver & Boyd, 1966.

———. "The Deuteronomic Theology of History in I and II Kings." In *The Problem of the Hexateuch and Other Essays.* New York: McGraw-Hill, 1966.

Walton, John H. "Psalms: A Cantata About the Davidic Covenant." *Journal of the Evangelical Theology Society* 34 (1991): 21–31.

Watts, James W. "Psalm 2 in the Context of Biblical Theology." *Horizons in Biblical Theology* 12 (1990): 73–91.

Weinfeld, Moshe. "The Covenant of Grant in the Old Testament and the Ancient Near East." *Journal of the American Oriental Society* 90 (1970): 184–203.

Weiser, A. "Die Legitimation des Königs David." *Vetus Testamentum* 16 (1966): 325–54.

———. *The Psalms: A Commentary*. Old Testament Library. Philadelphia: Westminster, 1962.

Westermann, Claus. *Isaiah 40–66: A Commentary*. Old Testament Library. Philadelphia: Westminster, 1969.

Wharton, J. A. "A Plausible Tale: Story and Theology in II Samuel 9–20, I Kings 1–2." *Interpretation* 35 (1981): 341–54.

Whedbee, William. "On Divine and Human Bonds: The Tragedy of the House of David." In *Canon, Theology, and Old Testament Interpretation: Essays in Honor of Brevard S. Childs*, edited by Gene M. Tucker, David L. Petersen, and Robert R. Wilson, 147–65. Philadelphia: Fortress, 1988.

Whitelam, Keith. "The Defense of David." *Journal for the Study of the Old Testament* 29 (1984): 61–87.

———. *The Just King: Monarchical Judicial Authority in Ancient Israel*. Sheffield: Almond, 1979.

Whybray, Norman. *Reading the Psalms as a Book*. Sheffield: Sheffield Academic Press, 1996.

Whybray, Roger Norman. *The Succession Narrative: A Study of II Sam. 9–20 and I Kings 1 and 2*. London: SCM, 1968.

Williamson, H. G. M. *Israel in the Books of Chronicles*. Cambridge: Cambridge University, 1977.

———. "'We Are Yours, O David': The Setting and Purpose of 1 Chronicles Xii 1–23." In *Remembering All the Way*, 164–76. OTS 21. Leiden: E. J. Brill, 1981.

Willis, J. T. "An Anti-Elide Narrative Tradition from a Prophetic Circle at the Ramah Sanctuary." *Journal of Biblical Literature* 90 (1971): 288–308.

———. "A Cry of Defiance: Psalm 2." *Journal for the Study of the Old Testament* 47

———. "Samuel Versus Eli." *Theologische Zeitschrift* 35 (1979): 201–12.

(1990): 33–50.

Wilson, Gerald H. *The Editing of the Hebrew Psalter*. Chico, Calif.: Scholars Press, 1985.

———. "Evidence of Editorial Divisions in the Hebrew Psalter." *Vetus Testamentum* 34 (1984): 337–352.

———. "The Shape of the Psalms." *Interpretation* 46 (1992): 129.

———. "Shaping the Psalter: A Consideration of Editorial Linkage in the Book of Psalms." In *The Shape and Shaping of the Psalter*, edited by J. Clinton McCann, Jr., 72–82. Sheffield: Sheffield Academic Press, 1993.

———. "The Use of the Royal Psalms at the 'Seams' of the Hebrew Psalter." *Journal for the Study of the Old Testament* 35 (1986): 85–94.

———. "The Use of 'Untitled' Psalms in the Hebrew Psalter." *Zeitschrift für die alttestamentliche Wissenschaft* 97 (1985): 404–13.

235

Wilson, Robert R. "Genealogy, Genealogies." In *Anchor Bible Dictionary*, 2:929–32. New York: Doubleday, 1992.

Wojcik, Jan. "Discriminations Against David's Tragedy in Ancient Jewish and Christian Literature." In *The David Myth in Western Literature*, edited by Raymond-Jean Frontain and Jan Wojcik, 13–35. West Lafayette: Purdue, 1980.

Yee, Gale A. "The Anatomy of Biblical Parody: The Dirge Form in 2 Samuel 1 and Isaiah 14." *Catholic Biblical Quarterly* 50 (1988): 565–86.

SCRIPTURE INDEX

241

243

HEBREW WORD INDEX

TOPIC INDEX